MW01620756

Perpetual Inventory

OCTOBER Books

Broodthaers, edited by Benjamin H. D. Buchloh

AIDS: Cultural Analysis/Cultural Activism, edited by Douglas Crimp

Aberrations: An Essay on the Legend of Forms, by Jurgis Baltrušaitis

Against Architecture: The Writings of Georges Bataille, by Denis Hollier

Painting as Model, by Yve-Alain Bois

The Destruction of Tilted Arc: Documents, edited by Clara Weyergraf-Serra and Martha Buskirk

The Woman in Question, edited by Parveen Adams and Elizabeth Cowie

Techniques of the Observer: On Vision and Modernity in the Nineteenth Century, by Jonathan Crary

The Subjectivity Effect in Western Literary Tradition: Essays toward the Release of Shakespeare's Will, by Joel Fineman

Looking Awry: An Introduction to Jacques Lacan through Popular Culture, by Slavoj Žižek

Cinema, Censorship, and the State: The Writings of Nagisa Oshima, by Nagisa Oshima

The Optical Unconscious, by Rosalind E. Krauss

Gesture and Speech, by André Leroi-Gourhan

Compulsive Beauty, by Hal Foster

Continuous Project Altered Daily: The Writings of Robert Morris, by Robert Morris

Read My Desire: Lacan against the Historicists, by Joan Copjec

Fast Cars, Clean Bodies: Decolonization and the Reordering of French Culture, by Kristin Ross

Kant after Duchamp, by Thierry de Duve

The Duchamp Effect, edited by Martha Buskirk and Mignon Nixon

The Return of the Real: The Avant-Garde at the End of the Century, by Hal Foster

October: The Second Decade, 1986–1996, edited by Rosalind E. Krauss, Annette Michelson, Yve-Alain Bois, Benjamin H. D. Buchloh, Hal Foster, Denis Hollier, and Silvia Kolbowski

Infinite Regress: Marcel Duchamp 1910–1941, by David Joselit

Caravaggio's Secrets, by Leo Bersani and Ulysse Dutoit

Scenes in a Library: Reading the Photograph in the Book, 1843–1875, by Carol Armstrong

Bachelors, by Rosalind E. Krauss

Neo-Avantgarde and Culture Industry: Essays on European and American Art from 1955 to 1975, by Benjamin H. D. Buchloh

Suspensions of Perception: Attention, Spectacle, and Modern Culture, by Jonathan Crary

Leave Any Information at the Signal: Writings, Interviews, Bits, Pages, by Ed Ruscha

Guy Debord and the Situationist International: Texts and Documents, edited by Tom McDonough

Random Order: Robert Rauschenberg and the Neo-Avant-Garde, by Branden W. Joseph

Decoys and Disruptions: Selected Writings, 1975–2001, by Martha Rosler

Prosthetic Gods, by Hal Foster

Fantastic Reality: Louise Bourgeois and a Story of Modern Art, by Mignon Nixon

Women Artists at the Millennium, edited by Carol Armstrong and Catherine de Zegher

"The Beautiful Language of My Century": Reinventing the Language of Contestation in Postwar France, 1945–1968, by Tom McDonough

The Artwork Caught by the Tail: Francis Picabia and Dada in Paris, by George Baker

Being Watched: Yvonne Rainer and the 1960s, by Carrie Lambert-Beatty

Robert Ryman: Used Paint, by Suzanne P. Hudson

Perpetual Inventory, by Rosalind E. Krauss

Perpetual Inventory

Rosalind E. Krauss

An OCTOBER Book

The MIT Press
Cambridge, Massachusetts
London, England

MIT Press books may be purchased at special quantity discounts for business or sales promotional use. For information, please email special_sales@mitpress.mit.edu or write to Special Sales Department, The MIT Press, 55 Hayward Street, Cambridge, MA 02142.

This book was set in Bembo by Graphic Composition, Inc. Printed and bound in the United States of America.

Library of Congress Cataloging-in-Publication Data

Krauss, Rosalind E.
Perpetual inventory / Rosalind E. Krauss.
p. cm.
"An October book."
Includes bibliographical references and index.
ISBN 978-0-262-01380-2 (hardcover : alk. paper)
1. Art, Modern—20th century. 2. Art, Modern—21st century. 3. Art criticism. I. Title.
N6490.K73 2010
709.04—dc22

2009028899

10 9 8 7 6 5 4 3 2 1

Contents

Acknowledgments

In 1973, recognizing the experience a practicing critic could bring to the campus, Dean Aaron Lemonick of Princeton University named me as director of their Visual Arts Program. It was in this context that I invited Richard Serra, Sol LeWitt, Mel Bochner, Robert Morris, Dorothea Rockburne, and Richard Tuttle to participate in the exhibition "Line as Language" by making works in situ at the Princeton Art Museum.

My practice as a critic of contemporary art had begun at *Artforum* in 1964 under the brilliant tutelage of Philip Leider, the magazine's editor-in-chief. The following year I joined the board of associate editors, until the beginning of the tenure of John Coplans in 1972. One of the first projects Coplans undertook was a tenth anniversary issue of the magazine, dedicated to Leider and intended as a retrospective of the magazine during his editorship. As such an overview, I wrote "A View of Modernism," meant to distance myself from the orthodoxy of Clement Greenberg and collected here under the rubric "Apostate."

Leider assigned me to review New York exhibitions, such as that of Donald Judd in 1966, and "The Cubist Epoch" in 1971 in Los Angeles. Coplans asked me to review Rauschenberg's 1974 exhibition, as well as Richard Serra's in 1972 and Paul Sharits's in 1973. Although my connection to *Artforum* was severed in 1976, when I resigned to found *October* magazine with Annette Michelson, it was resumed in 2007 when I published "The White Care of Our Canvas" under the new editor-in-chief, Tim Griffin.

The transition from Leider to Coplans was smooth at first, as witnessed by the anniversary issue's dedication to the former editor-in-chief. That it soon grew unmanageably stormy, leading to the near collapse of the magazine, is cannily recorded in the innovative oral history edited by Amy Newman, *Challenging Art: Artforum 1962–1974.* I am grateful for having been included in her project.

October has been a fulfilling experience, especially working with Annette Michelson and our editorial board: George Baker, Yve-Alain Bois, Benjamin H. D. Buchloh, Leah Dickerman, Hal Foster, Denis Hollier, Mignon Nixon, and Malcolm Turvey. I have benefited from their suggestions and criticism.

During his tenure as director of the Painting and Sculpture Department at the Museum of Modern Art, William Rubin was generously supportive of me, commissioning me to curate the Richard Serra exhibition in 1986 and asking me to present a paper at the symposium he organized to accompany his brilliant 1992 exhibition "Picasso and Braque." "The Motivation of the Sign" was collected among the papers from the symposium, as was the accompanying discussion, in a compilation edited by Lynn Zelevansky.

Roger Conover, my editor at the MIT Press, ventured into the rocky waters of the publishing world's disapproval of anthologies when he supported my *Originality of the Avant-Garde and Other Modernist Myths* (1986). For *Perpetual Inventory,* a sequel to that collection, he has shown the same welcome belief, for which my gratitude is immense.

To Adam Lehner, managing editor of *October,* who has dedicated time and attention to the book, my warmest thanks. *Perpetual Inventory* could not have been assembled without the perpetual care of Ryan Reineck, my research assistant at Columbia University and an intern at *October.* My greatest thanks to him.

Introduction

In a conversation with Barbara Rose, Robert Rauschenberg mused on the title for a future work. "I went in for my interview for this fantastic job," he said. "The job had a great name—I might use it for a painting—'Perpetual inventory.'"

During the years I wrote criticism for *Artforum* (1964–1976), I didn't think of it as a job; but nonetheless it had a great name: perpetual inventory. A critic constantly revises not only her conception of the direction and most important currents of contemporary art, but also her convictions about the most significant work within them. This entails a perpetual reassessment of the field she surveys and the demand that it be articulated in her writing.

The first collection of my inventory resulted in *The Originality of the Avant-Garde and Other Modernist Myths,* assembling essays that spanned the years 1976 to 1983. A second, *Bachelors,* performed a somewhat tongue-in-cheek collection of my essays on women artists—originally eight of them, but at the insistence of my editor at the MIT Press, Roger Conover, that there were in fact *nine* bachelors, a ninth was summoned into my introduction: Claude Cahun—another irony, because the bi-gendered French name Claude might mistakenly identify her as a male intruder.

Rauschenberg's own inventory was organized in files in his studio on Captiva Island, Florida. It primarily consisted of photographic illustrations, cut from newspapers and magazines and kept in reserve for the works he would later embark on, such as the *Dante's Inferno* series. Constructed entirely of image transfers, the works were made by saturating the illustrations with lighter fluid and then rubbing on them over drawing paper (Max Ernst's example of *frottage* comes to mind) so that the image plus the gesture of rubbing would leave a ghostly trace on the sheet below. This inventory was also the source for the photo-silkscreen paintings Rauschenberg had begun in the early 1960s, works that established his place within Leo Steinberg's important analysis "Other Criteria," in which the proliferation of images produced what Steinberg named a "shift from nature to culture" and called (in the first usage of this word) "postmodern." The writer's inventory requires a technical tool; mine was my constant companion, the typewriter. Whenever I look at the cover photograph for this collection, I think of Clement Greenberg's comment to me in 1974, "Spare me smart Jewish girls with their typewriters!"

By the late 1970s, two theoretical movements had begun to infiltrate my visual experience, with wide implications for my inventory. These were structuralism and its poststructural revision, both of which had already had an impact on my early essays, such as "Grids," "Notes on the Index," and "Sculpture in the Expanded Field." Poststructuralism's attack on self-identity (*le propre*) opened its reader to the influence of Georges Bataille in his work of dismantling form (by means of his destructive tool of the *informe*). Such a connection is explored in this volume in "Michel, Bataille et Moi," an essay on the work of Joan Miró as he absorbed the lessons of Bataille.

My connection to Rauschenberg's title has to do not only with the shift in and openness of my experience as a critic, but with the centrality of photography for the silkscreen works. Here I found myself, indeed, within the "postmodern condition," as Jean-François Lyotard called it—a situation I would come to name the "post-medium condition." Lyotard argues that *postmodernism* spells the end of what he terms the "master narrative," or the account of a broad sweep of history (such as the industrial revolution) in the light of a consistent worldview (such as utilitarianism) that shapes and interprets its meaning.

The master narrative of modern art turns on the importance of specific aesthetic mediums understood as simultaneously empowering artistic practice and leveraging the works' possibility of meaning. In charting the development of twentieth-century painting from cubism to abstraction to abstract expressionism, critics and historians follow Clement Greenberg who, in his essay "Modernist Painting," singled out *flatness* as the characteristic specific to painting because unshared by any of the other mediums, such as sculpture or drama.

This master narrative hit the wall of Lyotard's *Postmodern Condition* when certain aspects of artistic practice, such as conceptual art, jettisoned the use of a specific medium in order to juxtapose image and written text within the same work. The now-fashionable possibility of installation art followed in the wake of this dispatch of the medium. Installation is relentless in its refusal of specificity, filling galleries with mixtures of video images and taped narratives.

For the most part, *Perpetual Inventory* charts my conviction as a critic that the abandonment of the specific medium spells the death of serious art. To wrestle new mediums to the mat of specificity has been a preoccupation of mine since the inception of *October,* the magazine I founded in 1976 with Annette Michelson, the first issue of which carried my essay "Video and Narcissism" which attempts to tie the essence of video to the specular nature of mirrors. Photography is not a new medium, of course, but isolating its specificity in order to apply it to the understanding of its artistic practice led to my consideration of the index as the type of sign essential to camerawork.[1] The *index* proved its continuing analytic usefulness in my further treatment of Marcel Duchamp's work in *The Optical Unconscious.*

The onset of postmodernist practice in the 1980s saw the collapse of traditional mediums such as painting or sculpture. But the abandonment of the medium as the basis of artistic practice was not total. As a critic working in the 1980s and 1990s, I welcomed the perseverance of new artists in leveraging the meaning of their work in relation to what I came to call a "technical support." Mediums are specified by the material support they supply for artistic practice: the way canvas and stretcher support the images of traditional painting and plaster wall those of fresco, or the way metal armatures support the material of sculptural volume. The artists I observed persevering in the service of a medium had abandoned traditional supports in favor of strange new apparatuses, ones they often adopted from commercial culture—like Ed Ruscha's appropriation of the automobile ("'Specific' Objects," in this volume), Christian Marclay's importation of the movies' synchronous soundtrack ("Lip Sync," in this volume), William Kentridge's exploitation of cinematic animation ("The Rock," in this volume), or James Coleman's use of the commercial slide tape (now displaced by Power Point; see my essay ". . . And Then Turn Away?," *October* 81 [Summer 1977]). Calling such things "technical supports" would, I thought, allay the confusion of the use of "medium," too ideologically associated as the term is with an outmoded tradition.

The essays collected in *Perpetual Inventory* are for the most part concerned with the effort just sketched. If this effort works against the grain of the received ideas of contemporary criticism, I welcome this antagonism, which also characterized the work collected in *The Originality of the Avant-Garde and Other Modernist Myths.* I consider the "post-medium condition" a monstrous myth. If *Perpetual Inventory* can expose it by its example of an alternative, I will consider the book a success.

New York, 2008

I

The Post-medium Condition

The greatest challenge to a grasp of the art of the 1970s was the need to assemble the diverse threads of newly invented mediums (such as video, performance, body art, or the "dematerialization" of conceptual art) into coherent enterprises, related to one another by what could be understood as a common goal and a concerted projection of meaning. Video was certainly one of these, as was the proliferation of many new sculptural practices such as Bruce Nauman's video corridors or Richard Serra's use of the sheer weight of unattached lead plates. My efforts in this direction were tied to the founding and editing of *October* magazine in 1976. If Annette Michelson and I fled *Artforum,* where we were both advisory editors, it was because the new commitment of that magazine to art as social statement was increasingly hostile to the aesthetic concerns necessary to formulate the basis of formal coherence.

Video: The Aesthetics of Narcissism

It was a commonplace of criticism in the 1960s that a strict application of symmetry allowed a painter "to point to the center of the canvas" and, in so doing, to invoke the internal structure of the picture-object. Thus, "pointing to the center" was made to serve as one of the many blocks in that intricately constructed arch by which the criticism of the last decade sought to connect art to ethics through the "aesthetics of acknowledgement."[1] But what does it mean to point to the center of a TV screen?

In a way that is surely conditioned by the attitudes of pop art, artists' video is largely involved in parodying the critical terms of abstraction. Thus when Vito Acconci makes a videotape called *Centers* (1971), he realizes the critical notion of "pointing" by filming himself pointing to the center of a television monitor, a gesture he sustains for the twenty-minute running time of the work. The parodistic quality of Acconci's gesture, with its obvious debt to Duchampian irony, is clearly intended to disrupt and dispense with an entire critical tradition. It is meant to render nonsensical a critical engagement with the formal properties of a work, or indeed, a genre of works—such as "video." The kind of criticism *Centers* attacks is obviously one that takes seriously the formal qualities

First published as "Video and Narcissism," *October*, no. 1 (Spring 1976).

of a work, or tries to assay the particular logic of a given medium. And yet, by its very mise-en-scène, *Centers* typifies the structural characteristics of the video medium. For *Centers* was made by Acconci's using the video monitor as a mirror. As we look at the artist sighting along his outstretched arm and forefinger toward the center of the screen we are watching, what we see is a sustained tautology: a line of sight that begins at Acconci's plane of vision and ends at the eyes of his projected double. In that image of self-regard is configured a narcissism so endemic to works of video that I find myself wanting to generalize it as the condition of the entire genre. Yet what would it mean to say "The medium of video is narcissism"?[2]

For one thing, that remark tends to open up a rift between the nature of video and that of the other visual arts. The statement describes a psychological rather than a physical condition; and while we are accustomed to thinking of psychological states as the possible subject of works of art, we do not think of psychology as constituting their medium. Rather, the medium of painting, sculpture, or film has much more to do with the objective, material factors specific to a particular form: pigment-bearing surfaces; matter extended through space; light projected through a moving strip of celluloid. That is, the notion of a medium contains the concept of an object-state, separate from the artist's own being, through which his intentions must pass.

Video depends—in order for anything to be experienced at all—on a set of physical mechanisms. So perhaps it would be easiest to say that this apparatus—both at its present and future levels of technology—comprises the television medium, and leave it at that. Yet with the subject of video, the ease of defining it in terms of its machinery does not seem compatible with accuracy; and my own experience of video keeps urging me toward the psychological model.

Everyday speech contains an example of the word "medium" used in a psychological sense; the uncommon terrain for that common-enough usage is the world of parapsychology: telepathy, extrasensory perception, and communication with an afterlife, for which people with certain kinds of psychic powers are understood to be mediums. Whether or not we give credence to the claims of mediumistic experience, we understand the referents for the language that

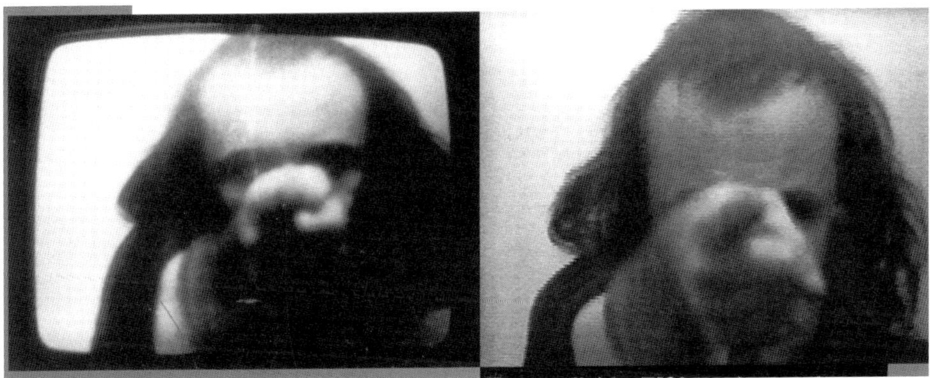

1.1 Vito Acconci, *Centers,* 1971. Courtesy the artist.

describes it. We know, for instance, that configured within the parapsychological sense of the word "medium" is the image of a human receiver (and sender) of communications arising from an invisible source. Further, this term contains the notion that the human conduit exists in a particular relation to the message, which is one of temporal concurrence. Thus, when Freud lectured on the phenomenon of telepathic dreams, he told his audience that the fact insisted upon by reports of such matters is that the dreams occur at the same time as the actual (but invariably distant) event.

Now these are the two features of the everyday use of medium that are suggestive for a discussion of video: the simultaneous reception and projection of an image; and the human psyche used as a conduit. Most of the work produced over the very short span of video art's existence has used the human body as its central instrument. In the case of work on tape, this conduit has most often been the body of the artist-practitioner. In the case of video installations, it has usually been the body of the responding viewer. And no matter whose body has been selected for the occasion, there is a further condition that is always present. Unlike the other visual arts, video is capable of recording and transmitting at the same time—producing instant feedback. The body is therefore centered, as it were, between two machines that are the opening and closing of a parenthesis. The first of these is the camera; the second is the monitor, which reprojects the performer's image with the immediacy of a mirror.

The effects of this centering are multiple. And nowhere are they more clearly named than in a tape made by Richard Serra, with the help of Nancy Holt, who made herself its willing and eloquent subject. The tape is called *Boomerang* (1974), and its situation is a recording studio in which Holt sits in a tightly framed close-up, a technician's headset on her ears. As Holt begins to talk, her words are fed back to her through the earphones she wears. Because the apparatus is attached to a recording instrument, there is a slight delay (of less than a second) between her actual locution and the audio feedback to which she is forced to listen. For the ten minutes of the tape, Holt describes her situation. She speaks of the way the feedback interferes with her normal thought process and of the confusion caused by the lack of synchronism between her speech and what she hears of it. "Sometimes," she says, "I find I can't quite say a word because I hear a first part come back and I forget the second part, or my head is stimulated in a new direction by the first half of the word." As we hear Holt speak and intuit that delayed voice echoing in her ears, we are witness to an extraordinary image of distraction. Because the audio delay keeps hypostatizing her words, she has great difficulty coinciding with herself as a subject. It is a situation, she says, that "puts a distance between the words and their apprehension—their comprehension," a situation that is "like a mirror reflection . . . so that I am surrounded by me and my mind surrounds me . . . there is no escape."

The prison Holt both describes and enacts, from which there is no escape, could be called the prison of a collapsed present, that is, a present time which is completely severed from a sense of its own past. We get some feeling for what it is like to be stuck in that present when Holt at one point says, "I'm throwing things out in the world and they are boomeranging back . . . boomeranging . . . eran-ging-ing . . . an-ginging." Through that distracted reverberation of a single word—and even word fragment—there forms an image of what it is like to be totally cut off from history, even, in this case, the immediate history of the sentence one has just spoken. Another word for that history from which Holt feels herself to be disconnected is "text."

Most conventional performers are of course enacting or interpreting a text, whether that is a fixed choreography, a written script, a musical score, or a sketchy set of notes around which to improvise. By the very fact of that relationship, the performance ties itself to something that existed before the given moment. Most immediately, this sense of something having come before refers to the specific text for the performance at hand. But in a larger way it evokes the more general historical relationship between a specific text and the history constructed by all the texts of a given genre. Independent of the gesture made within the present, this larger history is the source of meaning for that gesture. What Holt is describing in *Boomerang* is a situation in which the action of the mirror reflection (which is auditory in this case) severs her from a sense of text:

from the prior words she has spoken; from the way language connects her both to her own past and to a world of objects. What she comes to is a space where, as she says, "I am surrounded by me."

Self-encapsulation—the body or psyche as its own surround—is everywhere to be found in the corpus of video art. Acconci's *Centers* is one instance; another is his *Air Time* of 1973. In *Air Time* Acconci sits between the video camera and a large mirror which he faces. For thirty-five minutes he addresses his own reflection with a monologue in which the terms "I" and "you"—although they are presumed to be referring to himself and an absent lover—are markers of the autistic intercourse between Acconci and his own image. Both *Centers* and *Air Time* construct a situation of spatial closure, promoting a condition of self-reflection. The response of the performer is to a continually renewed image of himself. This image, supplanting the consciousness of anything prior to it, becomes the unchanging text of the performer. Skewered on his own reflection, he is committed to the text of perpetuating that image. So the temporal concomitant of this situation is, like the echo effect of *Boomerang,* the sense of a collapsed present.

Bruce Nauman's tapes are another example of the double effect of the performance-for-the-monitor. In *Revolving Upside Down* (1968), Nauman films himself through a camera that has been rotated so that the floor on which he stands is at the top of the screen. For sixty very long minutes, Nauman slowly moves, turning on one foot, from the depths of his studio forward toward the monitor and then back again, repeating this activity until the tape runs out. In Lynda Benglis's *Now* (1973), there is a similar leveling out of the effects of temporality. The tape is of Benglis's head in profile, performing against the backdrop of a large monitor that is replaying an earlier tape of herself doing the same actions, but reversed left and right. The two profiles, one "live," the other taped, move in mirrored synchrony with one another. As they do, Benglis's two profiles perform an autoerotic coupling, which, because it is being recorded, becomes the potential background for another generation of the same activity.

1.2 (*facing page*) Vito Acconci, *Air Time,* 1973. Courtesy the artist.

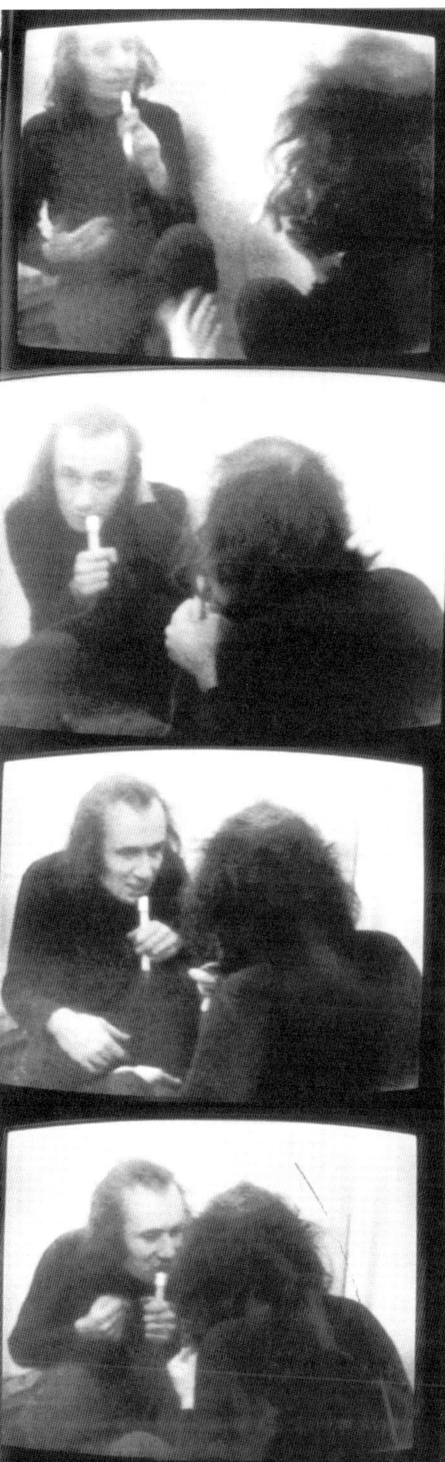

Through this spiral of infinite regress, as the face merges with the double and triple reprojections of itself merging with itself, Benglis's voice is heard either issuing the command "Now!" or asking "Is it now?" Clearly, Benglis is using the word "now" to underline the ambiguity of temporal reference: we realize we do not know whether the sound of the voice is coming from the live or the taped source, and if from the latter, from which level of taping. We also realize that because of the activity of replaying the past generations, all layers of the "now" are equally present.

But what is far more arresting in *Now* than the technological banality of the question "Which 'now' is intended?" is the way the tape enacts a collapsed present time. In that insistence it connects itself to the tapes by Nauman and Acconci already described, and ultimately to *Boomerang*. In all these examples the nature of video performance is specified as an activity of bracketing out the text and substituting for it the mirror reflection. The result of this substitution is the presentation of a self understood to have no past, and as well, no connection with any objects that are external to it. For the double that appears on the monitor cannot be called a true external object. Rather, it is a displacement of the self that has the effect—as Holt's voice has in *Boomerang*—of transforming the performer's subjectivity into another, mirror, object.

It is at this point that one might want to go back to the proposition with which this argument began, and raise a particular objection. Even if it is agreed, one might ask, that the medium of video art is the psychological condition of the self split and doubled by the mirror reflection of synchronous feedback, how does that entail a "rift" between video and the other arts? Isn't it rather a case of video's using a new technique to achieve continuity with the modernist ambitions of the rest of the visual media? Specifically, isn't the mirror reflection a variant on the reflexive mode in which contemporary painting, sculpture, and film have successively expressed themselves? Implicit in this question is the idea that autoreflection and self-reflexiveness refer to the same thing; that both are cases of consciousness doubling back upon itself in order to perform and portray a separation between forms of art and their contents, between the procedures of thought and their objects.[3] In its simplest form, this question would be the following: Aside from their divergent technologies, what is the difference, really, between Vito Acconci's *Centers* and Frank Stella's *Gran Cairo* (1962)?

Answer: The difference is total. Reflection, when it is a case of mirroring, is a move toward an external symmetry (screen and actor); while reflexiveness is a strategy to achieve a radical asymmetry, from within. *Gran Cairo* organizes a concentric nest of square stripes, each stripe the shape and width of the canvas stretcher on which the image is painted. As the squares diminish, they converge at the picture's center; and in this way, they "point" to it. Pointing to the center of the canvas distinguishes between the painting as a physical object (bounded by its framing edge) and the painting as a visual field (opening laterally from its fixed center).

Mirror reflection implies the vanquishing of separateness. Its inherent movement is toward fusion. The self and its reflected image are of course literally separate. But the agency of reflection is a mode of appropriation, of an illusionistic erasure of the difference between subject and object. Facing mirrors on opposite walls squeeze out the real space between them. When we look at *Centers,* we see Acconci sighting along his arm to the center of the screen we are watching. But latent in this setup is the monitor that he is, himself, regarding. There is no way for us to see *Centers* without reading that sustained connection between the artist and his double. So for us, as for Acconci, video is a process which allows these two terms to fuse.

One could say that if the reflexiveness of modernist art is a *dédoublement* or doubling back in order to locate the object (and thus the objective conditions of one's experience), the mirror reflection of absolute feedback is a process of bracketing out the object. This is why it seems inappropriate to speak of a physical medium in relation to video; for the object (the electronic equipment and its capabilities) has become merely an appurtenance. And instead, video's real medium is a psychological situation, the very terms of which are to withdraw attention from an external object—an Other—and invest it in the Self. Therefore, it is not just any psychological condition one is speaking of. Rather it is the condition of someone who has, in Freud's words, "abandoned the investment of objects with libido and transformed object-libido into ego-libido."[4] And that is the specific condition of narcissism.

By making this connection, then, one can recast the opposition between the reflective and the reflexive into the terms of the psychoanalytic project. Because it is there, too, in the drama of the couched subject, that the narcissistic reprojection of a frozen self is pitted against the analytic (or reflexive) mode.[5] One finds a particularly useful description of that struggle in the writing of Jacques Lacan. In *The Language of the Self,* Lacan begins by characterizing the space of the therapeutic transaction as an extraordinary void created by the silence of the analyst. Into this void the patient projects the monologue of his own recitation, which Lacan calls "the monumental construct of his narcissism." Using this monologue to explain himself and his situation to his silent listener, the patient begins to experience a very deep frustration. And this frustration, Lacan charges, although it is initially thought to be provoked by the maddening silence of the analyst, is eventually discovered to have another source:

> Is it not rather a matter of a frustration inherent in the very discourse of the subject? Does the subject not become engaged in an ever-growing dispossession of that being of his, concerning which—by dint of sincere portraits which leave its idea no less incoherent, of rectifications which do not succeed in freeing its essence, of stays and defenses which do not prevent his statue from tottering, of narcissistic embraces which become like a puff of air in animating it—he ends up by recognizing that this being has never been anything more than his construct in the Imaginary and that this construct disappoints all his certitudes? For in this labor which he undertakes to reconstruct this construct for another, he finds again the fundamental alienation which made him construct it like another one, and which has always destined it to be stripped from him by another.[6]

What the patient comes to see is that this "self" of his is a projected object, and that his frustration is due to his own capture by this object with which he can never really coincide. Further, this "statue" which he has made and in which he believes is the basis for his "static state," for the constantly "renewed status of his alienation." Narcissism is characterized, then, as the unchanging condition of a perpetual frustration.[7]

The process of analysis is one of breaking the hold of this fascination with the mirror; and in order to do so, the patient comes to see the distinction between his lived subjectivity and the fantasy projections of himself as object. "In order for us to come back to a more dialectical view of the analytic experience," Lacan writes, "I would say that the analysis consists precisely in distinguishing the person lying on the analyst's couch from the person who is speaking. With the person listening [the analyst], that makes three persons present in the analytical situation, among whom it is the rule that the question . . . be put: Where is the *moi* of the subject?"[8] The analytic project is then one in which the patient disengages from the "statue" of his reflected self, and through a method of reflexiveness, rediscovers the real time of his own history. He exchanges the atemporality of repetition for the temporality of change.

If psychoanalysis understands that the patient is engaged in a recovery of his being in terms of its real history, modernism has understood that the artist locates his own expressiveness through a discovery of the objective conditions of his medium and their history. That is, the very possibilities of finding his subjectivity necessitate that the artist recognize the material and historical independence of an external object (or medium).

In distinction to this, the feedback coil of video seems to be the instrument of a double repression: for through it, consciousness of temporality and of separation between subject and object are simultaneously evacuated. The result of this repression is, for the maker and the viewer of most video art, a kind of weightless fall through the suspended space of narcissism.

There are, of course, a complex set of answers to the question of why video has attracted a growing set of practitioners and collectors. These answers would involve an analysis of everything from the problem of narcissism within the wider context of our culture, to the specific inner workings of the present art market. Although I would like to postpone that analysis for a future essay, I do wish to make one connection here: and that is the connection between the institution of a self formed by video feedback and the real situation that exists in the art world from which the makers of video come. In the last fifteen years that world has been deeply and disastrously affected by its relation to mass media. That an artist's work be published, reproduced, and disseminated through the media has become, for the generation that has matured in the course of the last decade, virtually the only means of verifying its existence as art. The demand for instant replay in the media—in fact the creation of work that literally does not exist outside of that replay, as is true of conceptual art and its nether side, body art—finds its obvious correlative in an aesthetic mode by which the self is created through the electronic device of feedback.

There exist, however, three phenomena within the corpus of video art that run counter to what I have been saying so far, or at least are somewhat tangential to it. They are (1) tapes that exploit the medium in order to criticize it from within; (2) tapes that represent a physical assault on the video mechanism in order to break out of its psychological hold; and (3) installation forms of video that use the medium as a subspecies of painting or sculpture. The first is represented by Richard Serra's *Boomerang.* The second can be exemplified by Joan Jonas's *Vertical Roll* (1972). And the third is limited to certain of the installation works of Bruce Nauman and Peter Campus, particularly Campus's two companion pieces *mem* and *dor* (1974).

I have already described how narcissism is enacted in *Boomerang.* But what separates it from, say, Benglis's *Now* is the critical distance it maintains on its own subject. This is primarily due to the fact that Serra employs audio rather than visual feedback. As a result, the angle of vision we take on the subject does not coincide with the closed circuit of Holt's situation, but looks onto it from outside. Further, the narcissistic condition is given through the cerebrated form of language, which opens simultaneously onto the plane of expression and the plane of critical reflexiveness. Significantly, Serra's separation from the subject of *Boomerang,* his position outside it, promotes an attitude toward time that is different from that of many other video works. The tape's brevity—it is ten minutes long—is itself related to discourse: to how long it takes to shape and develop an argument; and how long it takes for its receiver to get the "point."

Latent within the opening situation of *Boomerang* is its own conclusion; when that is reached, it stops.

Vertical Roll is another case where time has been forced to enter the video situation, and where that time is understood as a propulsion toward an end. In this work, access to a sense of time has come from fouling the stability of the projected image by desynchronizing the frequencies of the signals on camera and monitor. The rhythmic roll of the image, as the bottom of its frame scans upward to hit the top of the screen, causes a sense of decomposition that seems to work against the grain of those 525 lines of which the video raster is made. Because one recognizes it as intended, the vertical roll appears as the agency of a will that runs counter to an electronically stabilized condition. Through the effect of its constant wiping away of the image, one has a sense of a reflexive relation to the video grid and the ground or support for what happens to the image.

Out of this is born the subject of *Vertical Roll,* which visualizes time as the course of a continuous dissolve through space. In it a sequence of images and actions are seen from different positions—both in terms of the camera's distance and its orientation to a horizontal ground. With the ordinary grammar of both film and video, these shifts would have to be registered either by camera movement (in which the zoom is included as one possibility) or by cutting. And while it is true that Jonas has had to use these techniques in making *Vertical Roll,* the constant sweep of the image renders these movements invisible. That is, the grammar of the camera is eroded by the dislocating grip of the roll. As I have said, the illusion this creates is one of a continuous dissolve through time and space. The monitor, as an instrument, seems to be winding a ribbon of experience into itself, like a fishing line being taken up upon a reel, or like magnetic tape being wound upon a spool. The motion of continuous dissolve becomes, then, a metaphor for the physical reality not only of the scan lines of the video raster but of the tape deck itself, whose reels objectify a finite amount of time.

Earlier, I described the paradigmatic situation of video as a body centered in the parenthesis between camera and monitor. Due to *Vertical Roll*'s visual reference through the monitor's action to the physical reality of the tape, one side of this parenthesis is made more active than the other. The monitor side of the double bracket becomes a reel through which one feels prefigured the imminence of a goal or terminus for the motion. That end is reached when Jonas, who has been performing the actions recorded on the tape, from within the coils of the camera/monitor circuit, breaks through the parenthetical closure of the feedback situation to face the camera directly—without the agency of the monitor's rolling image.

If it is the paired movement of the video scan and the tape reel that is isolated as a physical object in *Vertical Roll,* it is the stasis of the wall plane that is objectified in Campus's *mem* and *dor.* In both of the Campus works there is a triangular relationship created between (1) a video camera, (2) an instrument that will project the live camera image onto the surface of a wall (at life- and over-life-size), and (3) the wall itself. The viewer's experience of the two works is the sum of the cumulative positions his body assumes within the vectors formed by these three elements. When he stands outside the triangular field of the works, the viewer sees nothing but the large, luminous plane of one of the walls in a darkened room. Only when he moves into the range of the camera is he able to realize an image (his own) projected onto the wall's pictorial field. However, the conditions of seeing that image are rather special in both *mem* and *dor.*

In the latter, the camera is placed in the hallway leading to the room that contains the projector. Inside the room, the viewer is out of the range of the camera, and therefore nothing appears on the wall surface. It is only as he leaves the room, or rather is poised at the threshold of the doorway, that he is both illumined enough and far enough into the focal range of the camera to register as an image. Since that image projects onto the very wall through which the doorway leads, the viewer's relation to his own image must be totally peripheral; he is himself in a plane that is not only parallel to the plane of the illusion, but continuous with it. His body is therefore both the substance of the image and, as well, the slightly displaced substance of the plane onto which the image is projected.

In *mem,* both camera and projector are to one side of the wall plane, stationed in such a way that the range of the camera encompasses a very thin corridor-like slice of space that is parallel to, and almost fused with, the illumined wall. Due to this, the viewer must practically be up against the wall in order to register. As he moves far enough away from the wall in order to be able to see himself, the image blurs and distorts, but if he moves near enough to place himself in focus, he has formed such closure with the support for the image that he cannot really see it. Therefore in *mem,* as in *dor,* the body of the viewer becomes physically identified with the wall plane as the "place" of the image.

There is a sense in which we could say that these two works by Campus simply take the live feedback of camera and monitor, which existed for the video artist while taping in his studio, and recreate it for the ordinary visitor to a gallery. However, *mem* and *dor* are not that simple. Built into their situation are two kinds of invisibility: the viewer's presence to the wall in which he is himself an absence; and his relative absence from a view of the wall which becomes the condition for his projected presence upon its surface.

Campus's pieces acknowledge the very powerful narcissism that propels the viewer of these works forward and backward in front of the muralized field. And, through the movement of his own body, his neck craning and head turning, the viewer is forced to recognize this motive as well. But the condition of these works is to acknowledge as separate the two surfaces on which the image is held—the one the viewer's body, the other the wall—and to make them register as absolutely distinct. It is in this distinction that the wall surface—the "pictorial" surface—is understood as an absolute Other, as part of the world of objects external to the self. Further, the works specify that the mode of projecting oneself onto that surface entails recognizing all the ways that one does not coincide with it.

There is, of course, a history of the art of the last fifteen years into which works like *mem* and *dor* insert themselves, although it is one about which little has been written. That history involves the activities of certain artists who have made work that conflates psychologistic and formal means to achieve very particular ends. The art of Robert Rauschenberg is a case in point. His work, in bringing together groupings of real objects and found images and suspending them within the static matrix of a pictorial field, attempts to convert that field into something we could call the plane of memory. In so doing, the static pictorial field is both psychologized and temporally distended. I have argued elsewhere[9] that the impulse behind this move arose from questions that have to do with commodity fetishism. Rauschenberg, among many other artists, has been working against a situation in which painting and sculpture have been absorbed within a luxury market—absorbed so totally that their content has been deeply conditioned by their status as fetish prizes to be collected, and thereby consumed. In response, Rauschenberg's art asserts another, alternative, relationship between the work of art and its viewer. And to do this Rauschenberg has had recourse to the value of time: to the time it takes to read a text or a painting, to rehearse the activity of cognitive differentiation that that entails, to get its point. That is, he wishes to pit the temporal values of consciousness against the stasis of the commodity fetish.

Although responsive to the same considerations, the temporal values that were built into the minimalist sculpture of the 1960s were primarily engaged with questions of perception. The viewer was therefore involved in a temporal decoding of aspects of scale, placement, or shape—issues that are inherently more abstract than, say, the contents of memory. Pure, as opposed to applied psychology, we might say. But in the work of certain younger sculptors, Joel Shapiro for example, the issues of minimalism are being inserted into a space that, like Rauschenberg's pictorial field, defines itself as mnemonic. So that physical distance from a sculptural object is understood as being indistinguishable from temporal remove.

It is to this body of work that I would want to add Campus's art. For him, the narcissistic enclosure inherent in the video medium becomes part of a psychologistic strategy by which he is able to examine the general conditions of pictorialism in relation to its viewers. It can, that is, critically account for narcissism as a form of bracketing out the world and its conditions, at the same time as it can reassert the facticity of the object against the grain of the narcissistic drive toward projection.

II

Medium

Marshall McLuhan electrified cultural discourse with his 1964 pronouncement "The medium is the message," which shifted the discussion from aesthetic mediums to electronic media (in *Understanding Media: The Extensions of Man*). As a critic, I could not give up the idea of the medium as a continuing source of meaning; so in my own mind I converted McLuhan's slogan to "The medium is the memory." The essays in this part of the collection bear on this issue.

Fat Chance

Joan Simon opened her interview with Bruce Nauman—"Breaking the Silence"—by commenting on the range of mediums with which he had worked, in response to which Nauman said:

> In the '60s you didn't have to pick just one medium. There didn't seem to be any problem with using different kinds of materials—shifting from photographs to dance to performance to videotapes. It seemed very straightforward to use all those different ways of expressing ideas or presenting material. You could make neon signs, you could make written pieces, you could make jokes about parts of the body or casting things, or whatever.[1]

The discursive space of 1960s art was marked by the term "pluralism," an acceptance not only of many different mediums in operation at any given historical moment—as postminimalism expanded the palette of sculpture to include painting, performance, dance, and video—but, as well, of many different mediums cohabitating within the procedures of a single artist: we could think of the range of Robert Morris's palette, which included plywood, stone, felt, bronze, and mirrors.

Written June 2004; published for the first time in this volume.

As is clear from Nauman's remark, he was also committed to pluralism, not only in practice but as a point of pride. Yet I will be arguing that despite himself, Nauman's work explored the specificity of the various mediums—or technical supports—he adopted. From his corridors to his use of video, we see him engaging with the ontological question, that is, the essence—or what Roland Barthes would call the *genius*—of the material with which the artist worked.[2] Because this is also true of his 2001 video installation *Mapping the Studio,* I would like to explore that work a bit more here.

To get permission to contradict Nauman's own statements on this matter of medium, I need to take a short detour away from Nauman's practice and comment on the refusal by critics like myself to entertain the very possibility of pluralism. Basically, the argument went that history was not as permissive as it might seem and that not all options were open to any given individual at any one time. This was essentially a structuralist argument, and as such it insisted that possible practices were only a function of the history and structural logic of a given form.

If we take sculpture as an example, the argument began by looking for the structural principles of the medium. These it found (and here I am referring to my own analysis "Sculpture in the Expanded Field")[3] in the logic of the *monument* because, from its beginning, sculpture had functioned within the ritual form of marking the site of important burials, or ceremonial axes, or liturgical byways. The monument, I argued, operates by placing a representation atop a relevant site, either architectural (as in the case of the Vatican staircase for Bernini's *Conversion of Constantine*) or open-air (as in the courtyard of Rome's Campidoglio for the equestrian portrait of the emperor Marcus Aurelius in front of the Roman Senate). The hinge between the actuality of the site and the virtual condition of the representation is, of course, the pedestal of the work, which simultaneously ties the representation to its place and detaches it from its merely material condition.

If you have a structuralist turn of mind—which at the time I certainly did—the monument strikes you as a double negative—a combination of its material givens in their neutralized dimension, which is to say not-architecture

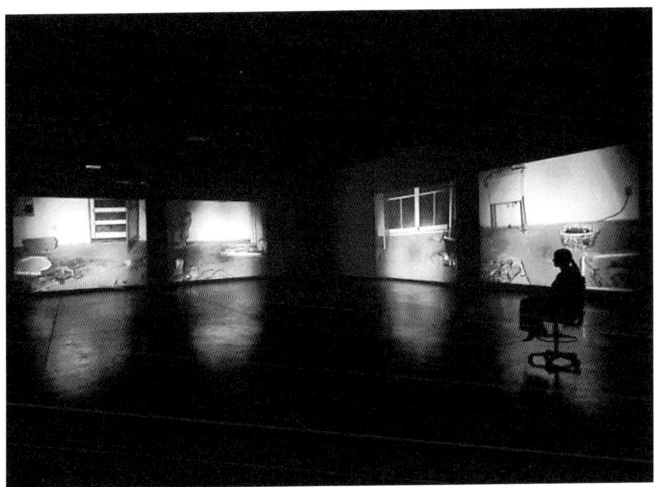

2.1 Bruce Nauman, *Mapping the Studio I (Fat Chance John Cage)*, 2001. Installation at Dia: Beacon, Beacon, New York. Lannan Foundation; long-term loan. Photo: Stuart Tyson. © 2009 Bruce Nauman/Artists Rights Society (ARS), New York.

plus not-landscape (the neither/nor of the virtual image). That neither/nor is the expansion in mirror form of the positive condition of the absolute binary that defines the field at large: that is, architecture versus landscape. This formation, called a Klein Group, is used by structuralists to move from the limited operations of a binary opposition (for example, *stop/go*) to the socially more supple possibilities of a quatenary or fourfold field (which, in this example, includes *caution*). The positive form of the opposition is located on what is called the complex axis, while the negative form defines the neutral axis. Two more combinations are possible within the quatenary—in this case, the combination of architecture and not-architecture plus landscape and not-landscape.

Part of the pleasure I derived from writing "Sculpture in the Expanded Field" came from illustrating that the apparent anything-goes pluralism of the 1960s exfoliation of sculpture into earthworks, performance, and institutional critique was in fact limited by the positions made possible by the fourfold structure itself and that the individual options available to any practitioner were likewise delimited. To take just a few examples, we might think of Smithson's *Buried Woodshed* as the complex axis's marriage of architecture and landscape; while any earthwork (here we might think of Heizer's *Double Negative*) would exemplify landscape plus not-landscape; the architecture plus not-architecture phenomenon was explored by artists such as Robert Irwin and Michael Asher; and the neutral axis's combination (neither/nor) gave rise to works such as Robert Morris's *Observatory.*

To return to Nauman, it is clear that the site for his expanded field throughout the sixties was his studio and, within that space, the endlessness of his pursuit of an idea for making a work. The pacing, the toe tapping, the finger strumming—all this activity of marking time characterizes the artist stalking his breakthrough. At some point Nauman decided to document this procedure, and what resulted were the videos *Beckett Walk* (1968), *Bouncing in the Corner* (1969), and *Walk with Contrapposto* (1968). The video corridors were the next extrapolation, which, as we might expect from the Klein Group, occupy the position architecture plus not-architecture.

Within the development of modern architecture, one of the problems posed by buildings with larger and larger scales was that of circulation: how to move ever greater numbers of people through the taller and longer spaces of skyscrapers and shopping malls while making such trajectories pleasantly habitable and not disorienting to those milling crowds. Gradually, architects made circulation itself into an autonomous form—we have only to think of Frank Lloyd Wright's solution at the Guggenheim Museum, where the spiral ramp as pure circulation is also the space of exhibition. The advantage of combining these two is the phenomenological payoff that, from the moment one moves onto the ramp, one can see the end point of the trajectory, so that circulation and its goal are combined with brilliant efficiency. All the ramps and spiral staircases of modernist architecture—as in the work of Le Corbusier—have this drive behind them, and the term used to mark the autonomously conceived axis of circulation was the designation "promenade." Promenade, made autonomous, emerged as a marker of the specificity of architecture itself.

Nauman's pacing within his studio was, of course, a form of promenade. The corridors he devised to mark this activity were thus continuous with the most modernist and highest forms of architecture. But with the video monitors added to them, they descended from the heights of promenade to the depths of surveillance—becoming the not-architecture of the merely anonymous hallways of office buildings or apartment complexes, within which televisual security measures are on constant alert.

By 1986 in Nauman's *Violent Incident,* the bank of monitors, through which the viewer oversees the onset and development of an altercation between two characters who eventually shoot one another, switches one's perspective from being the object monitored to the subject of surveillance. And with this switch, Nauman seems to have entered the uncertain terrain of locating the specificity of video as a medium.

It is possible, of course, to see video itself as the great destroyer of the very idea of medium specificity. For, with the introduction of the Portapak into the studios of artists of the early 1960s, video was understood as being no more engaged with the purity of the medium than a typewriter or a tape recorder; rather, it was seen as a recording device merely turned onto the activities within the studio itself. Its simplicity and economy stood as a rebuke to the expense and hard labor of American independent film through which artists like Hollis

Frampton, Michael Snow, and Paul Sharits were working to establish the specificity of the cinematic medium.[4]

Thus, not only did video itself have no specificity as an aesthetic support, but it seemed to void the whole modernist project of keying the meaning of a work of art to the revelation of the specific nature of its medium. This conceptual lacuna attracted attention during the 1960s and 1970s as critics and theorists took up the problem of video's elusive essence.

Fredric Jameson's response was to deal video into the dominant aesthetic form of late capital, which for him was, as we know, postmodernism. Adopting Raymond Williams's description of television as "total flow," Jameson was intent on characterizing the internal workings and structures of such continuous but uninflected sensory stimulation, a continuousness most theorists simply reduced to "boredom."[5] But postmodernism, Jameson retorts, is not boring. Rather, it is the stimulus of a constant sampling of tiny quotations, each of which bears with it the signal of a narrative as a kind of emblem or logo—the silent monolith in the landscape, for example, bringing with it in a flash the whole unfolding of *2001.* Postmodernism is a collage of such citational fragments, each become a signifier without any referent in the field of the Real. If video is the exemplary medium of postmodernism, Jameson concludes, it is because it has the capacity to stage such ceaseless reshuffling of the fragments of preexistent texts.

For Stanley Cavell the essence of television can also be found in the idea of "total flow," which he recodes as "a current of simultaneous event reception."[6] Such a current, he argues, is not perceived through what we ordinarily understand as viewing, but rather through the more passive activity of monitoring. It is surveillance, then, that essentializes television as the technical support of video. Nauman's activity in video has consistently developed within the terms of this argument, although I am sure it is not an argument with which he is familiar. I would say instead that he was instinctively attracted to the surveillance monitors, and this is why he used them consistently in his video corridors and finally in the work that concerns me here, *Mapping the Studio.* Before moving to the analysis of this extraordinary object, however, I'd like to review yet another theorization of the essence of video.

This is Sam Weber's brilliant essay "Television, Set, and Screen," which opens onto the question of ontology, or essence, by refusing it on the grounds that one must always respect what he calls "television's constitutive heterogeneity."[7] Television's defining condition, he argues, is difference. It is different from film, as well as being different from what is generally known as perception. "Above all," he concludes, "television differs from itself." This is because within the phenomenon signaled by the singular noun "television," there are secreted three different operations: production, transmission, and reception. If broadcast television means seeing at a distance, it can also be said to transport vision itself, placing it directly before the viewer. But no single body can perceive this vision, because it takes place, Weber argues, in three different places at once: the place of recording; the place of reception; and the place of transmission. To watch television, then, is to watch the invisible separation of the visual datum—split between its three places of habitation; and what the television screen does is to take this invisible separation and turn it into a gestalt. Carrying this idea of television's self-differing nature even further, Weber focuses on television's capacity for instant replay as a perceptual phenomenon in which original and copy are both indistinguishable and radically ambiguous. Weber's conclusion is that television has to be characterized through the term "differential specificity," which, though it sounds like a paradox, is necessary in order to respect the complexity of this form.

Mapping the Studio continues Nauman's investigations of video as a form of monitoring, as seven cameras mounted within his studio continuously recorded the invasion of the space by a horde of mice, itself repulsed from time to time by Nauman's cat. The mice, a shade of gray indistinguishable from the concrete floor, seem to explode into our field of vision by being perceptible only through their motion, that is, by becoming little furry blurs within the darkness. Barely visible, then, they are the support for a vision that is itself split between its site of recording and its site of reception, and the projection screen is precisely the field on which this invisible separation surfaces as gestalt.

LeWitt's Ark

It is appropriate to think of Sol LeWitt as a latter-day Noah, rounding up that half of the pictorial arts the Renaissance called *disegno* to distinguish its concentration on line from the other half—*colore*—the representation of atmosphere and rich texture. The flood from which Noah saved the travelers on his Ark was, indeed, concerted to wash away that linear half of pictorial expression, as so-called color field painting attacked linear contour's traditional hiving off spills of color by dissolving these cells into unbroken, lateral spreads of chroma.

LeWitt's commitment to line was not so much a matter of contour's compartmentalization of a flat field. Rather, it was an investment in that half of the twentieth century's practice of drawing which Benjamin Buchloh calls "matrix," to distinguish it from gesture. While gesture registers the artist's bodily and psychosexual energy, matrix is far less emotive; its intellecto-conceptual approach is to the object rather than the subject of the linear field—whether canvas, paper, or plaster wall. The ordinary grid is such a matrix, or any set of directions for linear inscription (such as LeWitt's "Ten thousand lines one inch long evenly spaced on six walls each of differing area") that is then scrupulously and repetitively executed. The evocative beauty LeWitt wrested from these exiguous means earned him the gratitude of many artists, whose work would not

First published in *October*, no. 121 (Summer 2007).

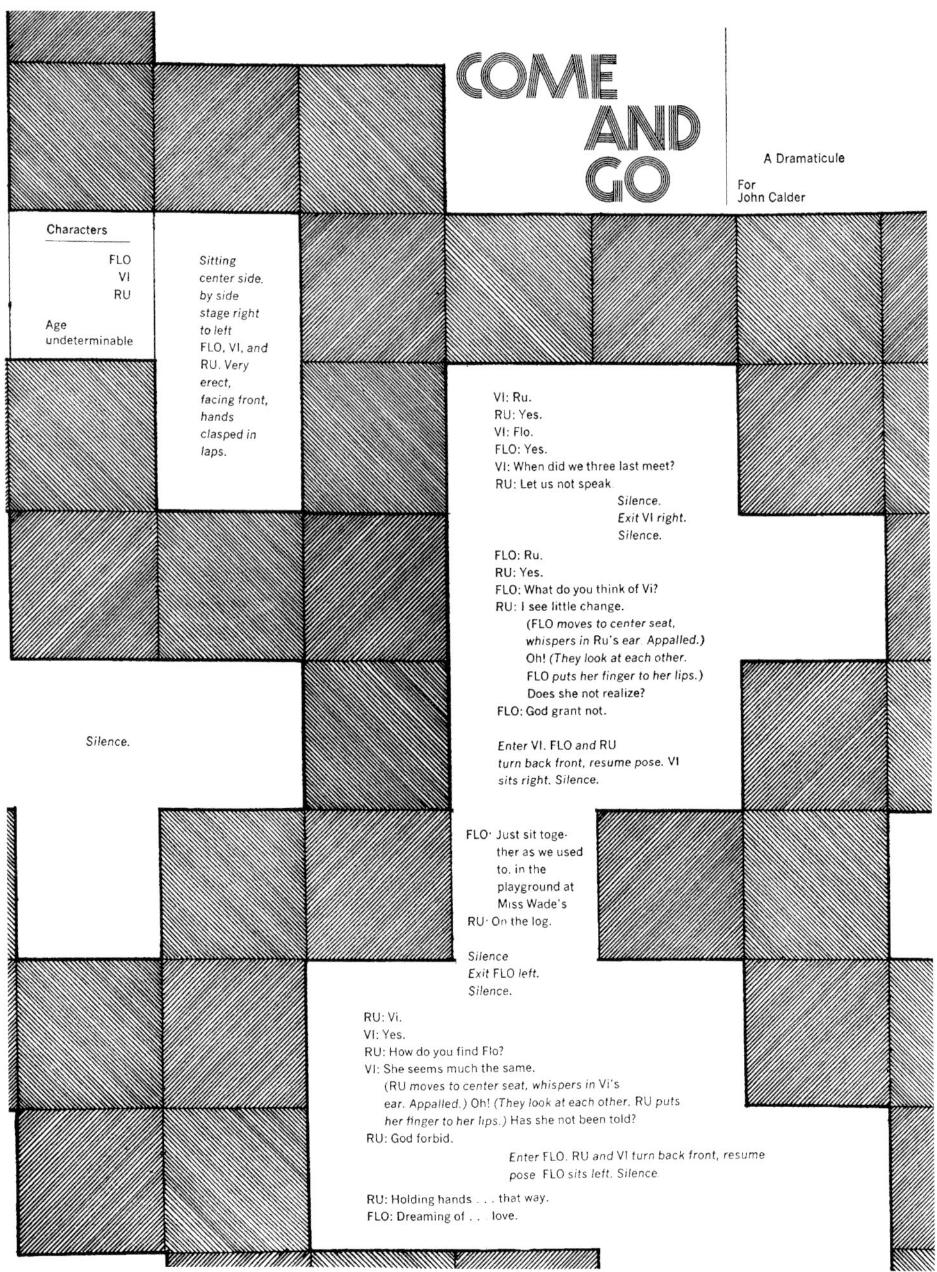

COME AND GO

A Dramaticule

For John Calder

Characters

FLO
VI
RU

Age undeterminable

Sitting center side by side stage right to left FLO, VI, and RU. Very erect, facing front, hands clasped in laps.

Silence.

VI: Ru.
RU: Yes.
VI: Flo.
FLO: Yes.
VI: When did we three last meet?
RU: Let us not speak.
Silence.
Exit VI right.
Silence.
FLO: Ru.
RU: Yes.
FLO: What do you think of Vi?
RU: I see little change.
(FLO moves to center seat, whispers in Ru's ear. Appalled.) Oh! *(They look at each other. FLO puts her finger to her lips.)* Does she not realize?
FLO: God grant not.

Enter VI. FLO and RU turn back front, resume pose. VI sits right. Silence.

FLO: Just sit together as we used to, in the playground at Miss Wade's.
RU: On the log.

Silence
Exit FLO left.
Silence.

RU: Vi.
VI: Yes.
RU: How do you find Flo?
VI: She seems much the same.
(RU moves to center seat, whispers in Vi's ear. Appalled.) Oh! *(They look at each other. RU puts her finger to her lips.)* Has she not been told?
RU: God forbid.

Enter FLO. RU and VI turn back front, resume pose. FLO sits left. Silence.

RU: Holding hands . . . that way.
FLO: Dreaming of . . . love.

3.1 Sol LeWitt, *Come and Go,* drawing for a play by Samuel Beckett, *Harper's Bazaar,* August 1969.

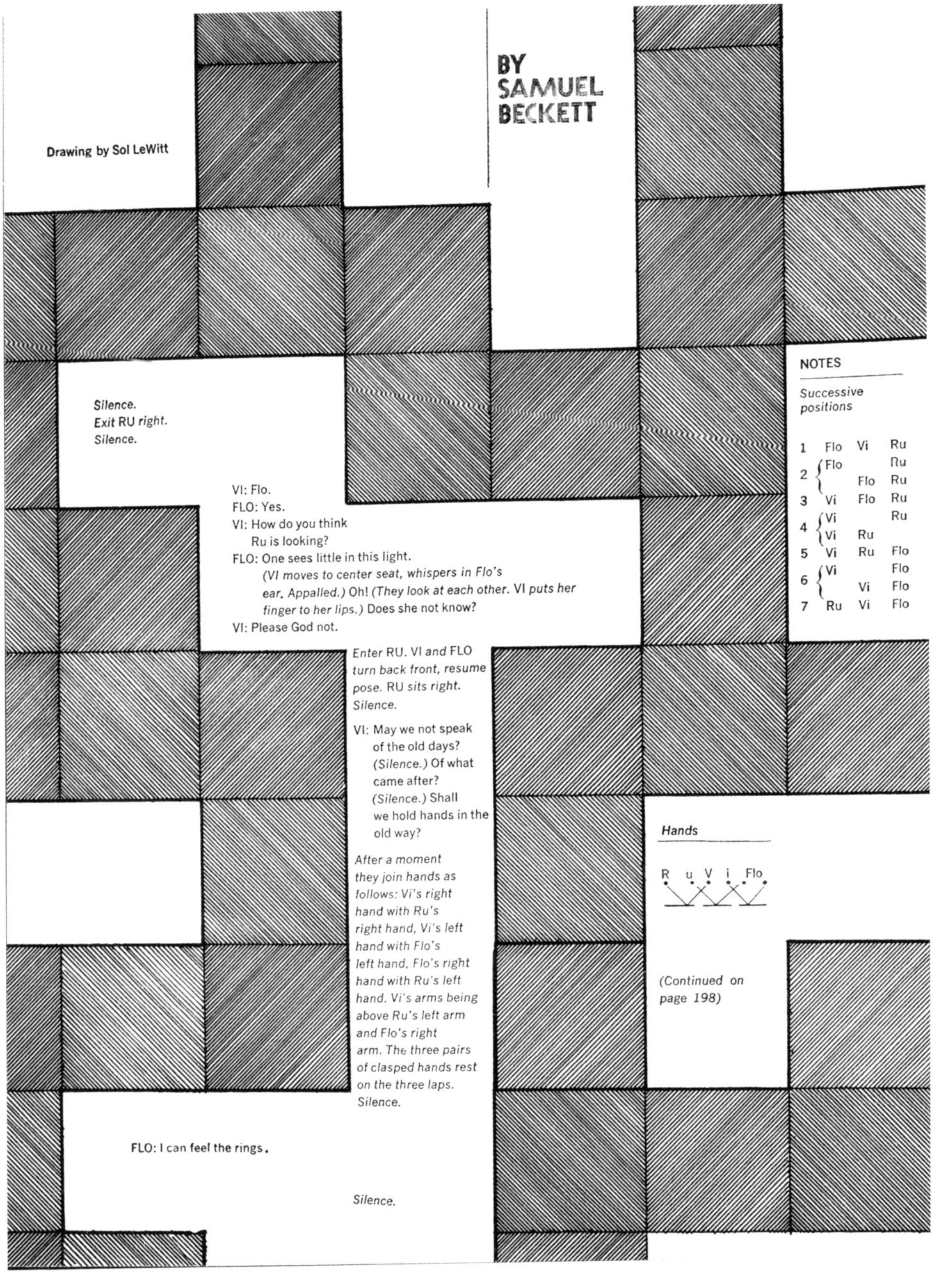

Drawing by Sol LeWitt

BY SAMUEL BECKETT

Silence.
Exit RU *right.*
Silence.

VI: Flo.
FLO: Yes.
VI: How do you think Ru is looking?
FLO: One sees little in this light.
(VI moves to center seat, whispers in Flo's ear. Appalled.) Oh! *(They look at each other.* VI *puts her finger to her lips.)* Does she not know?
VI: Please God not.

Enter RU. VI *and* FLO *turn back front, resume pose.* RU *sits right.*
Silence.

VI: May we not speak of the old days? *(Silence.)* Of what came after? *(Silence.)* Shall we hold hands in the old way?

After a moment they join hands as follows: Vi's right hand with Ru's right hand, Vi's left hand with Flo's left hand, Flo's right hand with Ru's left hand. Vi's arms being above Ru's left arm and Flo's right arm. The three pairs of clasped hands rest on the three laps.
Silence.

FLO: I can feel the rings.

Silence.

NOTES

Successive positions

1	Flo	Vi	Ru
2	Flo		Ru
		Flo	Ru
3	Vi	Flo	Ru
4	Vi		Ru
	Vi	Ru	
5	Vi	Ru	Flo
6	Vi		Flo
		Vi	Flo
7	Ru	Vi	Flo

Hands

R u V i Flo

(Continued on page 198)

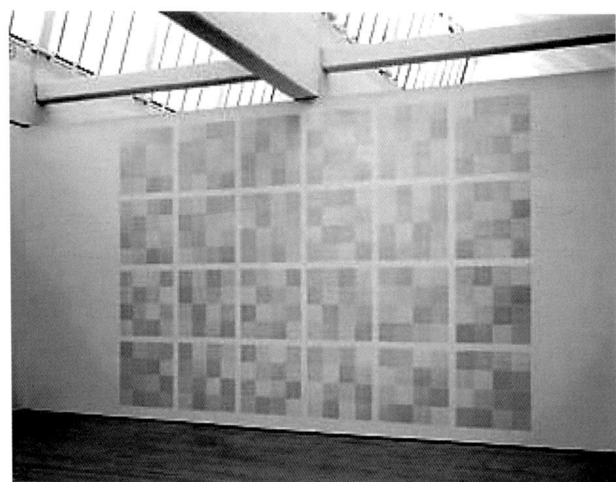

3.2 Sol LeWitt, *Wall Drawing #1085: Drawing Series—Composite, Part I–IV, #1–24, A+B* (detail), 1968/2003. Installation view, Dia: Beacon, Riggio Galleries. Photograph by Bill Jacobson. © 2009 The LeWitt Estate/Artists Rights Society (ARS), New York.

have been possible without him; Mel Bochner was certainly one of these, and Daniel Buren might be counted as another.

In speaking of LeWitt, Bochner stressed his deep connection to music, resulting in a massive musical library from which Marty Feldman used to borrow records. For both LeWitt and Bochner, the permutations of musical structure provided a foundation for their thinking about serialism. Another relation to the example of music was LeWitt's adoption of the role of a composer, creating works for others to "perform" or execute. LeWitt's example and support for Eva Hesse's emerging art is another example of the rewards of matrix. The extraordinary linear hive LeWitt conceived for the publication of Samuel Beckett's play *Come and Go,* in *Harper's Bazaar* (April 1969), must be counted among the expressions of LeWitt's interests that extended beyond the art world, and in the Beckett case might rest on a connection LeWitt made to this playwright's form of expression—its taciturnity, its intelligence—as comparable to his own.

Lip Sync: Marclay Not Nauman

Bruce Nauman's video *Lip Sync* (1969) mounts the artist's head upside down and close up, his inverted mouth at the bottom of the screen repeating the words "lip sync" as the sound gradually moves out of sync with the image, this drift transforming the engorged neck and pulsating mouth into a part object, erotically charged. The video clearly pays homage to the technical breakthrough in film history when, in 1929, synchronized sound did away with silent film and brought a new dimension to cinema. Technologically a later generation of motion pictures, video had synchronous sound available to it right from the start. It is to this dimension that Nauman points in *Lip Sync.*

Christian Marclay's magisterial work *Video Quartet* (2002) spreads four separate screens of DVD projection across forty feet of wall, each screen the unreeling of a compilation of film clips from well-known works of sound cinema. The four different tracks compete for attention for the most part, but occasionally quadruple each other to create synchronicity along the horizontal expanse of the work. The effect, not unlike Hollis Frampton's *Zorn's Lemma,* is a visual grid: the vertical axis is the unreeling narrative of the constitutive short segments of commercial films—such as Janet Leigh's scream in the shower from *Psycho,* or Ingrid Bergman's meditative singing of "As Time Goes By"

First published in *October,* no. 116 (Spring 2006); commissioned for *Christian Marclay: Replay* (Paris: Musée de la Musique, 2007).

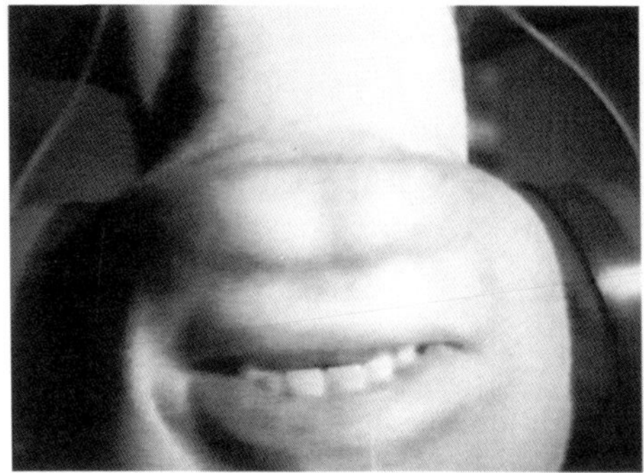

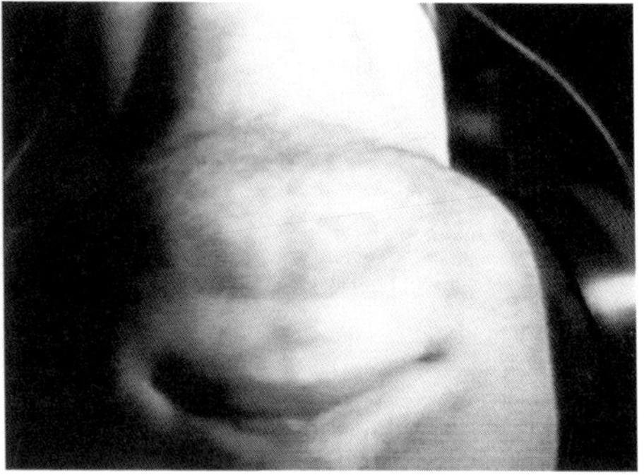

4.1 Bruce Nauman, *Lip Sync,* 1969. © 2009 Bruce Nauman/Artists Rights Society (ARS), New York.

from *Casablanca*—and the horizontal axis is the repetition of the visual fields or the competition among them for dominance. Repetition is, for the most part, a matter of analogy, as when the full-screen image of a spinning roulette wheel rhymes visually with a record on a turntable, as with the circles of drumheads seen from above. These turning disks, needless to say, create the kind of self-reference—here to the reels of film itself—familiar to us from modernist art.

But Marclay's prey goes deeper into the nature of his own medium by meditating on sync sound itself as the "technical support" of cinema. I am using the term "technical support" here as a way of warding off the unwonted positivism of the term "medium" which, in most readers' minds refers to the specific *material* support for a traditional aesthetic genre, reducing the idea of medium to what Michael Fried complains of as the basis of the "literalism" of the art he rejects: "Part of my argument with [Clement] Greenberg's reductionist, essentialist reading of the development of modernist art, was precisely this case history in minimalism of what happened if one thought in those terms."[1] Stanley Cavell seconds this objection by dismissing "medium specificity" as producing "the fate of modernist art generally—that its awareness and responsibility for the physical basis of its art compel it at once to assert and deny the control of its art by that basis"[2]—both of them thus rejecting the version of modernist "medium specificity" articulated by Greenberg.

"Technical support," on the other hand, has the virtue of acknowledging the recent obsolescence of most traditional aesthetic mediums (such as oil on canvas, fresco, and many sculptural materials, like cast bronze or welded metal), while it also welcomes the layered mechanisms of new technologies that make a simple, unitary identification of the work's physical support impossible (is the "support" of film the celluloid strip, the screen, the splices of the edited footage, the projector's beam of light, the circular reels?). Dziga Vertov's *The Man with a Movie Camera,* perhaps the most medium-specific film in the history of cinema, dramatizes the act of modernist self-reference that reveals the nature of the medium, as his own camera tracks the movie's cameraman through the city, while the latter films the urban landscape from various conveyances such as cars or horse-drawn carriages. All the while, Vertov's second camera performs an act of surveillance that provokes the viewer to reflect on the unseen cameraman who is even then filming the filmer. By dramatizing this normally invisible technician, Vertov forces into experience those parts of the cinematic medium—the camera and celluloid support of the filmic image—which are not usually exposed to view. Vertov's prey, in manifesting the medium of his art, is wider than the physical support of the representation. As well, he dramatizes the fact of editing—the normally invisible joining together of sequences of action to produce a narrative—by reversing the forward motion of such narrative, to generate the feeling that the spools of film are being wound back through the projector's gate onto the reels from which they originally issued—an effect Annette Michelson identifies with the poetic trope "hysteron proteron."[3]

If the traditional medium is supported by a physical substance (and practiced by a specialized guild), the term "technical support," in distinction, refers to contemporary commercial vehicles, such as cars or television, which contemporary artists now exploit.[4]

Marclay's focus on his technical support manifests itself early on in *Video Quartet* when the leftmost screen shows a clip of cockroaches running soundlessly across the keys of a piano, returning us thereby to silent film. In so doing, we have the sensation of looking at the projection on this field winding backward into the history of the movies to the onset of sound itself. The sensation is one of actually *seeing* the silence as well as the gridlike layering of the cinematic medium's additive condition of the soundtrack's audio edge running along the celluloid strip of the images. Himself a composer, Marclay has made quasi-sculptural works out of sound materials, such as skeins of audiotape, an unpleated accordion, or telephone headsets cast in series. None of this has the originality or focus of *Video Quartet,* as it unpacks the specificity of sync sound, making it *visible* to us and converting film's narrative continuum into a fundamentally visual simultaneity.

Marclay is not the first filmmaker to concern himself with sync sound. Besides the Nauman video mentioned at the outset, we might remember the American musical *Singing in the* Rain, in which the invention of the Hollywood soundtrack is dramatized by a love story that motivates the drive to make silent film obsolete.

That *Video Quartet* organizes its images within the geometry of the grid is not only an homage to the Frampton film *Zorn's Lemma,* and thus to the American independent cinema's concern with manifesting the foundational elements of the filmic medium (think of Michael Snow's *Wavelength,* with its temporal trajectory contracted into the single register of a progressive zoom, thereby making visible the capacity of the camera's lens; or of the "flicker" caused by Paul Sharits's use of interspersed frames of colored film interwoven with black leader, so as to make the joining of the pieces of celluloid that is entailed in the editing process the sole focus of the filmic experience). The grid goes further, to acknowledge the history of this important motif within the development of modernist painting: think of cubism, Mondrian, Malevich, Sol LeWitt, and many others. The grid's function, within this history, was to acknowledge—by repeating—the flatness of the pictorial support, as well as the physical limits of the canvas. Marclay's concern with the grid interweaves a reference not only to the flatness of the screen but to the edges of the celluloid strip, and to the diachronic unfolding of the narrative.

The Encounter: Ten [True] Stories

TRUTH—If art deals with illusion, modernism sought to ground the work of art in a reference to its material support that would make it "truthfully" express its medium. Hence Clement Greenberg's dictum that painting should refer to the flatness of its canvas surface. With the exhaustion of modernism, how is "truth" to be sustained? And under what conditions? Sophie Calle takes up this question in her recent work *True Stories* (1988–2003), where we find an attempt to secure "truth" after the end of modernism.

Under what circumstances are stories "true"? If they are autobiographical, is their truth secured by the mode of their recitation, as in psychoanalysis, where telling lies is pointless? Sophie Calle's "stories" are of dreams, love letters, fantasies, sex. They circulate around two photographs of Freud's couch, taken by Calle in his consulting room in the house where he lived and died in London. One of Calle's conceptual works is a photographic sequence of cathected objects she brought to Freud's house and placed on his couch—one of which was her wedding dress—spread out there, like a reclining body: undoubtedly imagined as hers.

First published in *Bing*, no. 4 (January–April 2007).

Truth is also the assumption underlying photojournalism—the modality of much of Calle's work. When she asks her mother to hire a detective to follow her, making a complete report of her daily itineraries, she also asks a friend to tail the detective and to photograph him on her trail. Meanwhile she keeps her own record on her itineraries, noting as well her fantasies about the man tracking her.

Exquisite Pain, the extended documentation of a failed love affair—with a man she associates with her father (where is Freud?)—intersperses the narrative with repeated images of the red telephone on her hotel room bed in New Delhi, while she fruitlessly awaits her lover's call. The object on the bed interfaces with Calle's personal objects placed on Freud's couch in London, half a world away from India.

Many of the true stories are analogues of *Exquisite Pain* in that they are accounts of nonconsummated or failed love affairs. Inevitably, Calle's wedding dress reappears in these, like the personal objects she had photographed on Freud's couch. She tells of her own staging of occasions to wear the dress and, distressingly, of spending the postceremonial night in her own bed, alone. This occurs in "The Dream Wedding," a ceremony to be performed at Roissy Airport just before the groom was to leave for military service in China. Another charade of marriage ceremonies, "The Fake Wedding," included not only the bridal dress but a formal photograph and a grand reception. She ends the account with the ironic pronouncement: "I crowned, with a fake marriage, the *truest* story of my life."

As in any analysis, Calle's father plays a prominent part in *True Stories.* Her "first love" was a man wearing the same bathrobe as his. He obeys her request never to let her see him naked from the front, but at the end of the affair, he leaves the bathrobe with her: another form of "wedding dress." Calle explains her phobic reaction to the sight of male genitals in "A Young Girl's Dream," named after a dessert she orders because its name intrigues her. When the plate comes, it turns out to be two balls of vanilla ice cream flanking a peeled banana. The waiter, serving it to her, laughingly says, "Enjoy."

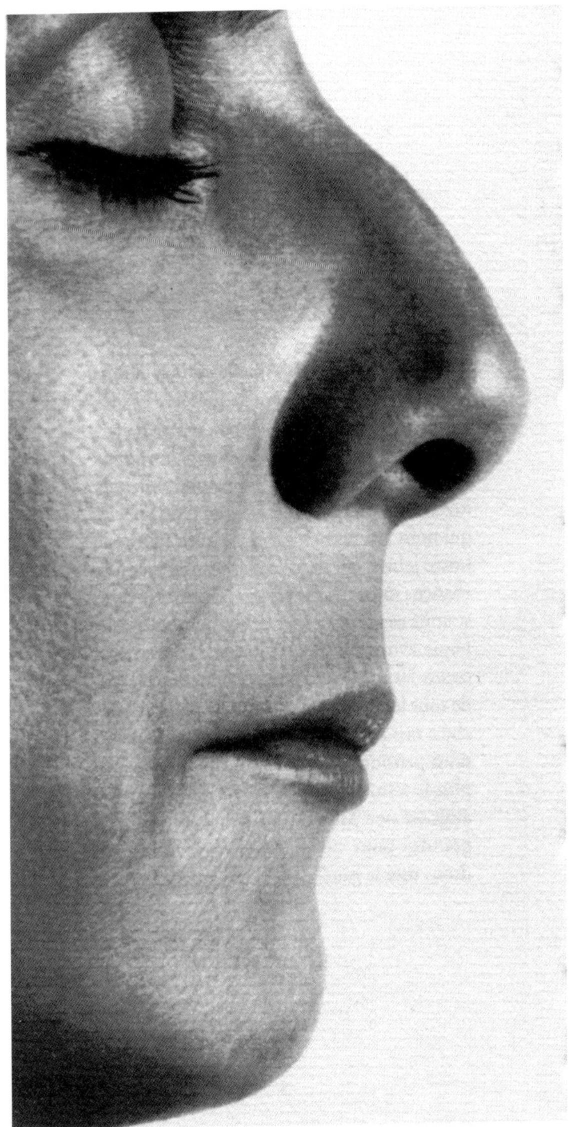

5.1 Sophie Calle, *Le nez*, from *Des histoires vraies*, 1994. © 2009 Artists Rights Society (ARS), New York/ADAGP, Paris.

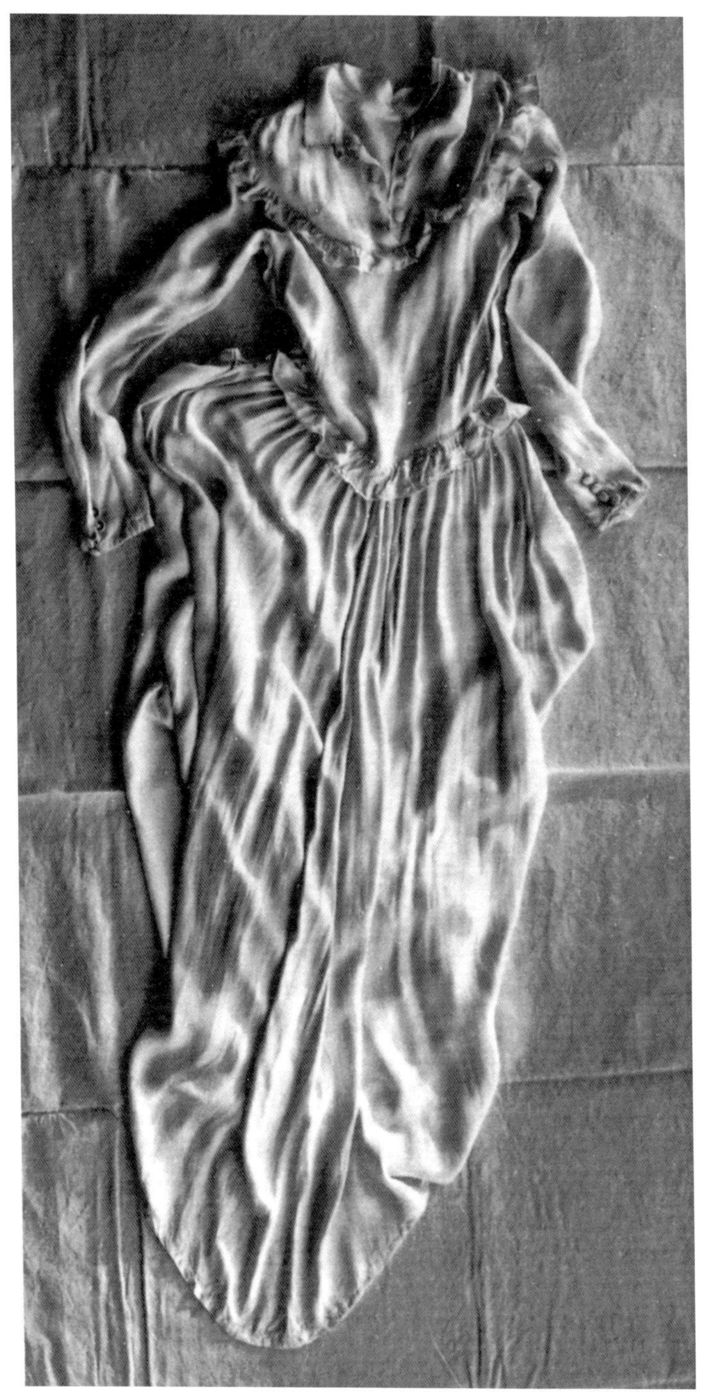

She explains that it was her father who enrolled her in psychoanalysis when he insisted she see a doctor because of her bad breath. Is her father's presence in her analysis the trace of the sight of his genitals viewed in the opening of his bathrobe?

This "truth," among all those spontaneously arising from the process of free association, presents us with the irony that it arrives prepackaged: just another psychoanalytic cliché.

5.2 (*facing page*) Sophie Calle, *La robe de mariée,* from *Des histoires vraies,* 1994. © 2009 Artists Rights Society (ARS), New York/ADAGP, Paris.

"Specific" Objects

A whole generation of artists has found itself wandering down a dusty path, mired in confusion and finally reaching a dead end, as its practitioners pursued the idea that in order for art to "think itself," it must be reconstructed as language, as proposition: thought only available as speech. "Art after Philosophy" was the bible of this diaspora and Joseph Kosuth its prophet. Viewing himself as an apocalyptic historian—the Oswald Spengler of aesthetics—Kosuth sketched the profiles of both philosophy and artistic practice in broad strokes.

Philosophy was seen as descending a slope that led precipitously from the heights of transcendentalist reflection to the depths of ordinary language: analytic philosophy's focus on the nature of the proposition having voided all metaphysical considerations. Art, Kosuth reasoned further, is the phoenix of this situation; it is the life that bursts into flower on the ashes of philosophy's exhaustion. Further, he argued, its bloom takes on the very form of the philosophical conflagration, since the rebirth of art will depend on its newly won configuration as language.

In Kosuth's account, the prophet who had come before him was Marcel Duchamp, the first artist to reconceive objects as statements, insofar as the readymade only exists as a form of ostensive definition: "This is art."

First published in *res,* no. 46 (Autumn 2004).

The readymade strategy overleaps the problem of the aesthetic medium with the single bound that takes it directly into the central question of aesthetics, by circumventing the "trivial" issue of specific artistic practice. As Kosuth expressed this: "Being an artist now means to question the nature of art. If one is questioning the nature of painting, one cannot be questioning the nature of art. If an artist accepts painting (or sculpture) he is accepting the tradition that goes with it. That's because the word art is general and the word painting is specific. Painting is a *kind* of art. If you make paintings you are already accepting (not questioning) the nature of art."[1]

Although Kosuth asked his readers to ignore the specific in order to achieve the general, he gave no advice about how this was to be done. Instead it was Donald Judd who, in his essay "Specific Objects," spelled out this strategy. "The best new work," he declared, is "neither painting nor sculpture," but, in Judd's view, a paradoxical hybrid, like "a picture [which] stops being a picture and turns into an arbitrary object."[2] The specific object only needs the third dimension in order to exist, he argued, since "Three dimensions are real space. That gets rid of the problem of illusionism and of literal space, space in and around marks and colors—which is riddance of one of the salient and most objectionable relics of European art."[3] In dispensing with illusionism as nothing more than an "objectionable relic," Judd could be thought to have been prescribing to his fellow artists in the 1960s, but in fact he was simply describing the impasse already reached by the medium of painting at that time. Cubism had reformed ambitious painting so totally that a newly hardened picture surface left no place for elements added to that plane to exist but on top of it in the real space of shallow relief. Judd's "specific objects" are acknowledgments of the relief (or sculptural) condition of postcubist paintings which now exist as slabs or shallow boxes affixed to the wall.

As Thierry de Duve has shown, however, Judd's analysis is misnamed, since what he is supporting cannot be the *specific* object but is, instead, the *generic* one: art-as-such, rather than painting, say, or sculpture.[4]

The third dimension, so imperative for the "specific object," has been garnered for conceptual art in either of two forms: through "installation" on the one hand and photography on the other. Installation folds the actual space of gallery or museum into the matrix of the assembled object such that, as the stage on which the object appears, it becomes essential to the object's very existence. Conceptual photography includes real space as the context for the objects the artist finds and reproduces in books of images, whether these be the industrial antimonuments of Bernd and Hilla Becher's *Anonymous Sculpture* albums or the gas stations and parking lots of Ed Ruscha's modest publications.

In the context of contemporary practice, however, it is important to challenge the conceptualist *doxa* about the status of books such as these and the "obviousness" of their renunciation of the aesthetic medium in the widest (but most naive) reception of them. Ruscha's case is particularly arresting since he himself so often invokes the concept of the medium, as when he says: "Right now, I am out to explore the medium. It's a playground or a beach so I'm going to send as much sand up in the air as I can! I think the next time I'll print with iodine. I have to be in control of the medium. The organic elements have to combine satisfactorily. What I'm interested in is the possible range; also in the use of a *processed* media." Or, again, when he says: "New mediums encourage me. I still paint in oil paint. But what I'm interested in is illustrating *ideas*. I'm not interested in color, if color suits me I use it intuitively. I'd prefer my painting to come to an end. . . . Painting for me is a tool."[5]

Ruscha is not sending sand "up in the air," so much as he is kicking it in the eyes of his admirers, who see him following the conceptualist strategy of abandoning the traditional mediums of the visual in favor of the textual one of the book. Nonetheless, one of his interlocutors recently detected a connecting thread that weaves its way through the varied directions of the books and links them as well to other parts of Ruscha's oeuvre. This is Henri Barendse, who comments to Ruscha: "You've said, half-seriously, I suspect, that you came to California because you like palm trees and hot rods. You've done the book of palm trees but never one of cars. It seems like cars are a missing link in the books, quite literally, since they would tie them together, be the conduit between the pools, apartments, and of course, the parking lots and gas stations. Perhaps I'm taking things too literally again."[6]

What Barendse is suggesting is that cars function as the "support" for all of Ruscha's practice. Ruscha himself understands that mediums are, in fact, supports for work, as when he says: "I'm painting on the book covers. I guess I'm just looking for another support. Maybe I'm moving away from the canvas, but I can't predict. I still paint on canvas, but I think there's another shift about to happen somewhere, maybe not so radical, but at least one that I know I will want to stick with."[7]

As Ruscha uses the word, "medium" either can mean the element in which color is suspended—traditionally oil, but for his *Stains* series, iodine, chocolate syrup, chutney, etc.—or it can be the technical support for the image, traditionally canvas, but for him, book covers like taffeta, or the photography of the books' contents. Besides the extravagance of his invention of matrices (axle grease and caviar is an example), Ruscha's interest in the idea of medium as a type of support also takes shape as a set of rules, as when he remembers: "I had this idea for a book title—Twentysix Gasoline Stations—and it became like a fantasy rule in my mind that I knew I had to follow."[8] So for him, "medium" has less to do with the physicality of the support than with a system of "rules." This is the system the philosopher Stanley Cavell wants to call "automatism,"[9] in an effort to get his readers to focus on the self-regulating character of traditional aesthetic mediums.

The Greek word for "self" shared by the prefix for *auto*matism and *auto*mobile not only restates the possible relation between car and medium but also turns "medium" in the direction of "medium-specificity," or the medium's power to represent it*self* that is so central to modernism. For Cavell, as for Ruscha, rules become necessary once the artist finds himself cut free of tradition and wandering haplessly in a field where "anything goes." In this situation the artist has to improvise, but it is only the rules—like the system of the fugue, or the resolution for the end of the sonata—that give his invention a goal, allowing him to gage whether his polyphonic improvisation on a melodic fragment or his impromptu cadenza called for by the score is successful or not.[10]

"Auto" does not merely express the isolation of the artist, then; it also suggests that the source of the "rules" comes from within the support: "twenty-six," for example, was derived from the number of refills necessary between California and Oklahoma and thus referred to the demands of driving and the exigencies of the car. In good modernist tradition, Ruscha's "Parking Lots" could refer to the flatness of the page, but it more probably marks the serial nature of the car, its existence as a multiple, like the printed book it*self*. In this form, "medium" is both specific, which is to say self-reflexive, and inventive, in that anything can be a medium, even the most common contemporary substance the artist—newly *auto*nomous—can imagine.

"Medium specificity" may ring strangely in the instance of Ruscha, but his very case promotes a sense of how eccentrically "medium" can be used to track this dimension of contemporary practice. If the car can become a medium, then anything might be pressed into such service. It only needs the set of rules that will open onto the possibility of artistic practice—like the musical goal in the example of improvisation. The very idea of the artist's invention of a medium, and thus his or her authoring a set of rules, will undoubtedly make us nervous. A medium is, after all, a shared language developed over centuries of practice so that no individual initiative, we would think, can either organize new sources of its meaning or change established ones. It is as though we were imagining the artist as playing a game of chess and announcing in the middle that the bishop moves orthogonally instead of diagonally. Ruscha's inventions are arbitrary, but not as eccentric as the one just mentioned. His *Stains* exult in the exoticism of his choices, but the very term "stains" pays homage to the recent history of painting in which staining provided what was felt to be a necessary alternative to drawing, such that from Pollock to Morris Louis and Helen Frankenthaler, laying down a stain was a way of avoiding the violence of a hardened contour. The rules for "stains" are thus "invented" within the context of a set of principles for abstract painting; these principles are presupposed for the possibility and pertinence of the invention of the rules themselves.

So remote is the idea of the medium from the center of attention of the contemporary viewer that concern for the medium is often confused with very different preoccupations. The work of the Irish artist James Coleman is a case in point. The medium he has "invented" is the slide tape, a sequence of exactingly projected slides synchronized with a taped soundtrack. The slide tape is familiar to most of us from the advertising projections we've seen in train stations and airports. It's part of the spectacle culture so widespread in the West—a public form of entertainment to distract commuters and relax shoppers. Coleman's version of the slide tape seems to have as one of its "rules" that it will acknowledge this condition as entertainment. To this end, his characters are often lined up across the visual field as though taking a bow at the end of a play. Altogether, its "rules" take the form of *auto*-reference; the staccato sound of the slides falling into place as the carrousels turn in sequence is imitated on the soundtrack of the work *I.N.I.T.I.A.L.S.*, as the narrator spells complicated words by rapping out the individual letters: e.s.o.p.h.a.g.u.s.

There is another "rule" Coleman has invented, which we might miss in a casual viewing, since we so often rely on a set of familiar ideas to explain this vivid work. The human subject, we have been taught, is constructed, a concatenation of social, ethnic, and even gender protocols to produce the roles each of us will play. Coleman's theatricality presents this project of construction and the way individuals bend to its demands, we might think. In our reading of what we take to be the "politics" of Coleman's work, we might neither notice nor ask about the curious choreography of his characters, who interact by facing the audience rather than one another. If we had taken the time, we would have thought of the way Roy Lichtenstein's lovers are always looking directly out of the frame even while their speech balloons project the most tender expressions toward each other ("It's, it's not an en*gage*ment ring?!!!"). We would have realized that the syntax of film is not open either to the comic book illustrator or to Coleman, since a film can jump back and forth between a speaker's face and the person to whom he or she is talking, the alternation (called "angle, reverse-angle" in cine-speak) happening in the blink of an eye.

For Coleman to imitate angle, reverse-angle would be more "realistic" but extravagantly distended in terms of the number of images needed to enact even the briefest of exchanges. It is both more simple and more economical for his actors to express their most fervent emotions as they both stolidly face the camera. So one of Coleman's rules could be called the "double face-out." He takes it from other forms of visual narrative: not only comic books, but photo novels and advertising (from which Lichtenstein had, himself, borrowed it). The double face-out supplies Coleman with a sense of the tragic temporal pressure that makes the voicing of emotion so impossible within the developed societies of the West. What it also furnishes is a reminder of the screen's surface as the underlying principle from which the "rule" derives. That the picture plane directly faces onto its viewer who, in turn, directly faces onto it is the convention that underwrites traditional painting, a convention that gives the double face-out its leverage on the condition of interpsychic connections within advanced consumer society.

Every space of luminous projection seems to supply proof that there is no field of "specificity," no surface against which to register the unity and extension of something like the picture plane. Because the picture plane had been, for many centuries, the cornerstone for "specificity," its erosion is the warrant, we believe, of these artists' indifference to the problem of the medium. More and more museums—in exhibitions such as the Whitney's "Beyond the Light" or the Guggenheim's "Moving Images"—are heralding the projected image as a new visual fashion worthy of examination in its own right.

From Coleman, our attention might be drawn to William Kentridge, a South African artist whose animated films pursue the problems of apartheid across the African veld with its mines and its slag heaps. Kentridge is another artist, however, who is inventing a set of "rules." His technique is erasure: every line is a potential pentimento, a mark to be modified, each modification recorded by a frame of film. This "rule" produces many of the sequences, such as a car ride in which the view of the landscape is constantly blurred by the windshield wipers, an image of the very act of erasure. The car's interior is then the site of the traumatic memory that forms the narrative climax of the work *History of the Main Complaint* (1996), with Kentridge's technique constantly narrativizing his own process. Erasure is to line what *Stains* is to drawing: two artists having converged within the grammar of modernist painting to discover the same set of "rules."

It is easy to miss this coincidence. But if our attention is on the blackness of the space of projection, we will overlook the aliveness to the issues of the medium that even this darkened field now promotes.

"The Rock": William Kentridge's Drawings for Projection

1. If it is true that William Kentridge's *Monument* (1990) is, as we are told, "loosely based" on Samuel Beckett's *Catastrophe* (1982), how are we to understand this relationship between film and play? Does it occur at the most manifest level, that of the utter subjugation of one man by another, the first turning the second into stone?

The bit of business, after all, that makes up *Catastrophe* concerns a stage director and his assistant as they "dress" a totally motionless figure for the play's final moment, its—to use the theatrical term—catastrophe. Raised on a pedestal, the object of this attention, initially clad in black, is gradually divested of his hat and coat to reveal his bald head and gray pajamas. The piecemeal adjustments demanded by the director then involve rolling up the pants and whitening the exposed areas of skin—the face, the pate, the partially bared chest, the legs. Monochrome and immobile, the figure is then ready for the final tableau in which a single spotlight isolates him from a now darkened stage and then slowly constricts itself to pick out the face alone. The director, viewing the effect from the audience, expresses his satisfaction. "Great!" he says, "We've got our catastrophe." Appreciation. Applause.

Is this the core around which Kentridge imagined his own "catastrophe"—South Africa's catastrophe? For in *Monument,* the mine owner Soho Eckstein is

First published in *October,* no. 92 (Spring 2000).

seen performing as civic benefactor when, with a flourish of media attention and to the applause of the crowd, he unveils the apparition of a dispossessed laborer whom we had seen walking at the outset of the film, now standing immobilized on a pedestal, his load still on his back. That it is the live man and not his representation is assured to us by a detail almost certainly drawn from the Beckett play. As the final shot irises-in on the face of the monument—in a parallel with Beckett's spotlight—the "statue" lifts its head and opens its eyes; the sound of its breathing continues over the blackened field of the credits. This had been the final moment—postcatastrophic, so to speak—of *Catastrophe,* as the figure, in defiance of the director, also raises his head and fixes the audience with his stare.

For Beckett, this last gesture is fully ambiguous. Slipping the bonds of total control, the figure's ultimate act of will would seem to open a chink of light onto a world beyond this walled-off stage, in order to allow a sign of freedom or redemption to enter, like the bird that arrives in *Endgame*. But if indeed there is nothing beyond this grip and its boundaries, nothing outside the totalizing system of the "director," then it would follow that this very act of voluntarism and the thought that propels it *is* the catastrophe.[1]

Kentridge has spoken about the danger for him, as for any South African artist, of addressing the catastrophe of apartheid head-on, of making a work either fixated on its record of dehumanization or invested in the image of a possible redemption. He calls apartheid "the rock"; and it is a rock on which art itself must always founder.[2] Writing in 1990, the same year he produced *Monument,* he says:

> These two elements—our history and the moral imperative arising from that—are the factors for making that personal beacon rise into the immovable rock of apartheid. To escape this rock is the job of the artist. These two constitute the tyranny of our history. And escape is necessary, for as I stated, the rock is possessive, and inimical to good work. I am not saying that apartheid, or indeed, redemption, are not worthy of representation, description or exploration,

> I am saying that the scale and weight with which this rock presents itself is inimical to that task. (WK 75)

But if the dehumanizing petrification represented in *Monument* clearly derives from "the rock," the indirect address to the problem urged by Kentridge—"you cannot face the rock head on; the rock always wins" (WK 75)—suggests that his attachment to Beckett's play might in fact have reached under the specifics of theme to find itself attracted to something else, something more formal in kind.

Most of *Catastrophe* is focused not on the immobile figure but on the space between it and the director, a space which is articulated by the constant movement of the assistant, who, notebook in hand and pencil at the ready, jots down the director's modifications even as she shuttles back and forth from the side of the stage to its center in order to carry out his commands on the body of the figure. She is the one who removes the hat, who takes the hands out of the pockets, who whitens the head, who rolls up the pants, each time moving back to the side of the director to join him in regarding their creation and to light his cigar and to note down his instructions on her pad. It is her traffic between the two points, that of command and that of execution, that makes up the business of the play or, as Gogo and Didi say to each other in Beckett's *Waiting for Godot,* that makes the time pass.

Now it is just this walking back and forth, this constant shuttling between the movie camera on one side of the studio and the drawing tacked to the wall on the other, that constitutes the field of Kentridge's own operation. The drawing on which he works is at all times complete and at all times in flux, since once he has recorded it from his station at his Bolex, he moves across the floor to make an infinitesimal modification in its surface, only then to retreat once more to the camera.[3] This is what he calls "the rather dumb physical activity of stalking the drawing, or walking backwards and forwards between the camera and drawing; raising, shifting, adapting the image" (WK 93). Working with no overall plan in mind, without the filmmaker's scenario or the animator's storyboard, he is instead dependent on this strange space of back-and-forth, at once mechanical and meditational, for the conception of his work: the individual images, their development, their interconnection that becomes, in the end, the "plot." It is a space which, as we have seen, is technical, dictated by an "animation" process in which a single drawing is gradually transformed through a combination of additions and erasures, each occurring a few millimeters at a time and each change recorded by exposing a single frame of film. The result is that an eight-minute film might be made through the modification of only twenty drawings. As opposed to the endless proliferation of drawings dictated by traditional animation, with each change of bodily position calling for a new rendering, and thus a separate graphic object, this is a technique of extreme parsimony and of endless round trips.

That the technical should open onto the conceptual leads Kentridge to associate a different notion of the wheel to this treadmill, one he calls *fortuna*. Caught up within the quasi-automatism of the process, he is strangely enough left free to improvise and to do this in the grip of agencies he characterizes as "something other than cold statistical chance, and something too, outside the range of rational control" (WK 68). The analogy he makes is to the way ordinary language, deploying itself in the course of conversation, is for the most part guided by habit, by learned patterns of speech, by rote formulations, by gambits and clichés. Thus, though we embark on our discourse knowing generally what we want to say, much of our activity of choosing the words and forming the sentences is preprogrammed, semimechanical, a form of automatism.

But this very fact also allows a kind of free association to what we are saying, as we are saying it, to occur. In midcourse, our remarks might, therefore, take off in an entirely unforeseen direction, one we could not have "meant" at the outset. In this sense, as Kentridge puts it, "in the very activity of speaking, generated by the act itself, new connections and thoughts emerge" (WK 69). And this new sense of automatism—the upsurge from the unconscious of the unanticipated, the unexpected—a sense that is the very opposite of the first, with its idea of the routinized and the programmed, is nonetheless folded together with it in the concept of *fortuna*.

Kentridge has given three examples of the operation of *fortuna* drawn from the opening stages of the conception of *Mine* (1991), the third of the series of works he calls "Drawings for Projection"—a rubric that holds open the possibility that there might be a problem, one to which we will return, in simply naming these works "animated films." The first example was the effort just to make an opening dent in the long process of conceiving the film, which in this case meant organizing an image whose changes would be wholly automatic, programmed from the outset, so that after a day's work at least something—several seconds of footage—would result. Accordingly, he drew a geological section of the black earth riven by the mine shaft within which the lift's slow ascension toward the top could be more or less mechanically shot and, bit by bit, erased and redrawn.

With the lift at the face of the earth, the emergence of a crowd of workers came next, the crowd itself another "automatism" of Kentridge's process. "With this charcoal technique," he says, "each person is rendered with a single mark on the paper. As more marks are added, so the crowd emerges. . . . It is far easier to draw a crowd of thousands than to show a flicker of doubt passing over one person's face" (WK 67). Kentridge next decided that this teeming landscape would acknowledge its own "possession" by the mine owner, Soho Eckstein; and so he depicted an "earthquake" that then transformed this field into Soho's bed covers, as he rolls over in awakening from sleep. This meant that the plot now contained Soho, in bed, on the one hand, and the mine with its workers on the other. The visual—and conceptual—link between the two was the next gift from *fortuna*.

While trying to figure out how to get Soho out of bed and into his office, from which he directs his industrial empire in the other films, Kentridge played for time by letting Soho have breakfast. The smoke from his cigar having transformed itself into a bell, the bell in turn was ready to metamorphose into a coffeepot so that the meal could commence. The kind of coffeepot Kentridge put in Soho's hand, however, was simply the accident of what happened to be in his studio that day, namely a *cafetière*: a glass cylinder with a metal plunger that compresses the grains of coffee within the pot.[4] "It was only when the plunger was half way down, in the activity of drawing, erasing it, repositioning it a few millimeters lower each time," Kentridge recounts, "that I saw, I knew, I realized (I cannot pin an exact word on it) that it would go through the tray, through the bed and become the mine shaft" (WK 68). And in this becoming, the whole of the film opened up for him: the meaning of the relationship between the mine and the bed, in which Soho will be seen "excavating from the earth an entire social and eco history. Atlantic slave ships, Ife royal heads, and finally a miniature rhinoceros, are dragged up through the miners embedded in the rocks to Soho having his morning coffee" (WK 60).

In characterizing this aspect of *fortuna,* Kentridge goes on: "The sensation was more of discovery than invention. There was no feeling of what a good idea I had had, rather, relief at not having overlooked what was in front of me." And he stresses the improvisational character of his discovery, along with the fact that he came upon it on the prowl: "What was going on while I was in the kitchen preparing something to drink? Was there some part of me saying 'Not the tea, there, you fool, the coffee, not espresso, the cafetière, you daft. . . . Trust me. I know what I'm doing.' If I'd had tea that morning, would the impasse of Soho in bed have continued?" (WK 68). That his prowl through the kitchen forms a parallel for him with his very process of "stalking the drawing," echoes in his remark: "It is only when physically engaged on a drawing that ideas start to emerge. There is a combination between drawing and seeing, between making and assessing that provokes a part of my mind that otherwise is closed off" (WK 68).

The generosity with which Kentridge opens his process, in all its minutia, to his listener—these comments come from a 1993 lecture called "'Fortuna': Neither Program nor Chance in the Making of Images"—would seem to be motivated by the desire to displace the focus on the general field of his activity from "the rock" and its ideological imperatives to the work and its routines. It is for this reason that the link between *Monument* and *Catastrophe* needs to be held in suspension between the thematics of outrage and the choreography of process, with neither given dominance, and with the possible understanding that the artist's leverage on the former is best exercised through the latter.

2. Let us then pursue that half of the connection that focuses on *fortuna,* with its stress on the automatic and automatism. It is related, as Kentridge himself admits, to the singularity of his process. Because that process arose from the

graphic medium and Kentridge's desire to track the course of his drawings as they evolved, it didn't begin with the problem of filmic animation; animation here—the run-on projection of the frames recording successive phases of the drawing, which thereby generates the sense of a single work in motion—is a kind of derivative of drawing. This is why the first of his films announced itself as *Drawings for Projection* before appending, as a subtitle, *Johannesburg, 2nd Greatest City after Paris* (1989). And this is why Kentridge has maintained the same master title for the developing series as a whole. And why it is important for him to hang on to the context of art—museum or gallery—as the place of exhibition for the films, insisting as well that they be screened alongside their constitutive drawings. This has annoyed certain commentators who, otherwise admiring Kentridge's work, don't see why he shouldn't just show them as animation films, entering them into the space of cinema and its particular theaters of display and competition. They find his resistance to this strangely arty, a tic.[5]

What these critics miss, however, is the uniqueness of Kentridge's medium and, with this, his desire to stress its specificity. Though they freely acknowledge the strangeness, even the perversity, of making animation not by addition but, so to speak, by subtraction, this peculiarity nevertheless remains for them a special case within that subset of film called animation. They do not see that for Kentridge animation is merely a technical support, like the slide tape James Coleman exploits. As such it brings along with it not only a set of material conditions, but also a dense layering of economic and social history that ranges from, on the one hand, its particular modes of commercialization and thus the need for industrialized production and mass dissemination, to the forms of serial repetition of its narratives and characters, on the other, as though it were the modern-day inheritor of the commedia dell'arte and the Grand Guignol, only now played entirely by animals.

But in Kentridge's practice, filmic animation is a support or ground for what takes place within or on top of it, namely a type of drawing that is extremely reflexive about its own condition, that savors the graininess of the clouds of charcoal or pastel as they are blown onto paper, that luxuriates in the luminous tracks of the eraser that open onto Turneresque fogs, that examines the particular form of the palimpsest as a graphically specific signifier, that delimits the frame within which the drawing's marks will appear and within that, ever smaller frames—drawing placing its own defining characteristic as contour *en abyme*. It is this very density and weight of the drawing, this way it has of producing the hiccup of a momentary stillness and thus dragging against the flow of the film, that opens up the gap between Kentridge's medium and that of film itself, a divide which produces the specificity of the thing that, like Coleman, he is "inventing."[6]

The connection between the specificity of a medium and something like Kentridge's *fortuna* has been wrought in a not unrelated context through the philosopher Stanley Cavell's decision to choose the word "automatism" to explore the very condition of mediums themselves. Arguing that the problem now posed by modernism is that the job its artists are asked to undertake "is no longer to produce another instance of an art but a new medium within it," Cavell alternatively describes this concern as "the task of establishing a new automatism."[7] In locating the idea of automatism in relation to what in traditional art might have been called the "broad genres or forms in which an art organizes itself (the fugue, the dance forms, blues) and those local events or *topoi* around which a genre precipitates itself (e.g. modulations, inversions, cadences)," Cavell clarifies: "In calling such things automatisms, I do not mean that they automatically ensure artistic success or depth, but that in mastering a tradition one masters a range of automatisms upon which the tradition maintains itself, and in deploying them one's work is assured of a place in that tradition" (WV 104).

The peculiarity of this verbal substitution—"automatism" for "medium"—is explained perhaps by the importance within an earlier discussion by Cavell of the concept of musical improvisation, which because it is undertaken against the backdrop—or rather with the support—of readymade formulae, is a peculiar blend of the kind of liberating release of spontaneity that we associate with, for example, the surrealists' invocation of the word "automatism" (as in psychic automatism) and the set of learned, more or less rote conventions (automatisms) contained within the traditional media that not only make it conceivable to improvise—as when Bach could improvise a single voice into the extraordinary complexity of a five-part fugue—but make it possible to test the validity of a given improvisation: the success or failure of a pianist's invention of the final cadenza for which a composer has called, for example. Arguing that one can imagine all music up to Beethoven as being, to a certain extent, improvised, Cavell says: "Reliance on formula seems to allow the fullest release of spontaneity. . . . The context in which we can hear music as improvisatory is one in which the language it employs, its conventions, are familiar or obvious enough that at no point are we or the performer in doubt about our location or goal."[8]

Cavell was driven to discuss improvisation because postwar music appeared to him to have produced the same dilemma to which Kentridge refers in his "Fortuna" lecture, namely the choice between two equally impossible alternatives: either the absolute mechanization of chance (John Cage) or the utter submission to total organization (Ernst Krenek's electronic programming). In either one of these options, not only are the results cut loose from a subject who can neither be said to have "intended" them nor be held responsible for them, but they are deprived of any way of being tested: there is no goal contained within the musical outcome against which it might be judged or appreciated, nor is there any condition within which chance itself might be seen to count. But because the taking and seizing of chance—which is another way of naming the capacity to improvise—now imposes itself as both the expression of the withdrawal of the traditional media and the alternative to that withdrawal, both improvisation and automatism thus take on a special weight within this argument. Improvisation now names both the freedom and the isolation of the artist operating without the guarantees of tradition.

In turning his attention from the tensions of modern music to the problem of modernism in film, Cavell adds a new layer to his use of "automatism." The photographic basis of cinema, he says, means that a certain automatism is naturally guaranteed to film. This is not just because the camera is a machine and thus its recording of the world, bracketing human agency, is produced "automatically," but because it mechanically assures that, as spectators, our presence to that world will be suspended: "In viewing a movie my helplessness is mechanically assured: I am present not at something happening, which I must confirm, but at something that has happened, which I absorb (like a memory)" (WV 26). It is this idea of the automatic conditions built into the medium's physical basis that issues into Cavell's global definition of film as "a succession of automatic world projections" (WV 72).

But the mechanical nature of film's guarantee of absence, and thus its automatic suspension of the modern problems of individuality and isolation, is not enough to raise this form of absence to the level of art. For if "film is a candidate for art through its natural relation to its traditions of automatism," then Cavell argues: "The lapse of conviction in its traditional uses of its automatism forces it into modernism; its potentiality for acknowledging that lapse in ways that will redeem its power makes modernism an option for it" (WV 103).

And it is here that the two automatisms layer over one another, the material basis on the one hand and the task of creating a new medium on the other, since as Cavell adds, "What gives significance to features of this physical basis are artistic discoveries of form and genre and type and technique, which I have begun calling automatisms" (WV 105). While it may seem perverse to use the same term for film's material support and for the conventions generated by it as a medium, this is necessitated in part by what he calls "the fate of modernist art generally—that its awareness and responsibility for the physical basis of its art compel it at once to assert and deny the control of its art by that basis." But then, standing at that crossroads imposed by the formalist implosion to which I have repeatedly referred,[9] Cavell goes on: "This is also why, although I am trying to free the idea of a medium from its confinement in referring to the physical bases of various arts, I go on using the same word to name those bases as well as to characterize modes of achievement within the arts" (WV 105).

The formalist implosion, through which in the 1960s mediums were understood as "essentialized" around a material condition—painting now read as having stripped away all superfluous conventions to reduce itself to the defining bedrock of its physical flatness—is thus resisted by Cavell. And the concept of automatism is the mode of this resistance. An artistic automatism is the discovery of a form—call it a convention—that will generate a continuing set of new instances, spinning them out the way a language does.[10] Further, it recognizes the need to take chances in the face of a medium now cut free from the guarantees of artistic tradition; finally, it implies the way in which the work so created is "autonomous," liberated from its maker.

Much of all of this is acknowledged in Kentridge's invocation of *fortuna*. The automatism he has discovered—"drawings for projection"—works itself out in a continuing series. Whatever else that series focuses on—apartheid, capitalist greed, eros, memory—the automatism of his process places procedure before meaning, or rather trusts to the fact that his new medium—his new automatism—will induce meaning: "The hope is that without directly plunging a surgeon's knife, the arcane process of obsessively walking between the camera and the drawing-board will pull to the surface, intimations of the interior" (WK 112).

3. If Cavell's automatism is revealing about what is at stake for Kentridge's aspirations for a medium—in all its invented specificity—the term also harbors a deep reservation about the possibility of that medium's seriousness. For Cavell is particularly unforgiving about animation, a reservation he expresses by insisting on referring to it as "cartoons." In being drawn—or in any event, in avoiding photography as its basis—animation is excluded from both the automatic (or mechanical) and the world (or realistic) parts of his definition of film as "a succession of automatic world projections." Indeed, one index of animation's specific release from the conditions of this definition is marked by the fact that cartoons are primarily inhabited by talking animals.[11]

This animistic world, Cavell argues, is essentially a child's world: "The difference between [it] and the world we inhabit is not that the world of animation is governed by physical laws or satisfies metaphysical limits which are just different from those which condition us; its laws are often quite similar. The difference is that we are uncertain when or to what extent our laws and limits do and do not apply (which suggests that [within the world of animation] there are no real *laws* at all)" (WV 170).

In this freedom from law, it is weightlessness and thus an eccentric relation to gravity that obtain; there, too, the conditions of both physical identity and physical destruction are suspended. Indeed, the fact that the bodies of cartoon characters never seem to get in their way makes them almost immortal. "Beasts which are pure spirits," Cavell says of these creatures, "they avoid or deny *the* metaphysical fact of human beings, that they are condemned to both souls and bodies. A world whose creatures are incorporeal is a world devoid of sex and death. Its creatures elicit from us a painful tenderness" (WV 171). And since what he sees as defining for film's development into the various movie genres is its opening onto a world we recognize as the one we inhabit, he concludes that "cartoons are not movies" (WV 168).

It could be objected that for Kentridge's purposes it is quite irrelevant whether or not animated cartoons qualify as "movies," and thus as a medium for film in Cavell's sense. For Kentridge is not pursuing film as such but is, rather, building a new medium on the technical support of a widespread and mostly mass-cultural cinematic practice, welcoming its condition as a popular rather than a high art, the way Barthes had turned to photo-novels and comic books as forms of support for what he was calling the "third meaning."[12] Further, Kentridge is patently interested in the conventions that cartoon animation developed, conventions that involve the serialized exploits of stock characters on the one hand and the possibility of physical metamorphosis on the other. Thus, he found himself not only generating a repertory of personae whose actions would be tracked within a continuing series of works but confronting the fact of how resistant such a set is to random expansion. (Kentridge describes how he imagined introducing another character—Liberty Eckstein—to the company he had developed in *Mine,* at that point consisting of Soho Eckstein, Mrs. Eckstein, and Felix Teitlebaum—introduced in *Johannesburg, 2nd Greatest City* and brought back as a group for *Sobriety, Obesity, & Growing Old* [1991]—but was unable to do so, because the principle of repetition that governs stock repertories such as the commedia dell'arte or animated cartoons applied equally to him.) And further, this rigidity of the cast finds its equal but opposite principle in the amazing elasticity of the forms.

This latter, of course, had been what most struck and excited Sergei Eisenstein as he theorized the phenomenon of Disney cartoons. Calling this "plasmaticness," he compared the freedom with which animated figures change identities—the mobility of their shapes, their endless metamorphic potential—to the phenomenon of fire. The universal fascination with fire, the libidinal energy associated with its formal flux, and the parallel to this presented by animation go part of the way to explain the grip cartoons exert. Another part, Eisenstein suggests, is produced by a kind of ontogenetic memory, the unconscious trace of the evolutionary transformations through which the human species itself developed; for a Disney figure presents its viewers with the sense of a being which "behaves like the primal protoplasm . . . skipping along the rungs of the evolutionary ladder."[13]

This elasticity of shape which, like the fascination with fire, he finds cross-culturally—in Carroll's *Alice in Wonderland,* in the illustrator Trier, in eighteenth-century Japanese etchings—leads Eisenstein to explain the power of this phenomenon as stemming from the desire for "a rejection of once-and-forever allotted form, freedom from ossification, the ability to dynamically assume any form." One example he gives to demonstrate how any part of the body might be submitted to this "plasmatic" principle focuses on Mickey Mouse's white-gloved hands: "How easily and gracefully these four fingers on both of Mickey's hands, playing a Hawaiian guitar, suddenly dissolve into . . . two pairs of extremities. The two middle fingers become little legs, the two outer fingers—little hands. The second hand becomes its partner. And suddenly there are no longer two hands, but two funny, little white people, elegantly dancing together along the strings of the Hawaiian guitar."[14]

But the most compelling explanation Eisenstein has for the attraction exerted by Disney is a socioeconomic one: given modernity's "mercilessly standardized and mechanically measured existence," Disney offers a "triumph over the fetters of form"; his spectacle of perpetual change is a revolt against the grayness of what Eisenstein identifies as both Fordism and "partitioning." He draws a parallel between Disney and the eighteenth-century protest the animal population of La Fontaine's fables could be seen as staging against seventeenth-century rationalization and mechanization. "The heartless geometrizing and metaphysics [in Descartes]," he writes, "here give rise to a kind of antithesis, an unexpected rebirth of universal animism."[15]

Is there not a sense, however, in which Disney's "triumph," along with that of the other Hollywood cartoonists, is not a revolt against the rationalization of the human body, but is its cast shadow, its dialectical underside now made to surface as comic? When the legs of little Jerry trying to escape from Tom are transformed into frantically turning wheels, they provide a picture of the human body not only endlessly available to mechanization, but fully opened to subdivision according to the requirements labor imposes on human motion—a Taylorist subdivision ("partitioning") that turns parts of the body into independent organisms of movement, just as Mickey's fingers become a tiny couple waltzing along the strings of his ukulele. Disney's "plasmaticness" may thus be not a twentieth-century version of the phenomenon of fire or the primitive idea of animism but, instead, an analogue of the principle of universal equivalence that reigns at the heart of capital. And if this is true, there is no real opposition in the end between Eisenstein's vision of Mickey Mouse (even Eisenstein cannot avoid saying of Disney's works, "because of the fleeting ephemerality of their existence, you can't reproach them for their mindlessness") and Cavell's condemnation of the weightlessness of cartoons.[16] The abstract condition of the general equivalent, the fluidity of its circulation and exchange, and the sense of its endlessly transformative power make the cartoon figure and money peculiarly apt mirrors of one another.[17]

Now it is precisely weight that is a continuing concern for Kentridge. It appears in the very names of his works—*WEIGHING and WANTING* (1998), *Sobriety, Obesity, & Growing Old*—and in the words he uses to name moral responsibility, as for example, he says of *The History of the Main Complaint* (1996): "here's a person who's in a coma because of the weight of what he's seen" (WK 179). And we find it in what he obviously intends for the physical character of his drawing, as captured by a critic's acknowledgement: "Unlike Daumier and Grosz, Kentridge is not a caricaturist, yet his drawings contain the same authority of line, the same contour and weight" (WK 178). But specifically concerning the "plasmaticness" inherent in animation, weight makes its appearance through his sense that this transformative power needs to have a certain drag placed on it, a certain resistance or pressure exerted against its weightless fluidity; hence the report of another critic who ends by quoting him: "[Kentridge] is wary of the threat of arbitrariness and guards against an underground series of chance images in which 'anything changes into anything else too easily, in which anything is possible without any pressure'" (WK 182).

This does not mean that Kentridge's films totally avoid the principle of universal equivalence; in a world inhabited by mine owners and bankers such avoidance would be peculiar. General equivalence is one of the conditions of the universe Kentridge is addressing. Hence, the *cafetière* becoming a mine shaft (*Mine*), the cigarette smoke becoming a typewriter (*Johannesburg*), the stethoscope becoming a telephone (*History of the Main Complaint*), the camera's tripod becoming helicopter blades or its lens a machine gun (*Ubu Tells the Truth*), and even more to the point, columns of numbers becoming office buildings or derricks (*Stereoscope*). But another condition that equally reigns within these films operates against the principle of anything changing into anything else, or at least works to dilate the time within which the change occurs and to underscore the impossibility of predicting the form it will take, thus investing that change with a kind of weight (emotional? moral? mnemonic?). As an example, in *Sobriety, Obesity, & Growing Old,* Soho pets the cat which lies in bed next to him in the absent Mrs. Eckstein's place, and the cat, leaping onto his face as though to comfort him, transforms itself into a gas mask, grotesque and terrifying.

If transformation is built into the very weft of animation—because they are drawn, the successive images can both render the variations in a moving figure's posture and by the same token can change the very nature of the figure, impossibly stretching or shrinking parts of its body or giving it a new identity altogether—pressure exerted against effortless transformation could also signal pressure exerted against animation itself, which is to say, animation's very illusion of movement. In this case, the momentary stillness interleaved between the frames, so to speak, the sense of a kind of rictus that brakes the forward motion, reinstating the stillness of a single drawing, would alter the conditions of Kentridge's support.

In theorizing the flow of cinematic illusion, which he calls "the movement-image," Gilles Deleuze opposes two types of photography:

time-exposure (*pose*) and snapshot (*instantané*). The former, which derives from the tradition of painting, strives after an idealization of its subject, the construction of a single posture replete with meaning. This possibility is not open to the snapshot, which merely nets what Deleuze calls "any-instant-whatever."[18] In its address to themes of movement, painting had always tried to precipitate out the pose that would constellate its idea, but in so doing, motion, which (as Zeno had long ago told us) occurs *in between* the possible postures, would always have escaped. For any given minute, however, the movie camera, in its total arbitrariness, captures twenty-four any-instants-whatever, none of them infected with the fatal stillness of the pose, each of them capable of ceding its place to its successor in the relay that constitutes the in-between of a motion that is never *in* the moving subject but is in the relay itself, in the space between two "nows," one appearing and one disappearing.

Given the importance of the mechanical—photographic—capture of these any-instants-whatever, Deleuze's theory would seem to make animation problematic for his definition of film, although in an entirely different way from Cavell's, since for him the drawn image would be not too light but too heavy for cinema. Deleuze, however, explicitly makes a place for animation:

> If [the cartoon film] belongs fully to the cinema, this is because the drawing no longer constitutes a pose or a completed figure, but the description of a figure which is always in the process of being formed or dissolving through the movement of lines and points taken at any-instant-whatevers of their course. The cartoon film is related not to a Euclidean, but to a Cartesian geometry. It does not give us a figure described in a unique moment, but the continuity of the movement which describes the figure.[19]

Indeed, to test their drawings for this continuity, traditional cartoon animators had recourse to the flip book, or flicker book, as a tool with which to guard against the pose:

> When an animator sketches out the scene in his flicker book, what is being expressed in the constant alternation between drawing and how it is seen as the book is flicked through is just this simultaneity of the pose and motion. Though the animator is only able to work from one to the other, what must nevertheless be captured in the flicker book, separated only by the thickness of the page or support itself, is the simultaneity of the pose and motion, the simultaneity—at once the same and different—of two poses.[20]

However technically primitive, then, the flicker book already projects the framework of film's mechanization of movement, as it also already implies the proliferation of images needed to construct it. If at nothing but the crudest, material notion of a medium's support, then, Kentridge's technical alternative, his eschewal of the flip book, sets his medium—his "drawings for projection"—at an angle to animation, one that seems "below" it, which is to say even less technologically invested than the flicker book itself.

One way of characterizing this quality of being "lower" or more regressed than the flicker book would be historical. One could say that, in the sense one has in his work of finished drawings substituting themselves for one another, Kentridge is invoking an earlier moment within the prehistory of animation, seeking among the optical toys through which a primitive version of the filmic was glimpsed for something even less apparatus-like than the whirling drum of the zoetrope, or the spinning wheel of the phenakistoscope. It is as though something even more primitively handcrafted is being appropriated as a model, something as moronically simple as the thaumatrope—that type of little disc whose sashes one twiddled between one's fingers so that as it spun, the image on the disc's back would optically marry itself to the image on its front, the bareback rider jumping thereby onto the galloping horse or the pictured canary finding itself within the image of its cage.

Alternatively, the idea of a "lower" form could be a matter of retrogression from what the Frankfurt School termed the "second nature" of technology, which film invokes through the mechanism of its apparatus, to the "first nature" not just of the handcrafted but of the bodily condition of the human subject. There is a sense in which the body's rhythms have penetrated Kentridge's support, to slow it down, to thicken it, to give it density. This occurs not just in the breathing that is thematized in so many of the works: the labored breath of the "statue" at the end of *Monument*; the rise and fall of the chests of the workers asleep in their terrible bunks in *Mine*; Soho's troubled wheezing through the gas mask of *Sobriety, Obesity, & Growing Old*; the open-mouthed rasping of the comatose Soho in *The History of the Main Complaint*. It also occurs at a deeper level of representation, in which the hesitations in the continuity of the movement seem the registration within the film's visual field of Kentridge's body "stalking the drawing," of his own movement both tracking and slowing that of the image.

Both these senses of "below"—as something more primitive that invests the procedures of animation which serve as Kentridge's technical support—converge in the relationship that this very crudeness bears to the primary matrix of the drawing itself. For the most striking character of the line generated by Kentridge's "altered" form of animation is that it exists as palimpsest. As the charcoal contours of one stage of the drawing are erased, they remain as ghosts through the next stage and the stage following that, to be joined by other ghosts and still others. So that the density of these pale tracks shadows the formation of each new drawing, like a leaf stuck to one's shoe.

4. Critics have not failed to describe the experience of Kentridge's work in terms of the palimpsest. The sense of the removal and redrawing of the line; the feeling of watching something having been peeled away or lightened while at another, almost contiguous spot something weighty has abruptly been added; the pale pseudo-cast-shadows that seem to underwrite the appearance of any line, each produced as the correction of a former one—all this has led to titles like "The Art of Erasure" for reviews of Kentridge's exhibitions. Indeed, since the early days of abstract expressionism, when an almost obsessional layering of contours, of the partial scraping away of undercoats and the addition of ever new versions of the same figuration—particularly obvious in the work of

de Kooning and Kline—never has the paradigm of the palimpsest so made its way into the discourse on modes of contemporary drawing. This most ancient of graphic phenomena—the residue of primitive markers on the walls of caves, as at Rouffignac with its visual braid of overlaid bison and mammoths not so much canceling each other out as providing an ever fresh ground for the formation of a new figure—is thus implausibly joined to the "second nature" of modern technology. The powdered pigment blown by the paleolithic artist onto the stone surface is now reprised by the equally powdery substance of charcoal, but this now hovers above the luminous ground of either projection screen or backlit monitor like a dense cover of black fog, sometimes greasily opaque, sometimes brokenly grainy, at other times a radiant mist.

It is this *form* of the drawing that one needs to hold at some distance from Kentridge's graphic style. As in Louis Hjelmslev's structuralist system, in which both the content and expression of a given sign are each subdivided into form and (material) substance, Kentridge's style of drawing, with its multiple art-historical references—to Max Beckmann, to Grosz, to Daumier, to Goya—belongs to the level of the works' content.[21] The semiologists would call these stylistic decisions "the form of the content," and indeed they project a set of concerns at the thematic level: the association with a lineage of political draftsmen; a type of strongly black-and-white rendering meant to connect with even earlier forms of popular protest such as woodcut broadsides or posters.

If these references are a manifestation of content, however, the palimpsest is a function of the support for that content, its "expression." And on this level, in which the substance of the expression is charcoal constantly modified by the application of the eraser, the form of the expression is the palimpsest. Which means that once again there is a gap in Kentridge's work between content and form—as was the case between the two types of "catastrophe" in *Monument*: that of the dehumanization of its depicted African subject, and that of the interminable shuttle set up by the act of "stalking the drawing." Yet once again this gap is not opened for the purpose of choosing, say, the formal over the political, but rather of seeing how the formal might indeed be invested by the political and how this in turn might reorganize one's sense of the political field itself.

As a "form of expression," the palimpsest could be usefully joined to the typology set up by Benjamin Buchloh for the analysis of graphic paradigms since the onset of modernism. Dividing the full range of drawing into two basic types, matrix and grapheme, Buchloh sees each of these as the condensed and abstracted rendering of the form of the "object" on the one hand and that of the "subject" on the other.[22] Whether grid or concentric structure, the matrix serves not only as the emblematic residue of those systems of projection, such as perspective, through which the objective world of three dimensions was formerly traced, but doubles and thereby manifests the infrastructure of the aesthetic object itself (the weave of the canvas, the armature of the sculpture). As for the grapheme, it is the precipitate of the universe of subjectively expressive marks now reduced to the pure trace of either the neuromotor or psychological-libidinal manifestations of a curiously voided subject. As examples of his dichotomy, Buchloh names Johns and Twombly, the first as the master of the matrix, the second as the producer of the grapheme.

But the palimpsest, graphically distinct from both grapheme and matrix, belongs neither to the world of the subject nor to that of the object. As an abstract form, it simply implies residue. As the possible deposit of many markers, it so disperses the field of the subject as utterly to depersonalize and thus denature it. And as the trace of a series of events, it eats away at the substance of anything we might call an object. The palimpsest, we could say, is the emblematic form of the temporal and as such it is the abstraction of narrative, of history, of biography—the latter implying a subject seen not from its own point of view but from that of a third, objectivized viewer, an outsider.

Buchloh's own typology was produced from the retrospective position necessitated by the efflorescence of drawing at the hands of Raymond Pettibon. For it is Pettibon, Buchloh argues, who forces onto this neat aesthetic distinction the disturbances wrought by mass-cultural incursions that have transformed both the world of the "object" and that of the "subject." If pop art had already challenged the matrix's presumption to access—in no matter how abstracted a form—to the objective world, by demonstrating how that very world has been permeated by the image system of media and thereby already reproduced as spectacle, Pettibon in turn challenges pop art's supposed objectivity with regard to spectacle itself. In opposition to the sinuous elegance of late pop drawings (Warhol, Lichtenstein) with their "placid acceptance of the cartooned forms of social interaction and articulation, Pettibon reinscribes the compulsive, fractured immediacy of notation made under duress." But equally, lest the authority of subjective expressiveness be allowed to resurrect itself on the basis of this felt pressure, Buchloh adds: "At the same time the purely corporeal grapheme of a draftsman like Twombly is recharged with a mass-cultural concreteness and circumstantial specificity that purges the corporeal notation of even its last remnants of bodily *jouissance*." In the grip of this dialectical intersection in which grapheme and matrix infect one another, the world of Pettibon is thus a choreography of "the entwining of public and private spheres" both, now, mass-culturally reorganized as "delusional systems."[23]

The joint presence of Pettibon and Kentridge within the art practice of the 1990s demonstrates the unlooked-for recrudescence of drawing, which is to say, the upsurge of the autographic, the hand-wrought, in an age of the mechanization and technologizing of the image via either photography or digital imaging. The extent to which each artist must acknowledge the penetration of drawing by technology and thus of the individual hand of the draftsman by mass culture is registered, however, by Buchloh's withering account of the shrunken domain left to Pettibon.

As I pointed out, Buchloh's bipartition of the graphic terrain omits the third term of the palimpsest, with all that it implies of the encoding of the temporal and thus its access to a kind of historical narrative otherwise left no place in a mass-culturally invested world of "delusional systems." But if Kentridge has recourse to the palimpsest, his practice—no less than Pettibon's—is cognizant of the ubiquitous force of mass culture and thus the precariousness of a narrative subject's claim to the position of historical reckoning. Indeed, it is this recognition that tends to be omitted by the unquestioning embrace of Kentridge's work as "about" memory and forgetting, "about" history and responsibility—a typical statement: "Kentridge's art stresses the importance of remembering and takes a stance against the risk of lapsing into amnesia and disavowal of historical memory, as well as of psychic removal, characteristic of society after traumatic events" (WK 31)—as though access to these things has not become incredibly complex. Kentridge himself cautions, "You cannot face the rock head on; the rock always wins," because in the age of spectacle, it is impossible for the memory of apartheid not to be itself spectacularized—as in the sessions of the Truth and Reconciliation Commission broadcast nightly on South African television.[24] As we are learning from the Holocaust, it is extremely hard for the business of memory not to be exploited to the point of becoming itself a business.

Hence the importance of admitting the penetration of the technological into the palimpsest, the invasion of a "first nature" by the "second." The technical support—animation—of Kentridge's medium might be alienated from itself by an incursion of the bodily, yet in an equal but opposite way, his graphic construction—the palimpsest—is infected by the mechanical.

This occurs at the most basic level of production, since Kentridge's reinvented version of the palimpsest depends for its very visibility on the intervention of the camera and the stop-shoot process. But the mechanistic also finds its way into the image field, as when the perceived erasures of a given contour move the experience of the palimpsest away from the reference to the caves and into the embrace of an entirely different primitivism, that of the early technology of movement. Thus, when we see the laborer at the beginning of *Monument* walking in a close-up in which each of his feet seems to be dragging a train of ghostly contours behind it, or when in *History of the Main Complaint* we watch the windshield wipers of Soho's car leave a sputter of spokelike effigies in their path, we feel ourselves in the presence of Etienne-Jules Marey's photographic motion studies, with each figure generating its trail of linear traces. And this permeability of the drawn palimpsest by the history of photographic technologies is echoed by the parallel Kentridge sets up in *History of the Main Complaint* between the handcrafted palimpsest, with its smudges and cloudiness, and the look of high-tech medical imaging such as CAT scans, sonar, MRI scans, and even X-rays. As he says, "there is a great affinity between the velvety grey tones of an X-ray and the softness of charcoal dust brushed onto paper" (WK 112).

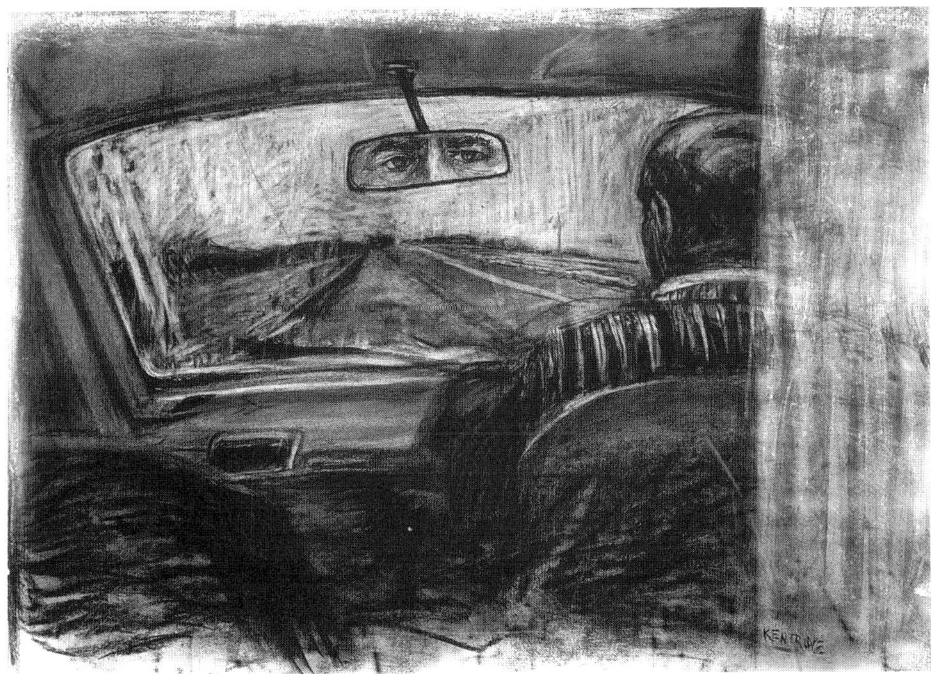

7.1 William Kentridge, *History of the Main Complaint,* 1996. Courtesy the artist.

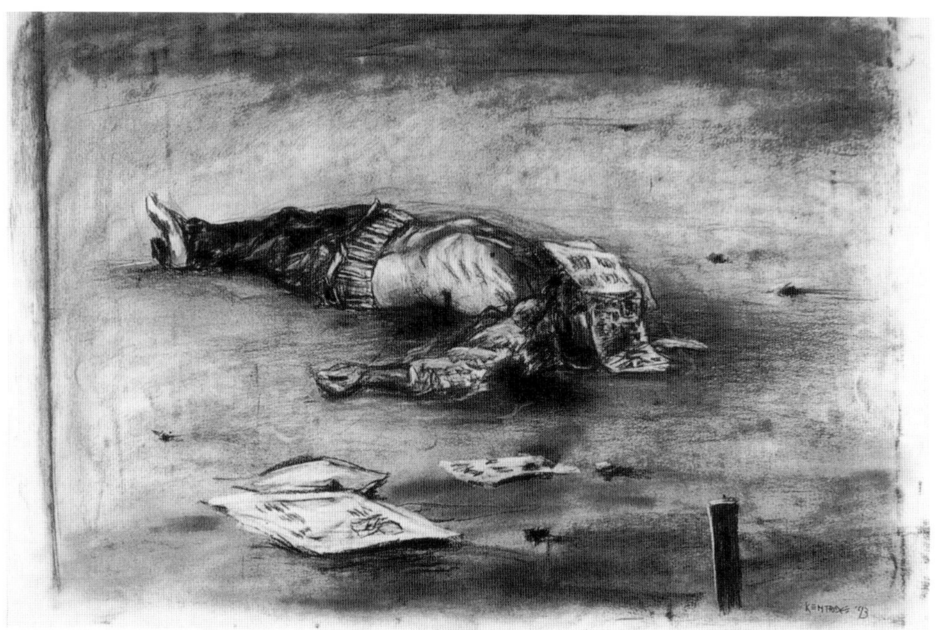

7.2 William Kentridge, *Felix in Exile,* 1993. Courtesy the artist.

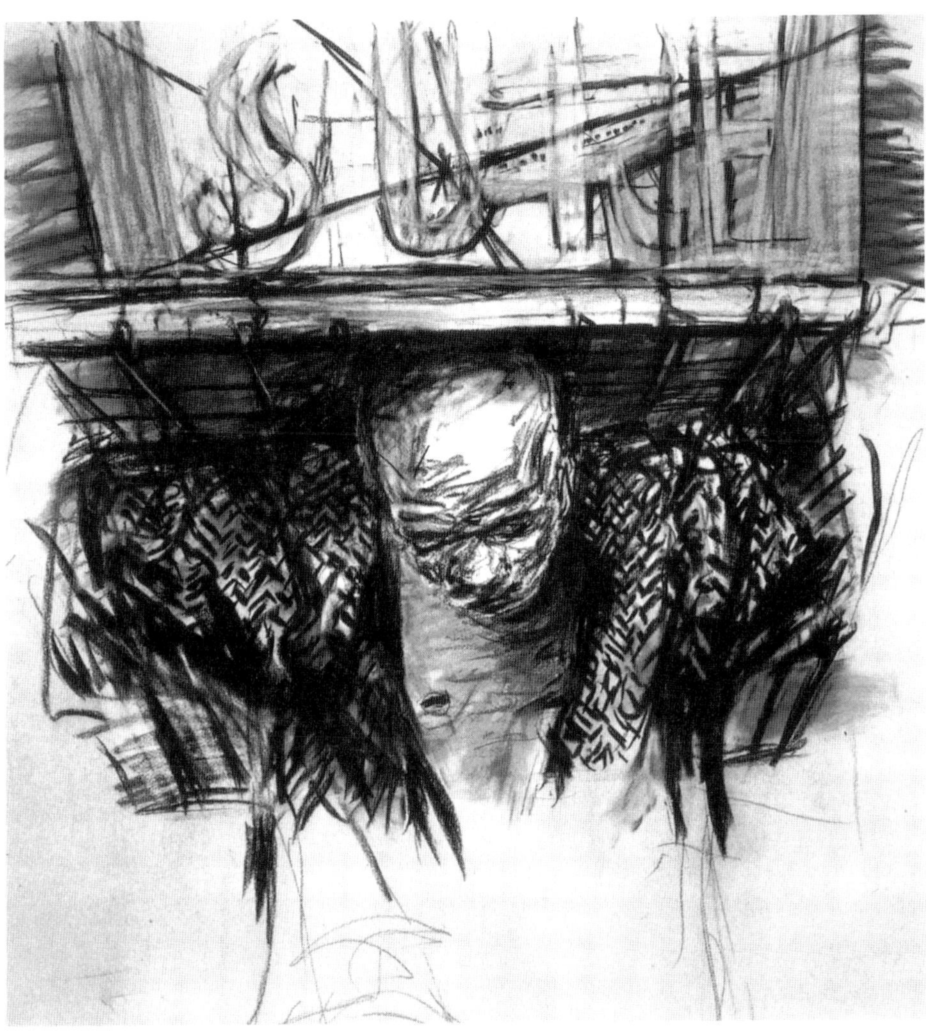

7.3 William Kentridge, *Monument,* 1990. Courtesy the artist.

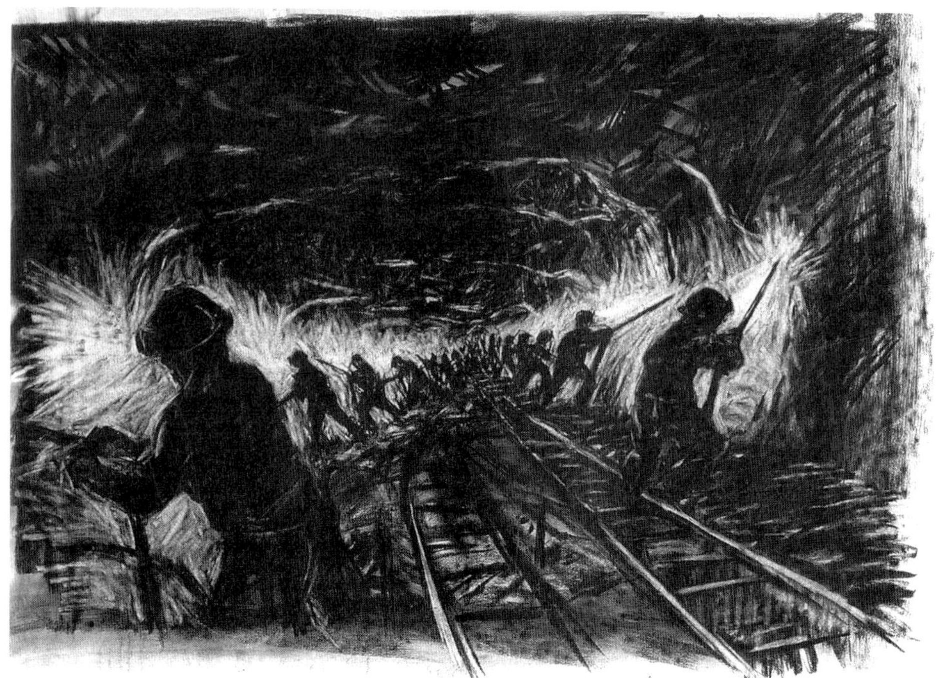

7.4 William Kentridge, *Mine,* 1991. Courtesy the artist.

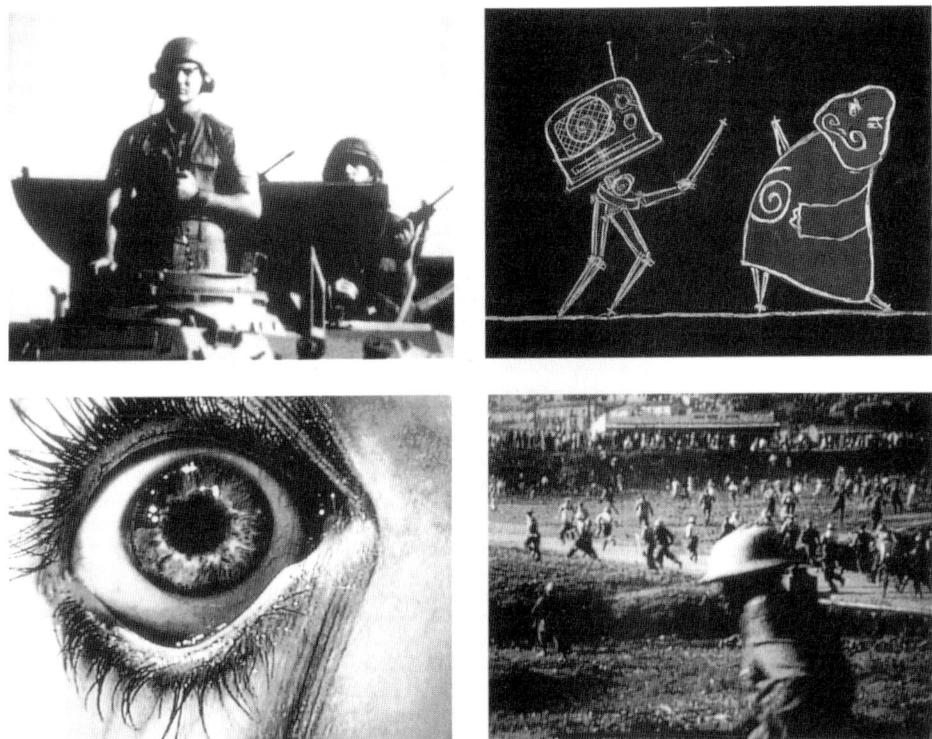

7.5 William Kentridge, *Ubu Tells the Truth,* 1996–1997. Courtesy the artist.

In the one film that is directly "about" drawing—*Felix in Exile* (1993), in which Felix Teitlebaum, in his hotel room in Paris, looks at the corpses scattered over the veld in the drawings made by the African woman Nandi which he carries with him—the narrative desubjectivizes this drawing by mechanizing it. Nandi is a surveyor and her graphic instrument is a theodolite. Furthermore, besides her registering of the theodolite's crosshairs, the only other lines we see her making belong to the world of impersonal traces—the forensic contours drawn around bodies at the scenes of crime.

This infiltration of the graphic by the technological also occurs at that level in which the expressive medium of drawing is taken as the stand-in for the subject him- or herself. When in *History of the Main Complaint,* for example, the exploration of Soho's bedridden, comatose body through the sophisticated imaging that will render it transparent yields up a succession of ticker-tape machines, telephones, hole punches, and typewriters, as the equipment of his consciousness, subjectivity itself is now portrayed as infected by "second nature." Or at the end of *Mine,* when Soho's state of intense satisfaction is signaled by his sweeping all his other possessions off his bed in order to play with the tiny rhinoceros just delivered to him through the mine shaft, the spontaneity of this "emotion" is already compromised by the degree to which this miniaturized animal resonates with associations not to Africa but to Disney.

5. To a degree equal to their attention to the presence of the palimpsest, Kentridge's critics have been struck by his recourse to the outmoded. The ringing of the Bakelite telephones, the clacking of the ribbon typewriters, the clanging of the trolley cars that drive a rift through the massing crowds, all call to us from the horizon of the 1940s. The political stage of these films may be choreographed by the chronological present of apartheid—its exceedingly recent dismantling and the painful national reconstruction it now necessitates—but its decor is that of the past.

The parameters of this pastness vary somewhat. Sometimes it is located in the decades of interwar modernism with its social-utopian cast, whether this be in the importation of Bauhaus architecture (Soho's International Style house in

WEIGHING and WANTING) or in the associations Kentridge's drawing style more generally makes to Weimar. Often it speaks from the late 1940s and early 1950s, that ambiguous moment just after World War II when, as the Bauhaus had predicted, technology had thoroughly reconceived the "furniture" of one's life—the telephones, the typewriters, the picture windows, the industrially designed china—but where the utopian frame that was to inform this reconstruction had all but receded, supplanted as it was by an ethos of consumption. At other times this reference to the past is shifted back to the late 1910s and early 1920s and the history of silent film, such as the use of vignetting in D. W. Griffith (as in the iris-in at the end of *Monument* or the irises-in and -out that punctuate *Johannesburg, 2nd Greatest City*) and the more general deployment of intertitles. In this latter case, the associations are to the progressive implications of mass culture as it was received by the surrealists, for example, or by Walter Benjamin.

Indeed, animation, the technical support for Kentridge's "drawings for projection," had itself been at stake in the argument Benjamin makes in "The Work of Art in the Age of Mechanical Reproduction," the thirteenth section of which—the one treating the optical unconscious—had originally been titled "Micky-Maus." That Disney's character was the product of animation meant on the one hand that he was not open to being reinfected by the "aura" that could regather around the human film actor become "star"; and on the other, that in Mickey's "plasmaticness" (to use Eisenstein's term), he offered the possibility of a release of subjectivity from its confinement to the human shape, rupturing, as Benjamin said, "the hierarchy of creatures predicated on the human being" (OMD 47).

In this latter idea, which he also called "the cracking of natural teleology," is contained part of the utopian possibilities Benjamin imputed to film in general, which he saw as preparing the human subject for a necessary and ultimately liberating integration with technology. Not only was film to release men and women from the confines of their private spaces and into a collective realm—"Then came film and exploded this prison-world with the dynamite of one-tenth seconds, so that now, in the midst of its far-flung ruins and debris, we calmly embark on adventurous travels"[25]—but it was to infiltrate and restructure subjectivity itself, changing damaged individual experience into energized collective perception. And in this idea of a newly organized psychological collective, the animating figure was Mickey Mouse. "Film has launched an attack against the old Heraclitean truth that in waking we share a world while sleeping we are each in separate worlds," Benjamin wrote in the first draft of "The Work of Art in the Age of Mechanical Reproduction." "It has done so, less with representations of dreams, than with the creation of figures of the collective dream such as the globe-orbiting Mickey Mouse" (OMD 31).

Specifically, Benjamin's recourse to Mickey Mouse revolved around the effects of collective laughter, which he saw as the antidote to the deadening of individual experience under the assaults of modern technology. To the individual anaesthetized by the shocks of contemporary life, this laughter would serve as a kind of countershock, a form of the same assault but now converted into "a therapeutic detonation of the unconscious" (OMD 31). In this sense, sufferers from the effects of technology could be protected by that same technology.

And this physiological conversion could also have a cognitive function. Benjamin spoke of the "possibility of psychic inoculation by means of certain films in which a forced articulation of sadistic fantasies or masochistic delusion can prevent their natural and dangerous ripening in the masses. The collective laughter signifies a premature and therapeutic eruption of such mass psychoses" (OMD 31–32). Imagining this as a process of transference by which individual alienation makes a leap into a form of collective, public recognition, Benjamin thus sees both the physiological and cognitive value of this laughter.

It is in this sense that film becomes a case of technology itself providing a homeopathic shock experience that would allow for a collective adaptation of and to technology. As Miriam Hansen puts it, Benjamin saw film as "a perceptual training ground for an industrially transformed physis." For, as he writes: "To make the vast technical apparatus of our time an object of human innervation [i.e., stimulation]—this is the historical task in whose service film has its true meaning" (OMD 38).

If Mickey Mouse vanished from the later versions of "The Work of Art," this was because Benjamin soon began to take seriously the note he had included in his first draft warning of the "usability of the Disney method for Fascism" (OMD 52). He now began to side with the opinion Adorno expressed in his letter responding to Benjamin's essay in which he warns, "The laughter of the audience at a cinema . . . is anything but good and revolutionary; instead, it is full of the worst bourgeois sadism."[26] Calling this laughter the "iron bath of fun" administered by the culture industry, Adorno saw it as persuading mutilated subjects to identify masochistically with the forces of social authority. And indeed, as Miriam Hansen points out in her discussion of the Benjamin/Adorno debate, the present-day variations on Benjamin's idea of "play versions of second nature," as in video games for example, "have become a major site for naturalizing violence, destruction, and oppression" (OMD 54).

With this reference to video games, however, we find ourselves in a very different technological field from that of Disney and CEL animation.[27] For video games, with their insertion of the computer chip into the field of action, heralded a wholesale shift in the visual media themselves. Having now become a matter of computer programming and digital imaging, animation has lost the kind of handcraft that had still survived even in its late forms of industrialization—something Chuck Jones, the animator of Bugs Bunny and Daffy Duck, underscored by saying, "The only thing all of us had in common was that we all could draw. We all could draw the human figure."[28] Benjamin similarly believed that technology doesn't altogether permeate the Disney characters' bodies, rendering them literalized figures of mechanization, but instead remains a "hidden figure," still permitting the sense of an imbrication of technology with natural beings out of which the transformations of the body seem to be improvised (OMD 42).

At the same time that the computer has rendered CEL animation utterly outmoded, it has also overtaken photographically based cinema, the kind of film that had declared its indexical connection to the contingencies of time and presence, the kind Cavell had called "automatic world projections." The digitizing of film means precisely that Cavell's distinction between "movies" and "cartoons" has utterly collapsed, so that just as animation increasingly penetrates photographically filmed material—not only in special effects, but in the integration of animated characters with live actors—the adult world of film invests the child's world of cartoons, projecting into the new breed of full-length animation the pornography and blood that Cavell had assumed this world could not support.[29] And for Benjamin's analysis this implosion means that, far from being a medium to "master the interplay between human beings and nature," the "leap into the apparatus" facilitated by film now constructs the subject as no more than one element "in a loop that processes information and sensory signals."[30]

The death knell that currently rings on all sides, as film is either infiltrated or replaced by digital technologies, signals its ever rapid slide into obsolescence. "This is why," Miriam Hansen warns, "taking Benjamin's imperative to 'actuality' seriously today means recognizing that the cinema, once celebrated for articulating the secret affinities among things in an age of accelerated obsolescence, may itself have become a thing of the past."[31]

Technoteleologists such as Friedrich Kittler or Norbert Bolz greet this rising cybernetic tide, in which all previous forms of media are now engulfed by digitization, as the inevitable course of progress, itself encoded within the logic of electronic systems.[32] In their eyes, Benjamin's technological pessimism from the late 1930s, and his reinvestment in forms of subjectivity utterly threatened by technology, render his own reflections on film no more than "beautiful ruins in the philosophical landscape."[33]

But in the matter of art Benjamin was very canny on the subject of ruins, for they allowed him to think an "outside" to the increasingly totalized system of "second nature." Thus his late considerations on photography leap over his 1935 "Work of Art" essay to cycle back to his thoughts from the opening of the decade and to reconsider the advantages of obsolescence.[34] Reflecting on the life cycles of technologies—the hopes with which they are born and the ignominious fates to which they are consigned at the moment of their obsolescence, moments which come with increasing speed as the pace of technology grows exponentially—he wondered whether photography had, like other technologies before it, released a fleeting image of the utopian promise it might contain at the moment when it was still an amateur pastime, still the medium of exchange between friends—the moment, that is, before it became commercialized and hardened into a commodity. Further, Benjamin believed that at the point when a technology is suddenly eclipsed by its own obsolescence, its armoring breaks down and it releases the memory of this promise. And here, he hoped, through the outmoded's creation of a chink in the armor, one could glimpse an outside to the totality of technologized space.[35]

The mediums that are now being "invented" are lodging themselves precisely in this space where obsolescence brackets technological determinism long enough for us to think our way back down the path of "progress" to the earlier, stranger forms of expressiveness contained in primitive technologies and to imagine mining these as just that source of "automatism" or "fortuna" that will yield the conventions necessary to a medium. If this has been true for Coleman's regression not just to the outmoded slide tape but to its ancestor, the magic lantern, it is true as well for Kentridge's insistence on the most primitive imaginable animation in the face of digital imaging. Kentridge's technical support is already obsolescent through and through, even before he renders it internally riven—self-different, self-differing—by the hesitations and contradictions encoded by the palimpsest.

Kentridge's recourse to the outmoded at the level of content—the old-fashioned telephones, typewriters, styles of architecture—is, then, like his recourse to the graphic styles of Weimar or of earlier political art. It operates on the form of the content of his work. To have it there at all runs a certain kind of risk. For the danger Kentridge courts in these references is one of "nostalgia," a kind of retro-fashionableness that produces the historical itself as a form of spectacle.[36] Kentridge is aware of this: "Of course the rough monochromatic drawings refer back to early black-and-white movie making. I am not blind to the nostalgia inherent in this" (WK 64–65). And acknowledging that this nostalgia might be "for a period in which political image-making seemed so much less fraught," he also understands that he has "to take responsibility" for such a choice.

But like the issue of the palimpsest in the matter of drawing, Kentridge's concern for outmodedness at the level of the support—his animation technique, which flaunts the hand-drawn in the very teeth of digital imaging, thus siding with the now obsolescent CEL production, in comparison to which his technique itself is also conspicuously more primitive—operates below the content. Instead it lodges itself in the domain of expression, becoming an aspect of the *form* of the expression: its imposition of stasis in the midst of movement; its investment of the traces of bodily production in the midst of the apparatus. Addressing itself to the specificity of the expressive level of the support (animation) in its historical dimension, this formal engagement is far from "nostalgic." It is, we could say, what attempts to undermine a certain kind of spectacularization of memory.

III

Art Criticism

My hostility to conceptual art was awakened by Joseph Kosuth's 1968 manifesto-like essay "Art after Philosophy." Arguing that art's new beginning dates to the work of Marcel Duchamp, Kosuth focused on the readymade as diverting the art object from aesthetic delectation by refocusing it into the bald statement "This is Art." In just the same way, he argued, analytic philosophy (as in the work of Wittgenstein, Ayer, and Quine) had shifted philosophical pursuits away from metaphysics and into a preoccupation with language. By refocusing artistic practice onto the general question "What is art?," conceptual art reoriented making from the specific (as in the specificity of the medium—of painting, of sculpture, of film, etc.) to the general. My theoretical address to what I call "the post-medium condition" constitutes the current focus of my critical energies; hence *Perpetual Inventory* includes examples of this work. Indeed, for those artists who needed to base aesthetic meaning on a medium to which their work could refer, reflexively, the postmodernist condemnation of painting and sculpture as specific mediums forced a turn to some other support than oil on canvas or plaster on metal armature. These innovative foundations I began to call "technical supports." The essays collected in part II, under the rubric "medium," began an investigation of technical supports, as in the work of Ed Ruscha, Christian Marclay, and Sophie Calle.

Part III collects the criticism I wrote (mainly for *Artforum*) based on the assumption that good work would have to refer, recursively, to the medium in which it is made.

Allusion and Illusion in Donald Judd

"... forms which do not depend on the balance and adjustment of one part to another for their meaning."

For some time Donald Judd has been a major spokesman for works of art which seek, as their highest attainment, total identity as objects. Last year in praise of a fellow sculptor's work, Judd wrote: "Rather than inducing idealization and generalization and being allusive, it excludes. The work asserts its own existence, form and power. It becomes an object in its own right." Thus object art would seem to proscribe both allusion and illusion: any reference to experiences or ideas beyond the work's brute physical presence is excluded, as is any manipulation (through the prescribed observation of that presence) of apparent as opposed to literal space. With this presumptive reduction of art from the realm of illusion—and through illusionism, of meaning—to the sphere of transparently real objects, the art with which Judd is associated is characterized as intentionally blank and empty: "Obviously a negative art of denial and renunciation."[1]

Approaching Judd's latest work from within this frame of reference, one is totally unprepared for the extraordinary beauty of the sculptures themselves, a beauty and authority which is nowhere described or accounted for in the

First published in *Artforum* 5 (May 1966).

polemics of object art and which leads one to feel all the more acutely the inadequacy of the theoretical line, its failure to measure up (at least in Judd's case) to the power of the sculptural statement.

In a recent article dealing with the phenomenon of object art, Barbara Rose emphatically recognizes the positive qualities, as opposed to the apparent blankness and denial, of this art, and suggests that these could be located in a mystical experience: "the blankness, the emptiness and vacuum of content is as easily construed as an occasion for spiritual contemplation as it is a nihilistic denial of the world."[2] One cannot here examine this notion as it applies to other sculptors Rose mentions, but at least in the case of Judd's work, which both compels and gratifies immediate sensuous confrontation, the suggestion that his sculpture is the occasion for an experience which completely transcends the physical object does not seem tenable. Nor does a description of Judd's art as meaning something only insofar as it embodies a negation of meaning ("the simple denial of content can in itself constitute the content of such a work")[3] seem to arrive at the richness and plentitude of the works, which are somehow not shorn and dumb, but, rather, insistently meaningful. As Maurice Merleau-Ponty writes, "It is easy to strip language and actions of all meaning and to make them seem absurd, if only one looks at them from far enough away. . . . But that other miracle, the fact that in an absurd world, language and behavior do have meaning for those who speak and act, remains to be understood."[4]

To get at meaning in Donald Judd's recent work necessarily involves brute description of the objects themselves, but significantly such a description cannot simply rest at an inventory of characteristics, even though many of the sculptors persuaded by object art maintain that such an inventory does indeed describe all that the works contain. Rose reports that the artists she deals with ask that their sculpture be taken as "nothing more than the total of the series of assertions that it is this or that shape and takes up so much space and is painted such a color and made of such a material."[5] But it would seem that in Judd's case the strength of the sculptures derives from the fact that grasping the works by means of a list of their physical properties, no matter how complete, is both possible and impossible. They both insist upon and deny the adequacy of such a definition of themselves, because they are not developed from "assertions" about materials or shapes, assertions, that is, which are given a priori and convert the objects into examples of a theorem or a more general case, but are obviously meant as objects of perception, objects that are to be grasped in the experience of looking at them. As such they suggest certain compelling issues.

One of the most beautiful of the sculptures in Judd's recent Castelli Gallery show was a wall-hung work (now in the Whitney Museum's collection) which is made of a long (approximately twenty feet) brushed aluminum bar, from which, at varying intervals, hangs a series of shorter bars enameled a deep, translucent violet. Or so it appears from the front. The assumption that the apparently more dense metallic bar relates to the startlingly sensuous, almost voluptuous lower bars as a support from which they are suspended is an architectural one, a notion taken from one's previous encounters with constructed objects and applied to this case. This reading is, however, denied from the side view of the object, which reveals that the aluminum bar is hollow (and open at both ends) while the purple boxes below it, which had appeared luminous and relatively weightless, are in fact enclosed, and furthermore function as the supports for the continuous aluminum member. It is they that are attached to the wall and into which the square profile of the aluminum bar fits (flush with their top and front sides), completing their own L-shaped profile to form an eight-by-eight-inch box in section. A view raking along the facade of the sculpture, then, reveals that one's initial reading was in some way an illusion: the earlier sense of the purple bars' impalpability and luminosity is reversed, and a clearer perception of the work can be obtained; but it is still one that is startlingly adumbrated and misleading. For now one sees the work in extension; that is, looking along its length, one sees it in perspective. That one is tempted to read it as in perspective follows from the familiar repetitive rhythms of the verticals of the violet boxes, which are reminiscent of the colonnades of classical architecture or of the occurrence at equal intervals of the vertical supporting members of any modular structure. Once again, then, Judd's work makes a reference to architecture, or to a situation one knows from previous experience—knowledge gained prior to the confrontation with the object. In this way, it seems to me, Judd brings a

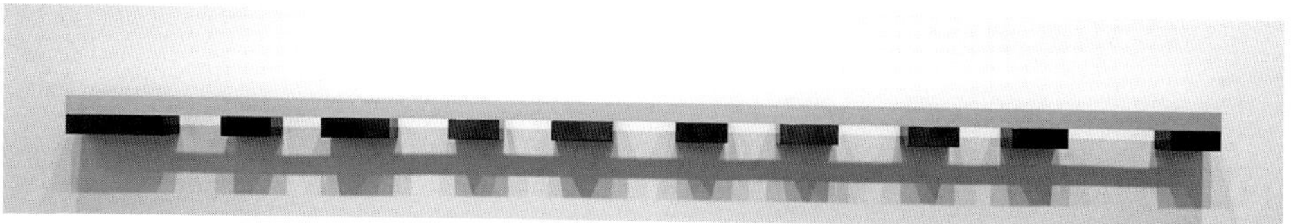

8.1 Donald Judd, *Untitled,* 1965. Whitney Museum of American Art, New York; purchase, with funds from the Howard and Jean Lipman Foundation, Inc. 66.53. Photograph by Sheldon C. Collins. © Judd Foundation/Licensed by VAGA, New York, NY.

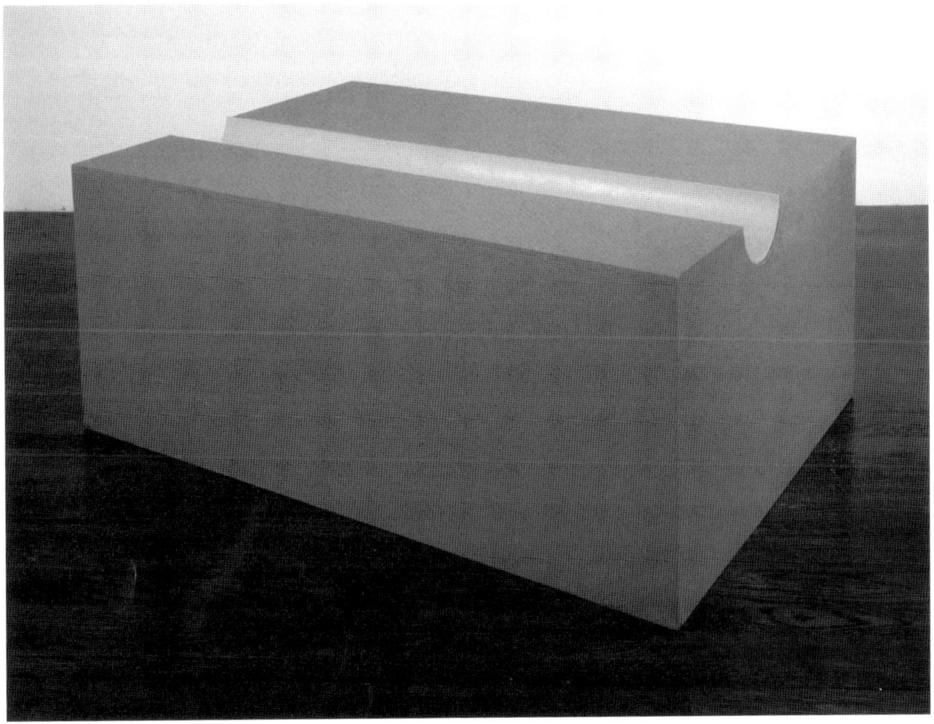

8.2 Donald Judd, *Untitled,* 1964. © Judd Foundation/Licensed by VAGA, New York, NY.

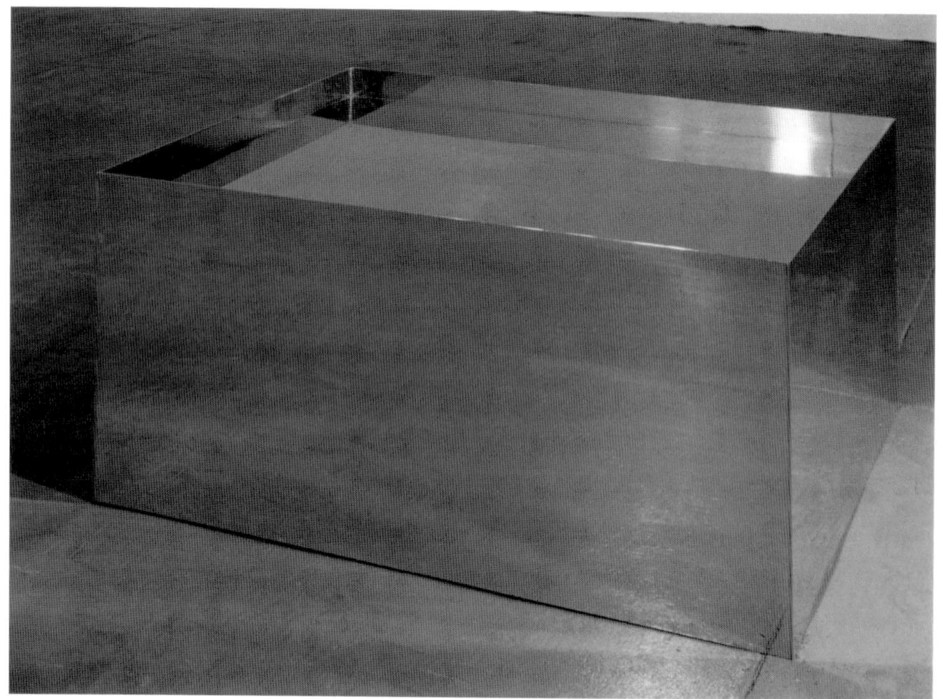

8.3 Donald Judd, *Untitled,* 1969. © Judd Foundation/Licensed by VAGA, New York, NY.

reference to a prior experience to bear on the present perception of the work. Or, to put it another way, the work itself exploits and at the same time confounds previous knowledge to project its own meaning. In Renaissance architecture, the even spacing of the colonnade is used to establish harmonious relationships as seen in perspective. The Renaissance mind seized on the realization that the same theorems of plane geometry unite proportion and perspective, and therefore assumed that a series of subjective viewpoints of a building (say, the sequence seen as one travels down the colonnade nave of Brunelleschi's San Lorenzo) would not invalidate an awareness of absolute measurement.[6] It was thus an optical space of measurable quantities that was involved in the Renaissance rationalization of space through perspective.

As was noted before, Judd's sculpture, unless it is seen directly from the front, which is difficult because if its extreme length, demands to be seen in perspective. Yet the work confounds that perspective reading which will guarantee a sense of absolute measurement through proportion, because of the obviously unequal lengths of the violet bars and the unequal distances which separate them. The work cannot be seen rationally, in terms of a given sense of geometrical laws or theorems evolved prior to the experience of the object. Instead, the sculpture can be sensed only in terms of its present coming into being as an object given "in the imperious unity, the presence, the insurpassable plentitude which is for us the definition of the real."[7] In those terms the French philosopher Merleau-Ponty describes perception which "does not give me truths like geometry, but presences." The "lived perspective" of which Merleau-Ponty speaks is very different from the rational perspective of geometrical laws: "What prohibits me from treating my perception as an intellectual act is that an intellectual act would grasp the object either as possible or as necessary. But in perception it is 'real,' it is given as the infinite sum of indefinite series of perspectival views in each of which the object is given but in none of which it is given exhaustively."[8]

It was noted at the beginning of this discussion that Judd's own criticism would seem to accept only that art which eschews both allusion and illusion. Yet his sculpture derives its power from a heightening of illusion—although not of pictorial illusion but of lived illusion. In the case of the sculpture described above, the work plays off the illusory quality of the thing itself as it presents itself to vision alone—which it does persuasively from a front view, in seeming to be a series of flat, luminous shapes; and from a raking view, in the optical disappearance created by its orthogonal recession—as against the sensation of being able to grasp it and therefore to know it through touch. The sculpture becomes, then, an irritant for, and a heightening of, the awareness in the viewer that he approaches objects to make meaning of them, that when he grasps real structures, he does so as meaningful, whole presences.

In constructing what is undoubtedly the most serious and fruitful description of the development of modern (as opposed to simply contemporary) art, Clement Greenberg and Michael Fried have insisted on the importance of that aspect of the artist's endeavor which involves a critical confrontation with the most vital work of the recent past. Judd's present sculpture can be situated, in this sense, in a critical relationship to the work with which David Smith was involved just before his death in 1965. This is of course not to say that the works contain some kind of veiled allusion to Smith or are only meaningful as seen in relation to his work; on the contrary, they are entirely meaningful on their own terms. Judd seems rather to have sensed in Smith certain sculptural possibilities which are as yet unrealized.

Smith's late *Cubi* pieces, especially *Cubi XXIV* and *Cubi XXVIII,* consist of large stainless steel cylinders and beams, which make up enormous rectangular "frames." Some of these frames are empty; others contain rectilinear volumes which are set with one broad side parallel to the viewer's plane of vision and are rendered further weightless and immaterial by the finish on the steel: a kind of calligraphic sanding of the metal so that the surfaces appear as a flickering, evanescent denial of the mass that supports them. The works wed a purely optical sensation of openness (the view through the frame) that is the presumed subject of the work, with an increased sense of the palpability and substance of the frame. Smith in this way embraced the modality of illusionism within pictorial space from painting, and used this to powerful sculptural advantage. Yet, to Judd, Smith's suspension of planes within the frame, one balanced off against the other, or even the composition of the frame itself of almost arbitrarily combined geometrical segments, must have seemed to rob the work of necessary lucidity. Smith's worrying of relationships between parts must have appeared to have clouded over the experience of the object with a kind of artiness which to Judd's eyes, at least, was irrelevant. In his work of the past few years, as in the pieces in this show, Judd arrives at sculptural forms which do not depend on the balance and adjustment of one part to another for their meaning.

That this departure from traditional modes of composition is also true of the work of Kenneth Noland has been demonstrated by Michael Fried in his various essays on that painter.[9] In Noland's case composition is discarded for what Fried has called "deductive structure": the derivation of boundaries within the pictorial field from the one absolute boundary given by the physical fact of the picture itself—its framing edge. The importance of Noland's decision to let the shape of the support serve as the major determinant of the divisions within the painting rests in part on its avoidance of an explicit affirmation of the flatness of the canvas, which would dilute the experience of the color by rendering it tactile (or merely the attribute of sculptural entities) rather than a sheerly visual or optical medium. Fried points to the large works of Barnett Newman from the early 1950s as establishing a precedent for a wholly optical statement conjoined with, or dependent upon, deductive structure.

In Noland's most recent exhibition, at the Andre Emmerich Gallery, a type of painting emerged which seemed to me to come from decisions by the painter which in part question the import of his earlier work. This type, found in *Across Center* (1966), a four-foot-high, twenty-foot-long canvas divided into four horizontal, evenly painted bands, has far greater affinities with Newman than anything else Noland has done until now. In *Across Center* color becomes more exclusively the basis of the experience than it had been in the diamond-shaped chevron paintings of the past year or so, for in those paintings the bounding shape itself had a limiting and closing effect on the color. Moving to a twenty-foot-long expanse of color points to a desire to combat the limits imposed by the shape itself and to promote an experience of the painting, either face-on, in fragment (from a vantage point far enough away to see the painting frontally and whole, the intensity of the colors would be somewhat reduced), or at an angle and therefore in perspective—a sensation promoted by the horizontal bands, which seem to increase the work's apparent diminution in size at the far end of one's vision. The sensation thus produced, that one cannot know absolutely the nature of the shape of the painting, that one's view is always adumbrated, that the work in its entirety is highly illusive, throws one more surely and more persuasively onto an immediate experience with color alone.

It is interesting that both Noland and Judd have arrived at formats that involve the viewer in an experience which is on the one hand more illusive than that of either a normal easel painting or an easily cohesive sculptural form, and on the other more immediate than both. But more important, from within this context of an increased sensuousness, neither artist will desert meaning.

The White Care of Our Canvas

In his short essay "The Storyteller," Walter Benjamin reflects on the impoverishment of soldiers returning from World War I, observing that they have "grown silent—not richer, but poorer in communicable experience."[1] At the root of such impoverishment, he says, is *Chockerlebnis*: the reduction of experience to naked information, wherein media ("every glance at a newspaper") does the work of shock. Today we might quickly grasp Benjamin's meaning by recalling, for example, the Vietnam War image of the young man with a pistol to his head, which reduced our experience of that conflict to the "shock" of a photographic image-bite.

The role for art in our engagement with such phenomena was the underlying subject of an important exhibition curated by Karina Daskalov in the summer of 2007 at the Marian Goodman Gallery in Paris. Titled "Invisible Colors," the show took its cue specifically from a crusade against the "regime of the image" launched recently by T. J. Clark in his books *Afflicted Powers: Capital and Spectacle in a New Age of War* (2005), coauthored with the political group Retort, and *The Sight of Death* (2006).[2] (A copy of the latter book was actually placed atop the gallery reception desk, testifying to its significance here.) As Clark puts it, the televisual clips played over and over since 9/11, as well as the autocratic

First published in *Artforum* 46 (October 2007).

power they have promoted, compose the political context and impetus for his aspiration to "make time for the opportunity for sustained attention, proposing that visual images carry within them the possibility of genuine difficulty, genuine depth and resistance." The result, he hopes, would be a way "of life in which the image-life of power could [at] once be derided or spoken back to."[3]

In *The Sight of Death,* Clark's refusal of media takes form in an elongated exploration and revisitation of a pair of Poussin paintings, which he seeks to see and resee in all the complexity of their compositional resonance. The book, he says, is intended to provide "the simple, central pleasure of looking that drives things forward—and the *astonishment* at what one or two pictures have to offer, if you give them half a chance."[4] Appropriately, then, the concern of "Invisible Colors" is *ritardando*—the slowing down of our perception, so accustomed has it become to image-bites (and this even within the art world, given the frantic pace of art fairs and biennials). Unfolding in three rooms, the show begins on the ground floor with works devoted to a kind of hallucinatory repetition, as, for example, Gabriel Orozco's *Ventilator* (1997) lazily fans three swathes of toilet paper hanging from the gallery's ceiling, and Oswaldo Macià's *Calumny* (2007) suspends five globular pendants, from which waft a variety of fragrances. Goodman's subterranean spaces then display two works, each one devoted to the constant revisiting of a single image. James Coleman's *Slide Piece* (1972–1973) projects the exact same Ektachrome—depicting a gas station in Milan where several cars are parked—through a slide-carousel-worth of "advances," which are accompanied by a taped commentary resembling the voice of a docent leading tourists through a museum. Marcel Broodthaers's 1974 film *A Voyage on the North Sea* fills the second room with an opulently obsessive survey of a nineteenth-century seascape.

The *pleasure* of looking incited by *Slide Piece* is owed to the formal analysis of its voice-over, which describes the repeatedly projected photograph in painful detail, often fixating on figure/ground reversals. For instance, the word "TOTAL," situated above the gasoline pumps, is initially viewed as an *O* encaged by the sides and struts of its two flanking *T*s; disengaged from this grid, the letter surfaces into the foreground of our visual focus. (Ironically, given its focused attention, Coleman says that he wrote most of this commentary until, exhausting his own patience, he advertised for writers to continue the analysis. Because Ireland is full of people sure of their own identity as writers, he adds, he had more offers for this job than he could handle.) In so confronting the fluctuation between figure and ground, *Slide Piece* clearly develops from Coleman's beginnings in Italian conceptual practice, where he responded in film and painting to Ludwig Wittgenstein's investigations into what it could mean to say that we see an *aspect* of an image—though the Gestalt psychologists also confronted this dilemma when they displayed the famous duck/rabbit diagram.

For its part, Broodthaers's *Voyage on the North Sea* is nothing but *astonishment*. Constantly panning his camera over the surface of an academic seascape painting he picked up at a shop on rue Jacob in Paris, the artist allows his film to unfold in a series of close-ups given different "page" numbers. The prow of a schooner under sail (page 12), say, accompanied by a dinghy filled with fishermen (page 13), churns up the green waves of the sea through which it cuts. It soon occurs to one that these pages of visual details could be offering a narrative of modernist painting, as a close-up of turbulent water recalls Manet's marinescapes, such as *The Battle of the Kersarge and the Alabama* (1864); and as a subsequent focus on a swathe of gray pigment pinning the billowing sail back to its mast (page 10) brings us forward in time, suggesting a vision of Manzoni's Achromes. The climax of this *musée imaginaire* is reached (on page 11) when nothing but the weave of the white sail is seen filling the entire screen with a magnificent monochrome, bringing to mind Mallarmé's poem "Salut," with its closing celebratory "toast [to] whatever was worth the white concern of our canvas."

Voyage was screened on a wall opposite Broodthaers's *Bateau tableau* (1973), a projected slide sequence synchronized with the film's details. This facing slide show could similarly be a lecture on the history of painterly modernism, from Manet's conception of pictorial flatness to Ryman's monochromes. Indeed, while the work's domination of the room might remind us of Broodthaers's earlier explorations of installation art—his *A Winter Garden* (1974), or *Museum of Modern Art, the Eagle from the Oligocene to the Present* (1972)—his works' double

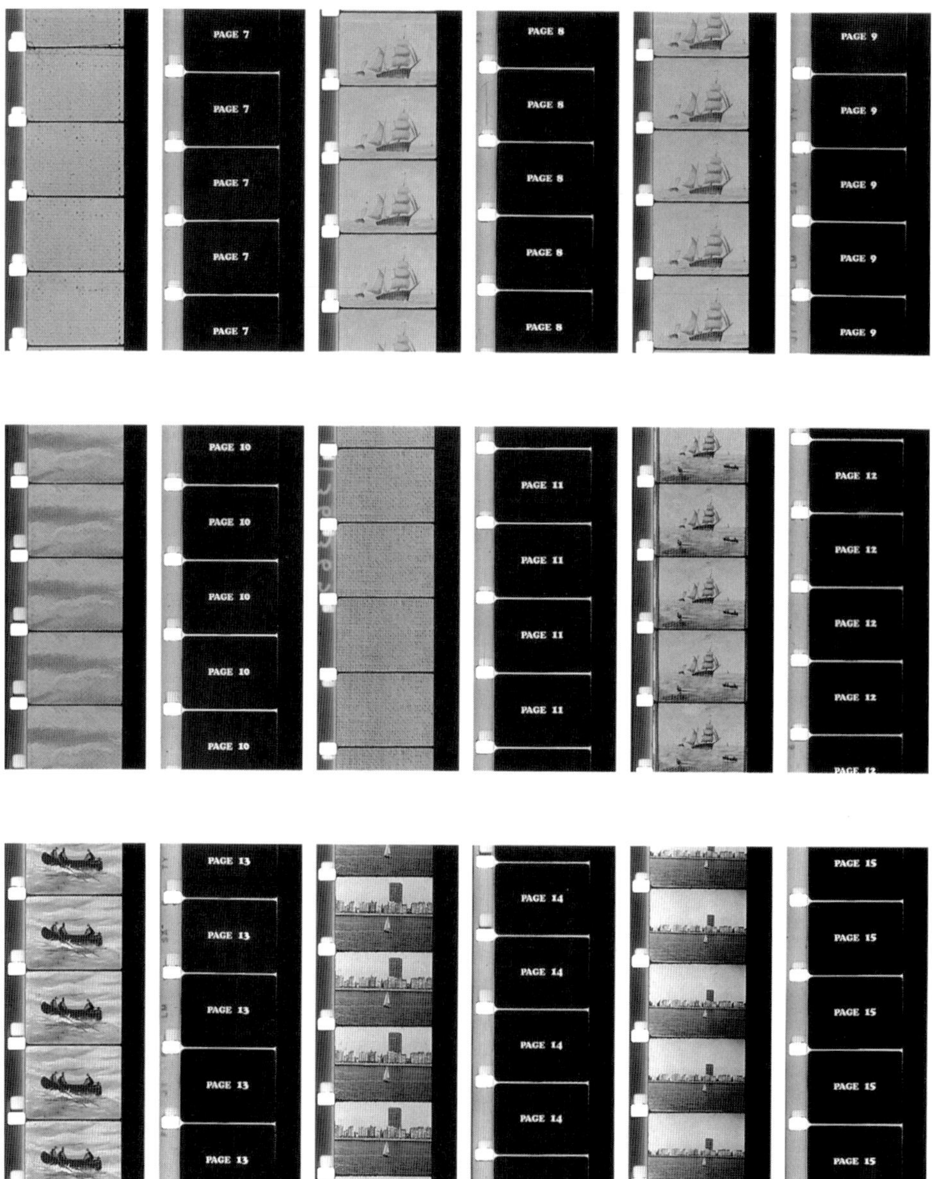

9.1 Marcel Broodthaers, *A Voyage on the North Sea,* 1974. © 2009 Artists Rights Society (ARS), New York/SABAM, Brussels.

commitment to painting as a specific medium and to a magnificently slow exfoliation of painting's history would argue against such an association.

The commitment to painting's specific history and "genius" (to use Barthes's term) parallels what a recent interviewer posed to T. J. Clark as his "heated response to contemporary 'image culture'; a critique of current trends in academic art history; and an impassioned argument for the value of time spent *looking* at works of art, making more than good on its claim that 'astonishing things can happen if one gives oneself over to the process of seeing again and again.' " As Clark eloquently responded:

> This pleasure and astonishment of looking are unnegotiable. Nothing the world can do to them will make them go away. And yes, I agree: the world does plenty. Pleasure and astonishment seem to me qualities that the world around us, most of the time, is conspiring to get rid of. Or to travesty . . . by which I mean the full range of human possibilities and sympathies that make up the human, as far as I'm concerned. Recognitions and sympathies, but also losses and horrors and failures of understanding. Everything the present ecstasy of "information" wants us to transfer to trash.[5]

Benjamin's shock results from media ("every glance at a newspaper"); Clark's "trash" is the effect of the televisual's control of our lives so that we "are accustomed from an early age to living in a constant flow of visual imagery." In other words, he says, "The imagery is designed not to be looked at closely, or with sustained attention."[6] Clark's reference to "flow" is impossible to read without thinking of Raymond Williams's characterization of television itself as "total flow,"[7] a description even more pertinent today. Clark focuses on the televisual as the enemy of his commitment to "sustained attention," and "Invisible Colors" proudly flies the banner of Clark's resistance.

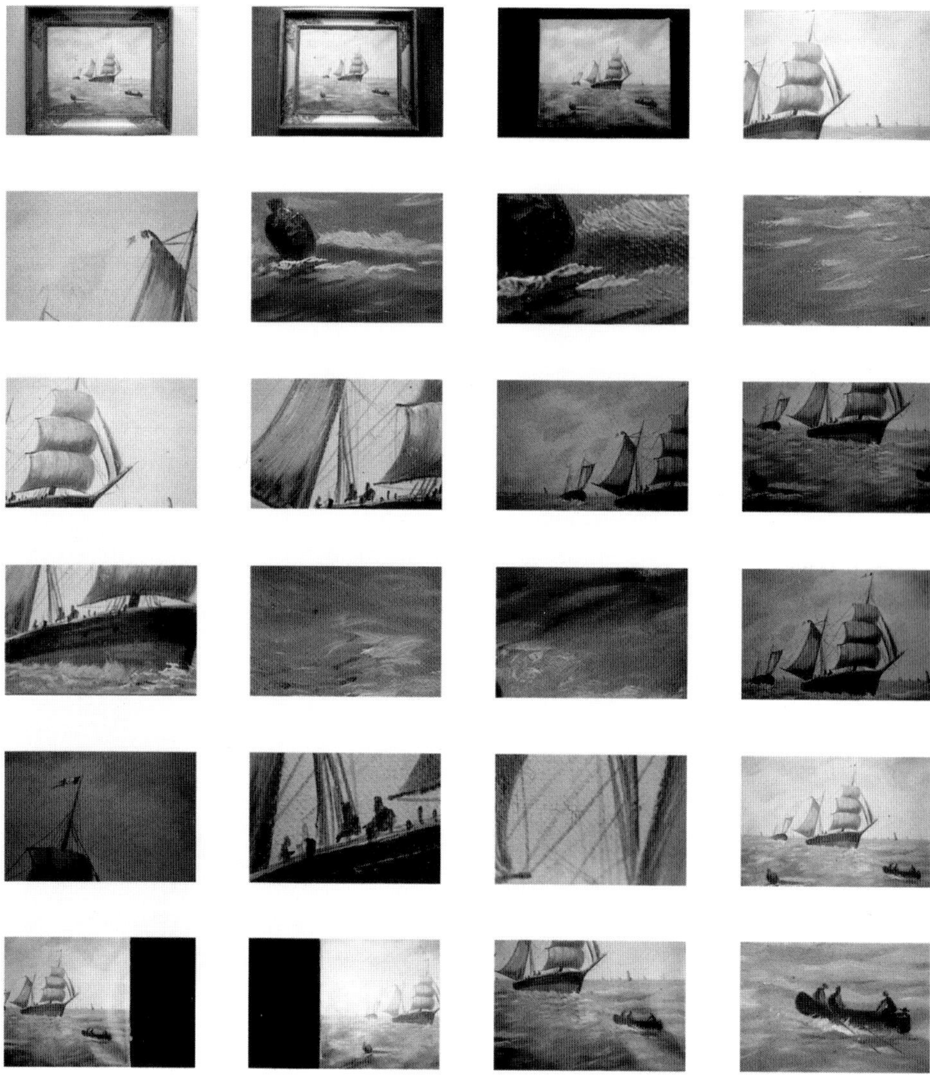

9.2 Marcel Broodthaers, *Analyse d'une peinture,* 1973. © 2009 Artists Rights Society (ARS), New York/SABAM, Brussels.

Mr. Clean-Up

During the 1990s, Daniel Libeskind catapulted himself to international renown as the Mr. Clean-Up of Modern Architecture, and this simply by internalizing two rules: (1) In the Beginning was the Word; and (2) Capitalism Abhors a Vacuum. Since these laws are given telegraphically here, perhaps a bit of unpacking is in order.

In the Beginning Was the Word

The commandment against graven images that is second nature to most Jews means that the power of rhetoric over reality functions for them as "a truth universally acknowledged." For architects this truth was driven home dramatically by a little David named Robert Venturi as he felled the heroes of his profession—giants such as Frank Lloyd Wright, Mies van der Rohe, and Le Corbusier—with the stone of a single word hurled from the sling of his 1966 book *Complexity and Contradiction in Modern Architecture*. That word was "duck."

On the Long Island road connecting New York and the Hamptons is to be found a roadside store selling ducklings, its place of business cleverly sculpted as a giant bird. Dismissing such buildings as the Guggenheim Museum, the United

Written 2003; published for the first time in this volume.

Nations, or the Seagram tower as so many "ducks," Venturi insisted on a return to what he called "the decorated shed," which meant architecture bearing the kind of ornament that would make the building's purpose self-evident, the way classical columns announce the presence of a bank or a town hall. Libeskind's generation of architects internalized this lesson in the whole profusion of buildings called "postmodernist," as practitioners such as Michael Graves looted the encyclopedias of architectural history for the designs of Egyptian peristyles or rococo follies. Libeskind's vocabulary has been far more limited, since his decorative choice has stayed with Russian suprematism (think Malevich and El Lissitzky), from which he borrows the flat slabs and tilted planes he uses to ornament the sides of his built volumes or his site plans. It is enough, however, to name any of these abstract figures with a palliative title to transform, utterly, the ground against which it appears.

Example: In a competition to urbanize Sachsenhausen, the former concentration camp at Oranienburg (forty kilometers from Berlin), Libeskind decided to challenge the topography of the site with a new channel of water that would symbolically purify the polluted earth. This giant oblong he called the "Hope Incision," describing it in his 1995 Raoul Wallenberg Lecture as "a new way of dealing ecologically with the land." Since his proposal did not provide for the 10,000 units of housing called for by the official program, Libeskind's project was disqualified; but due to its immediate appeal to the populace of Oranienburg, pressure was applied to the mayor to invite Libeskind into discussion with the building committee to explore the implementation of his ideas.

The lesson to be learned from this was not lost on Libeskind. The layperson does not understand or care about curtain walls or cantilevers; he cares about "hope," "consolation," and "despair." Consequently, the Jewish Museum in Berlin is a rhetorical feast: modeled on a Star of David, its very plan telegraphs "Jewish"; but in addition, the building is a charm bracelet of consolatory names: beginning with "Stations of the Star," it contains a "Holocaust Void" to lead to the "E. T. A. Hoffmann Garden"; and needless to say there is also a "Holocaust Tower."

The fate of modernist art is inscribed within the outlines of this story: the layperson who cares little for cantilevers cares even less for abstract art;

Kandinsky is nothing but a bunch of messy paint as far as he can see, but tell him that these are "really" landscapes with towers and horses and riders and he will feel instantly at ease. Architecture is such an abstract art, impenetrable to the person who doesn't read material structures and their principles or care about the problem of how to enter a building and how to make one's way through it (called "promenade" in archi-speak: the Guggenheim Museum, with its spiral ramp, is one long and brilliant exercise in "promenade").

Lesson one: "Form follows function"—this Bauhaus-bred rule of modernist architectural design was, ironically, the hatching ground for "ducks." Since Libeskind's function is consolatory and "ecological," his forms reach for the symbolic (hence the Star of David) and the disorienting. Most of us expect to find the structural stuff of a building at its corners—that's where, we think, the heavy lifting takes place. So it's usually at the corners of his volumes that Libeskind gets to work. He either slices right through the columns at the corner to produce a dramatic void, as at the Jewish Museum in Berlin, or he makes the corners narrow to an acute point, dispensing with the usual right angle. This use of geometry to put pressure on the visitor's body was undoubtedly a lesson Libeskind learned from the sculptor Richard Serra, whose works often squeeze the viewer's sensibility between massive sheets of steel. This is all the more ironic because Libeskind had the chutzpah to accuse Serra of plagiarism in the winning design Serra and Peter Eisenman submitted for the Berlin Holocaust Memorial—a sea of dolmen-like stelae that would fill Alexanderplatz—beating out Libeskind's own submission. Libeskind, deciding that he had a patent on one of the most widely used forms since Stonehenge, told *Die Welt* (January 2, 1999) that Serra and Eisenman had lifted their idea from his own E. T. A. Hoffmann Garden and that he intended to sue them.

Capitalism Abhors a Vacuum

If Gropius, Mies, and Corbusier were, indeed, giants, it is not because they limited their energies to constructing "ducks." They also focused on the massive problems of rebuilding and reconceiving whole cities after the devastation of world wars, and to this end they joined such organizations as CIAM which, along with urban planners, set architects to addressing the plight of cities and modern life. This effort was conceived of as finessing the power and self-interest of developers, and as such needs to be remembered as a model of professional responsibility and probity. (Historical accuracy alert: Mies was never a member of CIAM; Gropius's and Corbusier's work was a mixed blessing within the unfolding of architectural history since their concentration on rationalizing the plan of the city was opened to devastating criticism by postmodernism.)

The need for cleared land to exploit for commercial gain is so great that any tract, no matter how polluted, becomes valuable enough to support "ecological" renewal at a monumental scale. If thousands of yuppies will be happy to live in housing on the shores of the "Hope Incision" despite the fact that below it is the site of the first active crematorium in Germany, the lesson is obvious. No matter how toxic the pollution, language will make it pure.

Enter Mr. Clean-Up

In my view, Libeskind's strategy amounts to a pandering condescension that exploits the naiveté of the populations he addresses. He feeds their desire for narrative by a cynical recourse to language. Given my own abhorrence of this strategy, I would go one more step and say that should Libeskind be chosen as the rebuilder of Ground Zero, Al Qaeda will have doubly triumphed: first, in the massive loss of life that resulted from their leveling the site; second, in the conceptual decimation leading a whole population to abandon its cultural values.

Enter Buck Rogers

Now that Libeskind has produced a design for the renewal of Ground Zero, it is possible to put the analysis of his past performance to the test, and indeed nothing in his present project for downtown New York can be the least bit surprising, given his dependence on language (sure enough, there will be a Park of Heroes and a Wedge of Light) and his delight in the most banal symbolism—here, a monument to be rekindled on the solstice of the tragic events: Ground Zero as Stonehenge.

As his own best imitator, Libeskind is happy to repeat anything in his former practice that has seemed the least bit popular. In this case, the peculiar circumstances for the Jewish Museum in Berlin (which forced him to zag into the site of the new building through the inviolate, existing structure of the Museum of the City of Berlin—which he did by tunneling into the basement of the old museum to create a chthonic entrance into the new one) were suggestive for downtown New York, giving Libeskind the idea once more of creating an entry by burrowing deep into the very bedrock of destruction.

Libeskind's formal palette continues to be slavishly suprematist, so that his spaces are imagined as straight out of El Lissitzky's *Story of Two Squares* (a comic book for [Communist] adults) and resemble spaceships from either *2001* or Buck Rogers; so that we are made to feel that, ultimately, the most prescient designer of the twentieth century was Stanley Kubrick and that our fundamental imaginative project is the adolescent dream of "a space odyssey."

IV

Apostate

Artforum's tenth anniversary was conceived as a reflection on how the magazine had developed since its inception. In all honesty, I felt my own contribution had to be an analysis of the distance I had by then staked out from the historical assumptions and theoretical categories of Clement Greenberg, the most powerful critical voice and eye of postwar American art. This distance had already appeared in my assessment of cubism and was further articulated in "A View of Modernism."

A View of Modernism

One day while the show "Three American Painters" was hanging at the Fogg Museum at Harvard, Michael Fried and I were standing in one of the galleries. To our right was a copper painting by Frank Stella, its surface burnished by the light which flooded the room. A Harvard student who had entered the gallery approached us. With his left arm raised and his finger pointing to the Stella, he confronted Michael Fried. "What's so good about that?" he demanded. Fried gazed back at him. "Look," he said slowly, "there are days when Stella goes to the Metropolitan Museum. And he sits for hours looking at the Velázquezes, utterly knocked out by them and then he goes back to his studio. What he would like more than anything else is to paint like Velázquez. But what he knows is that that is an option not open to him. So he paints stripes." Fried's voice had risen. "He wants to be Velázquez, so he paints stripes."

I don't know what the boy thought, but it was clear enough to me. That statement, which linked Stella's needs to Velázquez's in the immense, broad jump of a single sentence, was a giant ellipsis whose leap cleared three centuries of art. But in my mind's eye, it was more like one of those strobe photographs in which each increment of the jumper's act registers as a single image. I could see what the student could not, and what Fried's statement did not fill in for him.

First published in *Artforum* 11 (September 1972).

Under the glittering panes of that skylight, I could visualize the logic of an argument that connected hundreds of separate pictorial acts into the fluid clarity of a single motion, an argument that was as present to me as the paintings hanging in the gallery—their clean, spare surfaces tied back into the faint grime of walls dedicated to the history of art. Though Fried had not chosen to give the whole of that argument to the student, he had tried to make the student think about one piece of the obvious: that Stella's need to say something through his art was the same as a seventeenth-century Spaniard's; only the point in time was different. In 1965, the fact that Stella's stripes were involved with what he wanted to say—a product, that is, of *content*—was clear enough to me.

I am thirty-one. Eight years ago I began writing art criticism. I was living in Cambridge then, so I frequently came to New York to look at art. Sometimes, on those trips, I would meet people who had known me before only through my writing. Phil Leider was one of these; I met him shortly after *Artforum*'s offices moved from the West Coast to New York. His reaction to me was typical. "You're Rosalind Krauss?" he said. "I had expected that you'd be at least forty."

Although I heard what he said, I did not really notice it—or rather notice the implications of it. It did not strike me at the time that there was anything really peculiar about sounding almost twice one's age, or at least that there was anything wrong with that, when what one was writing about was art.

At that same time, Donald Judd published a piece in *Studio International* on the then-current situation in art—including criticism. In that article he spoke disparagingly of Michael Fried and me. Referring to the intellectual debt which we, among many other writers, continually acknowledged to Clement Greenberg, he called us "Greenbergers." Beyond its wit, Judd's remark implied the danger of self-objectification inherent in our position, mine and the others', in espousing a doctrine, the doctrine to which we were committed, which was "modernism." But it was a danger which I suppose I was willing to run in the service of describing as objectively as possible my responses to works of art and in attempting to account for the sources of power that certain art possessed, to create or elicit those responses. Far from bothering me, the charge of being a "modernist" critic was something I was proud of.

One of the things about holding ideas or beliefs in common with a group of people is that it cuts down on the amount of explanation one member of the group has to make to the others. So once when Clement Greenberg remarked to me that "formalism" was one of the most intellectually vulgar notions he knew of, I did not really ask him to explain what he had said, because it seemed pretty clear to me what he meant. Shortly afterward he said the same thing in print. He said, "Whatever its connotations in Russian, the term [formalism] has acquired ineradicably vulgar ones in English. . . . No proper literary critic would dream of using it."[1]

Before, when he had said this to me, I had taken the expanded meaning of it to be something like the following: Clive Bell and Roger Fry had often expressed hostility toward the content of works of art, suggesting at times the usefulness of turning paintings on their sides so that their apparent subject matter would not get in the way of one's seeing their design quality. Further, they held that this design quality was purely the function of formal relationships: the intervals of color and shape and the arrangement of those intervals on the surface of the picture. What they seemed to be saying was that the only relevant judgments one could make of a work of art were those made by assessing that design quality. But it seems clear that good design will not yield much more than good design; that it will not yield works of art. The experience of a work of art is always in part about the thoughts and feelings that have elicited—or more than that, entailed—the making of the work. And if the work is not a vehicle of those emotions, in no matter how surprising a form, then what one is in the presence of is not art but design. I assumed that the vulgarity Greenberg was talking about was the imputation that anyone could or would confuse the experience of art with the confrontation with contentless good design. And that, further, there could only be two reasons for doing so. Either the person who imputed it was himself or herself confused about the difference between design and art, and thus did it out of the poverty of his or her own aesthetic experience; or, it was an imputation out of bad faith: the person was fully aware of the meaning of aesthetic experience but was simply not willing to credit Greenberg with an equal awareness of it. Whether it came from ignorance or bad faith made it no less vulgar. "Formalism" had become a peculiar stick for attacking other people, and to wield it against the "modernist" critics simply meant that the person who did it was either too hostile or too lazy to read what they wrote. Minus the Fry and Bell part, all of that is pretty much what Greenberg said in print: "that the quality of a work of art inheres in its 'content,' and vice versa. Quality is 'content.' "

The content question has always been just under the surface of the writing of most "modernist" critics. So when Michael Fried wrote the extended essay for his exhibition "Three American Painters," he of course called attention to his experience "that both Noland and Olitski are primarily painters of *feeling* and that what I take to be their preeminence among their contemporaries chiefly resides not in the formal intelligence of their work, which is of the very highest order, but in the depth and sweep of feeling which this intelligence makes possible."[2] In characterizing the "passion, eloquence and fragile power" of Noland's painting, or in speaking of Noland as "a tense, critical, almost hurting presence in his work," Fried pointed to both color and design (or structure) as the sources of these impressions. But he confined his analysis to the structure and not the color because structure, being the result of rational decisions, could be usefully described, while color, being arbitrary, could not. And the partialness of this analysis was not seen as a kind of cheating or shying away from the responsibility to confront the total work, because it was precisely in that very mixture of rationality and arbitrariness that the work's meaning was seen to reside. Fried saw Noland's painting as a response to a general "crisis of meaning" generated by a particular history—one that made imperative the invention of a self-evident, reflexive structure and drove lyricism onto an increasingly narrow highland of color.

That whole story, beginning with Greenberg's remark to me, is offered in evidence of the fact that most people who attack the "modernist" critical position do so by omitting or distorting various parts of that position. Of course,

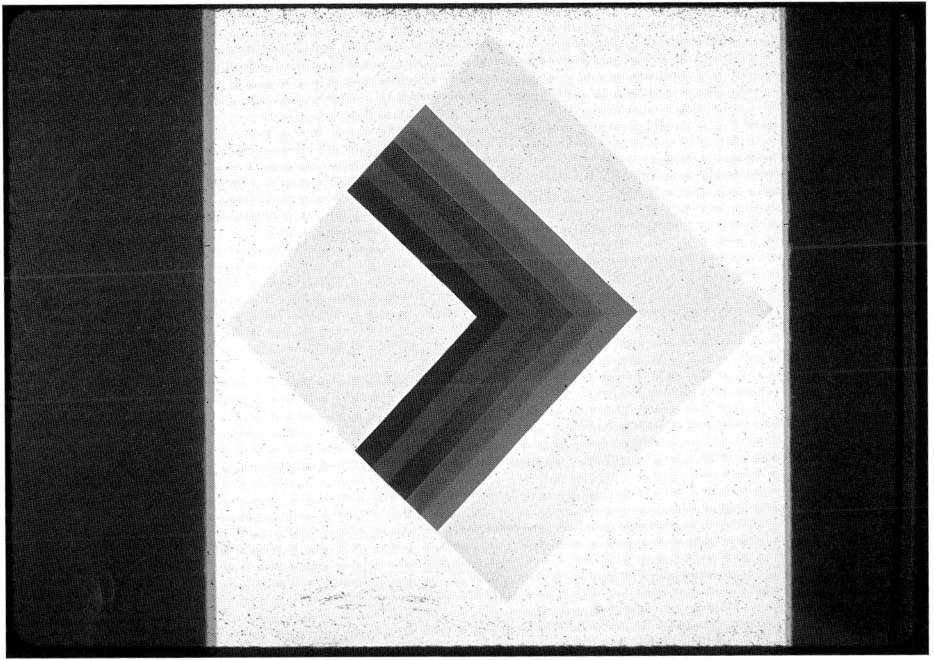

11.1 Kenneth Noland, *Go,* 1964. © Kenneth Noland/Licensed by VAGA, New York, NY.

11.2 Jules Olitski, *Tin Lizzie Green,* 1964. © Estate of Jules Olitski/Licensed by VAGA, New York, NY.

they could reply that they cannot be expected to take into account what is left out of most "modernist" writing; that if questions of content and feeling really are central to "modernist" critics, the critics themselves are keeping it a secret since such questions are never really up front in what they write. But upfrontness is rather a tricky criterion when discussing a large body of theory. It's a bit like saying that the philosophical position of Wittgenstein is an argument for behaviorism because that's what is up front in his writing. Yet anyone reading the late Wittgenstein must realize that his work taken as a whole offers an impassioned and profound attack on behaviorism, along with idealism. It is simply a method of argumentation that is up front.

With "modernism," too, it was precisely its methodology that was important to a lot of us who began to write about art in the early 1960s. That method demanded lucidity. It demanded that one not talk about anything in a work of art that one could not point to. It involved tying back one's perceptions about art in the present to what one knew about the art of the past. It involved a language that was open to some mode of testing. That that language was also something I could hide behind, that it accounted for why I wrote like a forty-year-old, for why I, along with some of the other "modernist" critics, adopted that curiously dissociated tone, did not strike me at the time. For I was being carried by an idea of historical logic, buoyed like the others by the possibilities of clarity.

In the 1950s we had been alternately tyrannized and depressed by the psychologizing whine of "existentialist" criticism. It had seemed evasive to us—the impenetrable hedge of subjectivity whose prerogatives we could not assent to. The remedy had to have, for us, the clear provability of an "If x, then y." The syllogism we took up was historical in character, which meant that it read only in one direction; it was progressive. No *à rebours* was possible, no going backward against the grain. The history we saw from Manet to the impressionists to Cézanne and then to Picasso was like a series of rooms *en filade.* Within each room the individual artist explored, to the limits of his experience and his formal intelligence, the separate constituents of his medium. The effect of his pictorial act was simultaneously to open the door to the next space and to close out access to the one behind him. The shape and dimensions of the new space were discovered by the next pictorial act; the only thing about that unstable position that was clearly determined beforehand was its point of entrance. In 1965, it followed logically that to work at the level of Velázquez, Frank Stella had to paint stripes; and that Noland's choices about structure had narrowed to what Michael Fried termed "the deductive logic of the framing-edge."

We saw the aching beauty of those works in their constant invention of formats that collapsed into one instantly perceived chord the sounds of all those doors to the past closing at once, managing in the space that was left to lodge powerful evidence of the feeling of their makers. One part of what we were seeing was a kind of history, telescoped and assessed; and the other part was the registration of feelings generated by that historical condition. I never doubted the absoluteness of that history. It was out there, manifest in a whole progression of works of art, an objective fact to be analyzed. It had nothing to do with belief, or privately held fantasies about the past. Insofar as modernism was tied to the objective datum of that history, it had, I thought, nothing to do with "sensibility."

Obviously modernism *is* a sensibility—one that reaches out past that small band of art critics of which I was a part, to include a great deal more than, and ultimately to criticize, what I stood for. One part of that sensibility embraces analysis as an act of humility, trying to catch itself in the middle of the very act of judgment, to glimpse itself unawares in the mirror of consciousness. The attention to self-reflexivity, or what the structuralist critics term *dédoublement,* is thus one of the most general features of the larger modernist sensibility. And because of that attention, another part of the modernist sensibility feels extreme wariness over the question of perspective.

I look at a painting. The landscape opens out before me in the measurable increments of a systematic perspective. I know what comes next after the closest thing, and how much distance separates it from the thing that comes after that. As de Kooning, describing Renaissance space, said: "It was up to the artist to measure out the exact space for a person to die in or be dead already. The exactness of the space was determined, or rather, inspired by whatever reason the person was dying or being killed for. The space thus measured out on the original plane of the canvas surface became a 'place' somewhere on the floor."[3]

Perspective is the visual correlate of causality—that one thing follows the next in space according to rule. In that sense, despite differences of historical development, it can be likened to the literary tradition of the omniscient narrator and the conventional plot. As de Kooning described it, perspectival space carried with it the meaning of narrative: a succession of events leading up to and away from this moment; and within that temporal succession—given as a spatial analogue—was secreted the "meaning" of both that space and those events. And it is that very prior assumption of meaning that the larger modernist sensibility abhors. If Robbe-Grillet speaks of "the destitution of the old myths of 'depth,'" it is because he sees the traditional narrative as the representation of an order:

> This order, which we may in effect qualify as natural, is linked to an entire rationalistic and organizing system, whose flowering corresponds to the assumption of power by the middle class. . . . As the technical elements of the narrative—systematic use of the past tense and third person, unconditional adoption of chronological development, linear plots, regular trajectory of the passions, impulse of each episode toward a conclusion, etc.,—everything tended to impose the image of a stable, coherent, continuous, unequivocal, entirely decipherable universe. Since the intelligibility of the world was not even questioned, to tell a story did not raise a problem. The style of the novel could be innocent."[4]

We can no longer fail to notice that if we make up schemas of meaning based on history, we are playing into systems of control and censure. We are no longer innocent. "For if the norms of the past serve to measure the present, they also serve to construct it."[5]

If someone asks us what's so good about a painting by Stella and our answer is that he has to paint stripes because of Manet, etc., etc., and impressionism, etc., etc., and then cubism, and then we move on to a history of the necessity of flatness, we have made the Stella painting into a particular kind of screen onto which we project a special form of narrative. The flatness that modernist criticism reveres may have expunged spatial perspective, but it has substituted a temporal one—i.e., history. It is this history that the modernist critic contemplates while looking into a vortex of, say, Stella's concentric stripes: a perspective view that opens backward into that receding vista of past doors and rooms, which, because they are not reenterable, can only manifest themselves in the present by means of diagrammatic flatness.

Modernist criticism is innocent. And its innocence obtains on three counts: it refuses to see the temporality which it never tires of invoking—"the entire history of painting since Manet"[6]—as that perspectival armature on which it structures the art in question (and on which that art has increasingly tended to structure itself); it thinks of that history as "objective"—beyond the dictates of sensibility, beyond ideology; and it is unself-critically prescriptive. Failing to see that its "history" is a perspective, *my* perspective—only, that is to say, a point of view—modernist criticism has stopped being suspicious of what it sees as self-evident, its critical intelligence having ceased to be wary of what it has taken as given. Although its disclaimers to being a prescriptive position are sincerely meant, it has failed to put a check on the ways that its belief in the "reality" of a certain version of the past has led it to construct (in its coercive sense) the present.

For example, Michael Fried can acknowledge the importance of Stella's, Noland's, and Olitski's working in series, holding that the series provides "a context of mutual elucidation for the individual paintings comprising a given series";[7] he can even go on to say that for Noland the series serves something like a linguistic function, signifying "related transformations of syntax in the interest of saying something new (or perhaps in the interest of saying something at all)." Yet Fried can also maintain that it is an essential feature of a modernist work to declare itself in terms of a "continuous and entire presentness, amounting, as it were, to the perpetual creation of itself, that one experiences as a kind of *instantaneousness*."[8] Surely these two notions are mutually contradictory, or at least in apparent conflict. A series simply is diachronic in character—the experience of it is entirely temporal—and as such it is at odds with Fried's demand for "presentness."

If a work's meaning depends on comparison with things that exist outside it, then that meaning cannot be seen to be entirely present in the perception of a single work. And this is not simply a conceptual matter, but a matter of experience. It became my experience of modernist painting-in-series in the late 1960s (specifically that of Stella and Noland)—a reaction that was especially disturbing due to the reliance of those paintings on a sensuous experience of color.[9] Then too, it is my experience that by the late 1960s the ability of a given modernist work to make its connection of the past perceptually immediate—to make that connection, in Fried's term, "perspicuous"—became increasingly attenuated. With that attenuation, the sense of historical necessity that had been part of the content or meaning of modernist painting no longer appeared at the moment of perception of the work itself. And the effect of this for me was to reveal the inherently narrative character of that meaning, and to heighten and exacerbate its temporal quality.

What this whole business about series and perspective adds up to is a set of anomalies which does not fit, and cannot comfortably be explained by, modernist critical theory. And they are not, of course, the only anomalies. Another is that modernist theory has never been able to come up with a satisfactory history of sculpture. Whatever power the modernist history of painting has had to convince comes mainly from the fact that it was able to explain as a comprehensible progression the most important pictorial evidence of the last one hundred years. But this is not the case with sculpture. The conception of modernism in sculpture depends exclusively on describing the developments within constructed sculpture rather than work which is carved or cast. What this has meant is that modernist critics find themselves tactically cut off from acknowledging the work of Arp, as well as most of Brancusi. In the case of Brancusi, the open carved pieces like the *Prodigal Son* are admitted to the canon, while the monolithic carved and cast pieces are not; and clearly, on the grounds of sheer quality, such a distinction is untenable. And on this end of the line, modernist critics appear to have cut themselves off from what is most energetic and felt in contemporary sculpture. Their inability to deal with Richard Serra, or Michael Heizer, or Keith Sonnier, or Robert Smithson is anomalous in the extreme. Further, these critics have continually balked at admitting film to the status of a "modernist art."[10] Given the quality of recent advanced film, this position is simply no longer admissible even for critics who confine themselves to dealing just with painting and sculpture, for film as a medium has become increasingly important to sculptors themselves; Serra and Sonnier are only the most obvious examples.

Recently Clement Greenberg published an essay entitled "The Necessity of Formalism." When I opened the journal in which it appeared I assumed, because of our discussion of a few years ago—about "formalism" as an intellectual vulgarity—that Greenberg meant this title ironically, but I was wrong. Greenberg still sees "modernism" as not exactly "coterminous with formalism," but he does argue now that formalism must set the terms of "modernism," that technical preoccupations "must be [modernism's] essential, defining side, at least in the case of painting and sculpture."[11] In a "Post-postscriptum," Greenberg speaks, as he had earlier, of aesthetic value originating in content; but the "necessity of formalism" underscores the way that such content arises out of technical preoccupations "when searching enough and compelled enough." Yet, given the rest of Greenberg's text, this search and this compulsion are so tightly tied back into form, or what he calls "artisanal considerations," that all I understand by this notion of content is something like, for example, that sculpture should be about the exigencies of making sculpture. Since most of contemporary sculpture is about the problems of sculpture itself, that notion no longer seems to discriminate much of anything; and further, it fails to note the obvious: that *some* sculpture is about more than that. Some sculpture has shared the need to find and express a structure that will no longer be "innocent." When Robbe-Grillet charges conventional narrative with innocence, this does not mean that he wants or even thinks it possible to dispense with narrative. His own novels are intense, continual, even compulsive narrations. Yet his stories are constantly eclipsed by the point of view of the teller, holding up this point of view, turning it around, examining it, taking responsibility for it, never allowing either himself or the reader at any moment to be innocent about it.

Richard Serra's sculpture is about sculpture: about the weight, the extension, the density and opacity of matter, and about the promise of the sculptural project to break through that opacity with systems which will make the work's structure transparent both to itself and to the viewer who looks on from outside. But beyond any of that there is an attention to narrative that suffuses the work, subordinating structure to a point of view. This is true of *Strike* (1969–1971) and of the five-plate piece he showed in New York this winter. It is true of *Circuit* (1972), Serra's most recent sculpture, installed at Documenta, which I have not seen but which I know about from drawings and descriptions. It is also true of the large outdoor piece that he did for Joseph Pulitzer (1970–1971) (published in *Artforum,* May 1972). The narrative quality of Serra's work demands that a given sculpture be seen successively—and that each moment of its perception supersede in affective importance the viewer's intuition of the work's actual structure, whether cruciform, or fan-shaped, or whatever. The strategy employed in Serra's work is to create a point from which the viewer can sense the logic of the work's structure—can feel it fanning outward from her, like the extended perimeters of her own body—although it is exactly at this point that the material visibility of the work is most depleted. Thus, the point from which one gets the "logic" of the work is one of extreme tension with the external, perceptual facts of which the work is composed. Again and again, Serra's sculpture makes a viewer realize that the hidden meanings she reads into the corporate body of the world are her *own* projections and that interiority she had thought belonged to the sculpture is in fact her *own* interiority—the manifestation, from the still point, of her own point of view. The successiveness to which Serra's sculpture resorts is no longer there by default or innocence; it is there by searching, almost savage, design.

As I thought about this, I remembered something else Greenberg had said in that earlier essay where the statement about the vulgarity of "formalism" appeared. He had said, "Why bother to say that a Velázquez has 'more content' than a Salvator Rosa when you can say more simply, and with directer reference to the experience you are talking about, that the Velázquez is 'better' than the Salvator Rosa?"[12] Which is to say that it matters what the content of a work of art is, that some content is "more" than others, better than others.

Which is also to say that I am still stuck with believing that "formalism" is a vulgarity; that I began as a modernist critic and am still a modernist critic, but only as part of a larger modernist sensibility and not the narrower kind. Which is further to say that what I must acknowledge is not some idea of the world's perspective but simply my own point of view; that it matters who one sounds like when what one is writing about is art. One's own perspective, like one's own age, is the only orientation one will ever have.

The Cubist Epoch

Not long ago I was involved in a discussion of Marx's essay on "The Civil War in France" in which one of the participants expressed his dissatisfaction with Marx's account—given Marxist theory. Because in the light of a Marxist economic analysis, there is no reason on the face of it why those events (the war of 1870) should have given rise to that outcome (the Paris Commune). This sense—that between a theory which is supposed to account for the structure of a given occurrence and the actual constellation of detail which makes up that occurrence there lies a disturbing opacity—nags at any writer of history who wants to analyze as well as record events. And for the art historian concerned with twentieth-century painting, the phenomenon of cubism offers just this kind of resistance to explanation.

The cubists, we are told, were intent on representing the fullness of the freestanding, volumetric object on the flatness of the picture surface. If, in doing so, the ties between representation and resemblance were progressively severed, this was a logical consequence, we are assured, of a need to attest either to the superior access which consciousness has to reality or to the process of picture making, or both. The first position—which differentiates conception from brute vision, pointing to the way in which all six sides of a cube are transparent

First published in *Artforum* 9 (February 1971).

to the mind in a way that they never are to perception—is largely the theoretical property of the early writers on cubism.[1] The second—that the cubist analysis is a critique of the pictorial functions, dismembering the image into its constituent aspects of flatness, illusionism, and sign, and in the process revealing the limits of each mode of description—begins with Kahnweiler in 1915 but owes its elaboration to a postmodernist interpretation of the work of Picasso and Braque.[2] Yet if one comes to the paintings of these two men armed with these theories, one has the sense of being rudderless in the actual encounter. It is as if a cloud of intellectual dust has settled on these works, a cloud which a glimpsed, sensuous detail will suddenly disperse, if only in patches.

In what sense are Picasso's 1909 Horta landscapes subservient to the laws of picture making, when at their centers they are gashed by deep canyons down through which vision plunges in a free fall toward a hypothetical vanishing point? There is, of course, no single projective system which reconciles the perspective of each of the houses in the paintings. But there *is* the sense of a single perspective: vision caged and focused into a single beam before which the volume of objects gives way, desiccating into a crumpled array of shapes. How are we to understand the terrible pit that opens up between the crooked arm and side of the 1910 *Fanny Tellier,* making us feel the breast as something mutilated because, like a flap of dead skin, it seems stranded at the surface of the deep wound that rends the picture? Why in the *Ma jolie* of 1911–1912, his most hermetic image of the female nude, does Picasso hold on to that same terrifying sense of the breast as an impotent shape nailed to the picture surface by a nipple-turned-spike? If, as I recently read, cubism obsessively encircles the object so that "the object of common use" becomes the "Object of Knowledge,"[3] why does Picasso devote his large and ambitious canvases to the people to whom he was linked emotionally—his friends and lovers—acknowledging their individuality through a fragmented tracery of signs, but dispersing them as perceptual sets into figures that in no sense can be known? In front of Picasso's pictures one has very little sense of a man in touch with a theory he wished to research, but rather of someone in the grip of a compulsion he had to explore.

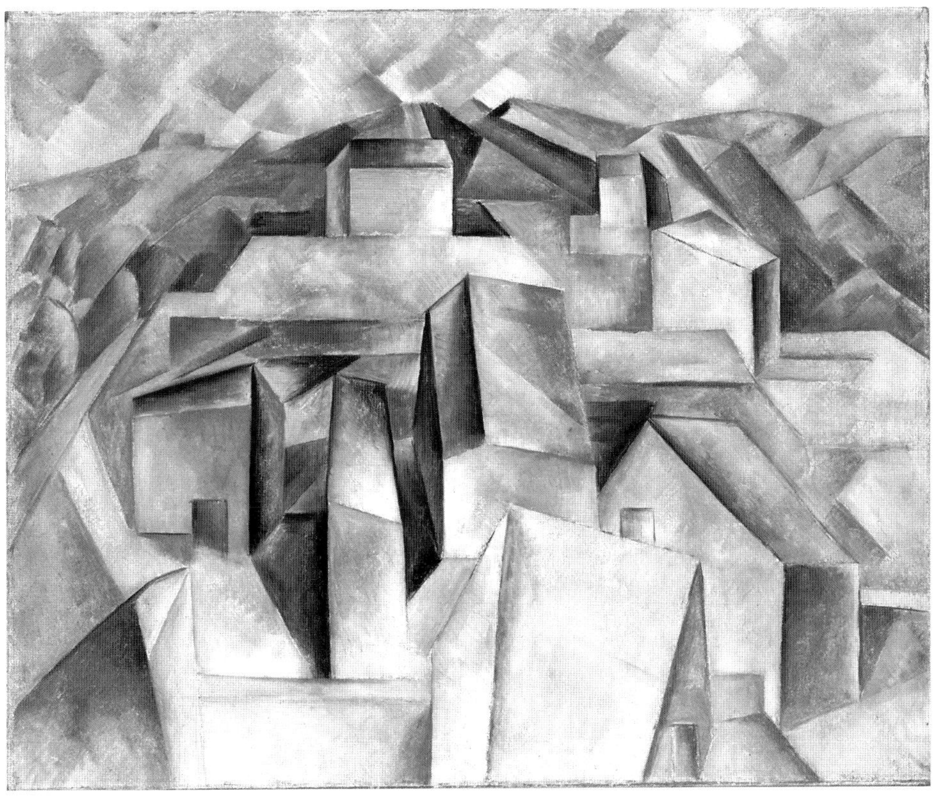

12.1 Pablo Picasso, *Houses on the Hill, Horta de Ebro,* 1909. Bildarchiv Preussischer Kulturbesitz/Art Resource, NY. © 2009 Estate of Pablo Picasso/Artists Rights Society (ARS), New York.

Picasso has been fanatically secretive about the ideas that preoccupied him during those years, and the accounts of eyewitnesses have been less than revealing about his ambitions with regard to the development of cubism. But in the pictures themselves, in the repertory of detail and the way detail is treated, I find evidence that in these years Picasso was plagued by a kind of skepticism about vision from which there was more fear than pleasure to be derived—especially for a painter. And the fear seems to have come from the question about whether there can ever be direct access to depth through vision—whether anyone can really see depth.

We can imagine a pencil held parallel to our plane of vision. What we see is a bar with a pointed end—a shape given to us as simple extension. If we turn the pencil ninety degrees, so that it is perpendicular to our visual plane, what we see is not the five or so inches that begins closer to our eyes at one end and terminates at the far end of the object; what we see is a point into which that distance has been compressed.[4] The skeptical argument about depth reasons that vision registers extension only; that depth, because it is not a shape spread laterally across our visual field, is forever invisible. The mass of a given object, according to this argument, may be accessible to touch, but for a stationary viewer, it will forever remain the phantom property of a consciousness that must reconstruct it from intermediary sets of evidence. In Picasso's paintings of the houses at Horta de Ebro one begins to see precisely this tension between the frontality of all shape as such and the meaning of the oblique. In these works, the houses are located in terms of ineluctably ambiguous shapes that must remain mute on the question of the mass or volume of the objects for which they serve as masks—and therefore noncommittal on the problem of how each shape is to be read within three-dimensional space. It is like the trapezoid which we can regard either as a shape in its own right or as a square seen in perspective—but to do the latter we must have some way of testing or establishing our independent orientation toward the object. The modeling of the forms—the pictorial surrogate for touch—seems in these works to be dissociated from the houses' contours so that one feels in the paintings the coexistence of two warring sets of perceptual cues which are no longer fused in the object.

From the Horta landscapes on forward in time, Picasso begins to make the picture surface itself more and more the metaphor for a consciousness which would be the locus of fusion between visual and tactile cues, between separately given modeling and shape. The picture plane in its wholeness, its unity, its instantaneity, is seen as that entity which can be known without doubt. In this sense it is equated to consciousness as that medium through which a world exists at all and is constituted. In the hermetic pictures, touch and sight, the two warring faculties of sense, are increasingly fused or processed through the independently given reality of the picture surface.

But in this equation of the picture surface with the medium of consciousness, there is lodged a residual uncertainty, and this has to do with orientation: for a totally constructive consciousness is completely fluid in its orientation to the object and to space. This fact seems to register in the way that when one looks at the modeling in the Horta landscapes, one feels suspended above the ground of the painting and looking down into a kind of pit, whereas when one looks at the contours of the houses—at shape—one feels oneself to be confronting a set of elevations set like stage flats parallel to one's own upright body. It is as though sight presupposes a projection out from the body toward a horizon so that the visual field is conceived of as parallel to the plane of the body; but touch orients the body to the ground beneath its feet—that is, to a plane perpendicular to the visual one. And even though the picture surface can integrate these two functions, it cannot determine the orientation a viewer must take toward it.

This sense that the newly constituted picture surface remains indeterminate on the question of how the viewer is to orient himself to it—whether he is to look down onto it as though viewing the objects it bears in plan, or face it in elevation—continues well into Picasso's and Braque's work with collage. The collages repeatedly take the oval as a format, either for the picture or as a whole, or as a bounded field suspended within a larger rectangle. And, as is made clear from the outset in the 1912 *Still Life with Chair Caning* (by the rope frame that doubles as carved furniture molding), this oval can be alternatively interpreted as a literal tabletop down onto which one looks at objects in plan, or as an upright frame which fans the contents of the visual field across its enclosed surface.

The authority possessed by Picasso's and Braque's early cubist masterpieces comes neither from a game about picture making nor from a dispassionate examination of the object. Throughout the 1910–1912 pictures there resonates a tragic sense of loss, as one feels one is confronting an increasingly dissociated set of pictorial cues to the most elusive constituent of the experienced world: depth from a fixed vantage. As the congruence of descriptive shape with literal flatness closes out and makes ever more precarious the latitude in which modeling can render up a sense of the depth that is necessary to endow images with their affect, one feels Picasso and Braque struggling with the poverty of a constructive view of consciousness. The *Fanny Tellier* exudes this acute sense of emotional cost, as shards of the most sensuously affective parts of the body—like the breast or the junction of the neck and shoulder—are stranded as desiccated shape above voluptuous chasms of a depth which can no longer be wedded to the contours that would give depth meaning.

"The Cubist Epoch," an ambitious exhibition organized by Douglas Cooper at the Los Angeles County Museum of Art (to travel in a more expanded version to the Metropolitan Museum in February), gives one an opportunity to reexamine some of these supreme pictures by Braque and Picasso; but it also leads one to a sense of extreme discomfort in front of the mass of evidence for how stupidly the two men's efforts were betrayed by their epigones. The show wishes to demonstrate the international spread of the style during the time that its major practitioners, Picasso, Braque, and Gris, were developing its premises and consolidating its language—that is to say, from 1908 to 1921. The exhibition includes the work of sixty painters and sculptors from ten different countries, its international scope arising from the by now standard thesis that cubism represents a reorientation of artist to reality unparalleled since the onset of Renaissance art. But it seems to me that "The Cubist Epoch" does more to damage that view than to support it—at least in the form in which the exhibition itself sets up the argument.

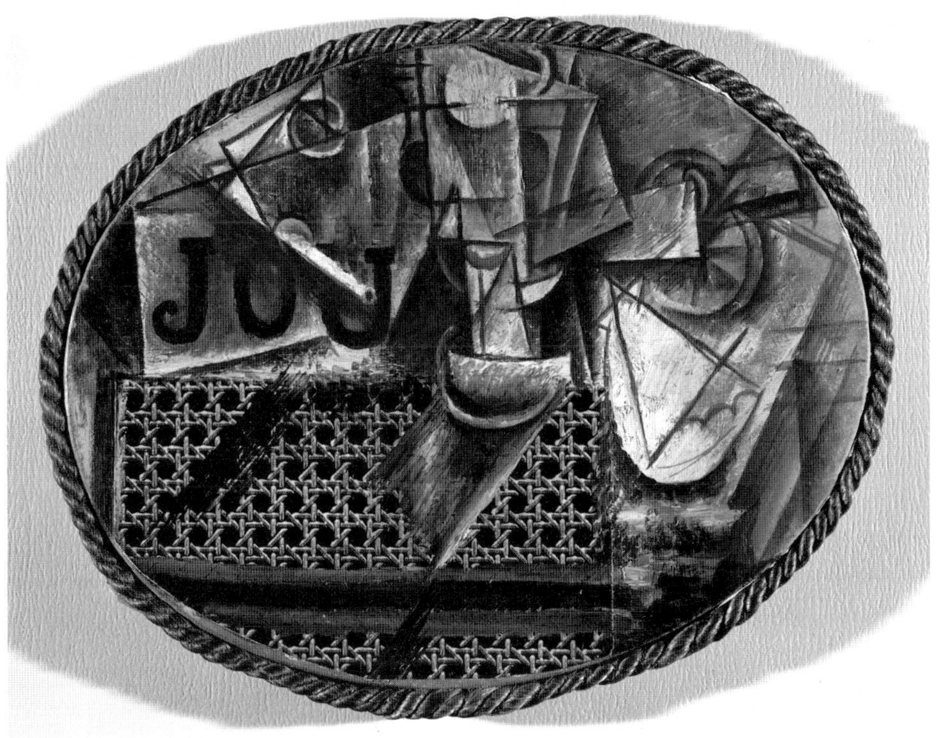

12.2 Picasso, *Still Life with Chair Caning,* 1912. © 2009 Estate of Pablo Picasso/Artists Rights Society (ARS), New York.

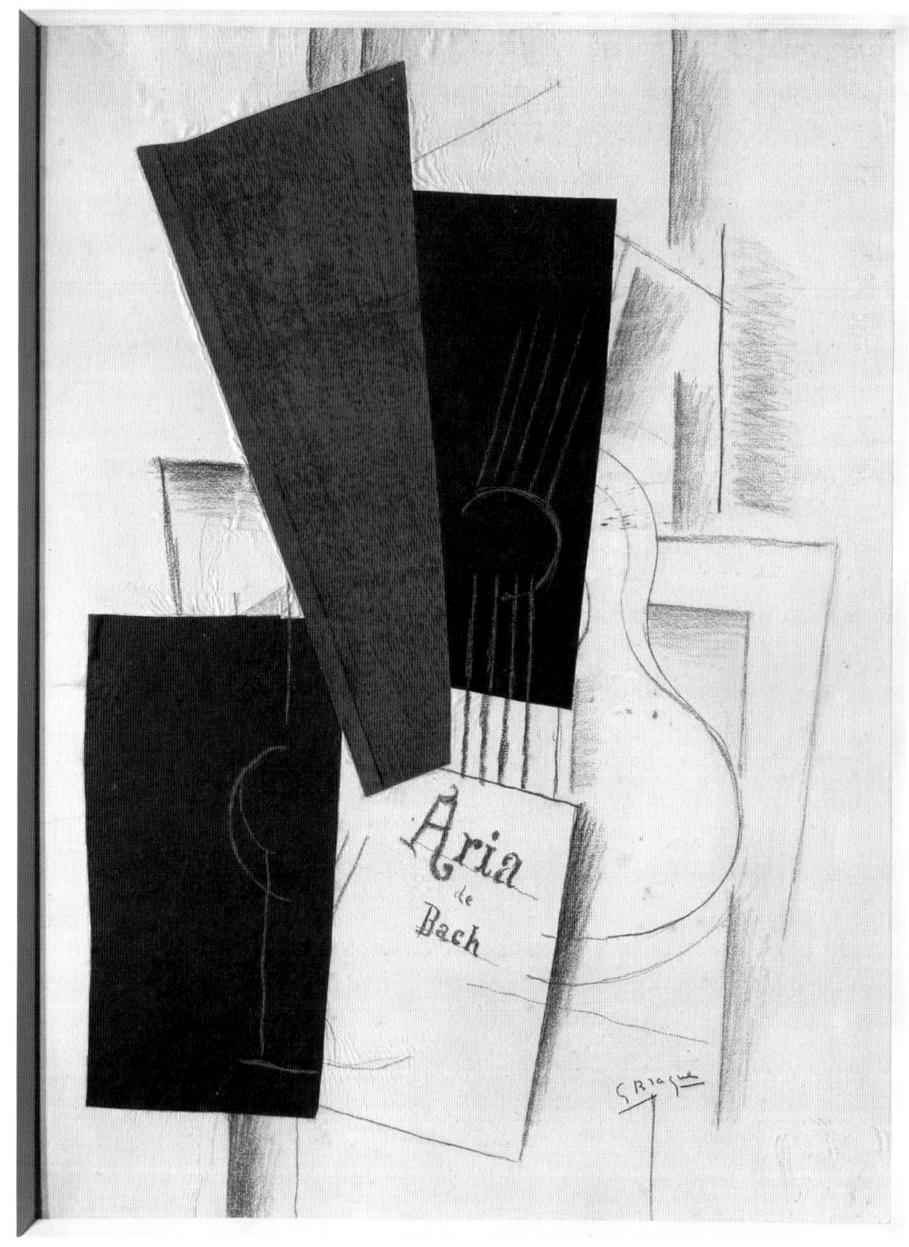

12.3 Georges Braque, *Homage to J. S. Bach*, 1912. © 2009 Artists Rights Society (ARS), New York/ ADAGP, Paris.

For me, the most moving painting in the exhibition was Braque's *Homage to J. S. Bach* (1912). The asceticism of Braque's vision, with a dusting of color that is puritanical both in the limitation of its range (from ochre to gray to white) and in the reticence of its facture, nonetheless produces a quality of pearly light emanating from the remains of a shallow depth, creating a sense that each part of the painting is a transparent plane that opens onto every other part. Next to this, his *Still Life with Pipe* (1912), a much smaller work that seems to be closely reliant on Picasso both in the descriptive language of its images (the particular pipe one finds there is a Picasso invention) and in the un-Braque-like opacity of the planes which close out the space, comes off as a minor, almost failed work. Indeed, in the first section of the exhibition, where a sampling of the two men's hermetic pictures are assembled, there is a high percentage of second-rate paintings. Braque's *Still Life with Clarinet and Violin* from 1912–1913 is surely one of the worst pictures he ever painted, and Picasso's *Clarinet Player* of 1911 must rank among the most enervated of all his figure paintings. What comes across most strongly in this section is a quality of fecklessness in the selection of objects, and this is matched by the slovenly handling of information about the pictures in the catalogue text accompanying the exhibition.

Cooper's ambitions in this text seem to have been to write a book that could compete with Rosenblum's *Cubism and Twentieth-Century Art.* It is a 265-page essay on the movement, lavishly illustrated in color, including plates of many pictures that Cooper never even hoped to include in the exhibition. The critical treatment of what he terms "true Cubism" is a strange mélange of interpretation, in which Greenberg's ideas of the formal import of collage (which Cooper never acknowledges) find themselves curiously juxtaposed with the quite different interpretations of Rosenblum and Golding (likewise unacknowledged). The carelessness about documentation extends to small but significant details about the pictures. For instance, Cooper refers to Picasso's first collage (not in the exhibition) as *Still Life with Caned Chair,* when it has always been titled *Still Life with Chair Caning.* Since Cooper's version implies a positive identification of the rectangular patch of oilcloth as an object set apart from the table's surface, while the other title does not, one wonders what his authority was for introducing this particular nomenclature. He also speaks of Braque's 1911 *Portugais* (not in the exhibition) as the first cubist painting to employ stenciled letters, while in the show itself there is a Picasso dated 1910 with "CORT" stenciled in letters three inches high across its upper left corner *(Absinthe Glass, Bottle, Pipe and Musical Instruments on a Piano)* (1910–1911). Since this is the only Picasso before the end of 1912 to use stenciling at all, and since the figuration in the picture itself seems impossible before the summer of 1912, one wonders why Cooper saw no reason to take issue with the date assigned to the work in the Zervos catalog of Picasso's oeuvre, or at least to revise his assessment of Braque's *Portugais*.

But the intellectual poverty of the catalog is small change compared to the aesthetic disaster of the exhibition itself as a whole. Except for the first section and a later small section of magnificent collages by Picasso, Braque, and Gris, the walls are awash with wave after wave of bad painting, as the syntax of the original language of cubism was siphoned off from every pictorial meaning with which it had initially been invested. In addition to cubist exercises by Marcoussis, Lhote, Villon, Herbin, Metzinger, Picabia, and Férat, that are uniformly overworked and overblown, there are seventeen works by the Czech adepts Filla, Kubišta, Procházka, Beneš, Gutfreund, and Čapek that attest to the orgy of academicism that the new style unleashed on European art. In the Russian section of the show were two brilliant pictures, *The Looking Glass* by Goncharova and the *Scissors Grinder* by Malevich, both from 1912. The vigor of the former issued from a primitivism that set a vertiginous sense of space against the stolid iconic quality of the image, the power of the Malevich from a directness of high color and symmetrical design that overwhelmed the depicted object. But the closer the Russians and Italians drew to a strictly cubist style, the more shackled and precious their art seemed to become; and wherever one turned in the exhibition, this was the case. The three groups of pictures which seemed eloquently to take up and extend certain of the issues raised by Picasso and Braque were the cathedral facades by Mondrian, the collage-paintings by Gris, and the cityscapes by Delaunay. In these works all three men examine on their own terms the problem of whether there can be any synonymy between one's orientation to a vertical plane and the position that must be assumed in

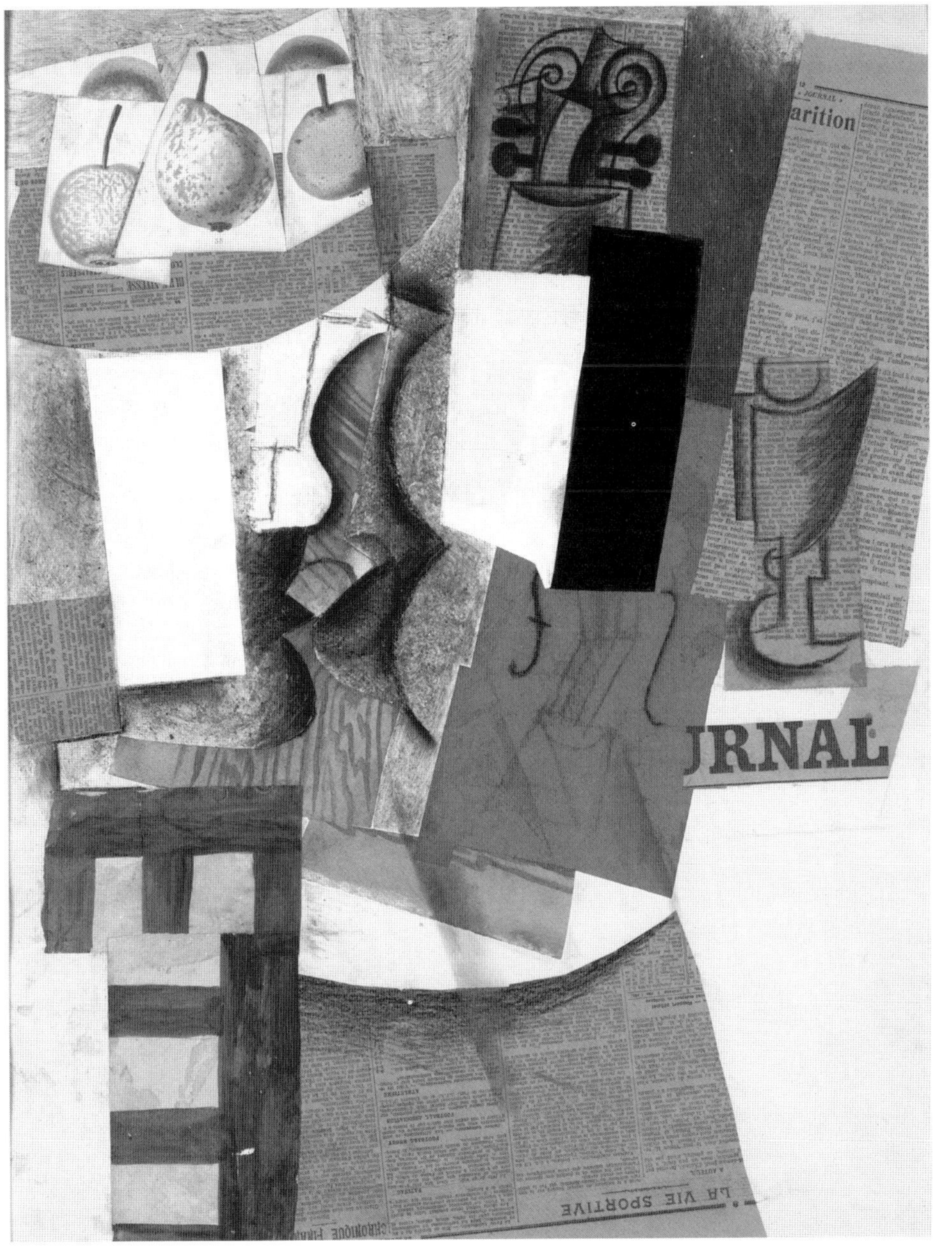

12.4 Pablo Picasso, *Bowl with Fruit, Violin, and Wineglass,* 1912–1913. © 2009 Estate of Pablo Picasso/ Artists Rights Society (ARS), New York.

order to grasp objects arranged on a ground perpendicular to that plane. In Delaunay's 1911 *The City Seen from an Open Window,* a decoratively wrought pointillist screen establishes for the viewer both the fact of the vertical fall of the picture surface along the plane of the wall on which it hangs and the irreconcilable notion that whatever she hopes to see beyond that surface cannot be seen *from there*—that is, from the angle of vision she must maintain with regard to the upright plane. With a kind of hopeless irony, the atmospheric meaning of pointillism is emptied out. The original neo-impressionist ambitions to recreate retinal excitation are confronted here by Delaunay with an understanding of the retina as a flat screen which itself registers no more than a flat array of light and dark points; and thus the painting becomes a poignant admission that, because depth cannot be visually accounted for, it cannot in fact be seen.

In Gris's 1914 collage-paintings, like *Fruit Dish and Carafe,* there is likewise the superimposition of the tactile world of the factual surface and a phantom visual world of objects. Gris's use of the isometric perspective to project these objects, like Delaunay's pointillism, promotes the sense that there is no way of determining for the viewer the position from which these objects are to be seen, since the isometric view is utterly indeterminate on the question of vantage.

"The Cubist Epoch" confirmed my sense of the difference between the kind of critical examination that was the burden of the early work of Picasso, Braque, Gris, Delaunay, and the pre-1921 Mondrian—an examination of the possible meaning of a literal plane transecting vision—and the attitudes of the devotees of the style who exploited the picture surface merely as a decorative matrix. It made me feel more strongly than ever that the pressing questions raised by the originators of cubism—questions of the inexplicable gulf between signified and sign, between resemblance and representation, between depictive and literal shape, questions of where one could possibly find ultimate sanctions for compositional decisions—had to wait for a postwar group of painters like Hofmann, de Kooning, Pollock, Johns, or Stella, to take them up and extend them.

Rossellini's film *The Rise to Power of Louis XIV* ends with a scene in which the king is seated alone at a raised banquet table, consuming an endless meal and contemplating the crowd of courtiers who silently and respectfully watch him eat. They, in all seriousness, believe themselves to be attending a meaningful ritual. But he, from the position of regal aloofness to which he has sentenced himself, knows that what he is both promoting and enduring is an extreme act of foppishness for an audience of impotent slaves. And he does it in order to renew their condition of servitude continually, to bind them wordlessly to him as he consolidates to himself the powers of state. It is as if the tragedy of a self-inflicted isolation and the absurdity of a mass loss of self-consciousness meet across the space of the banquet table. One feels that same thing along the course of "The Cubist Epoch." For the first time, I understood the contempt the surrealists felt for the aesthetic epidemic of academicism known as "cubism."

Richard Serra: Sculpture Redrawn

In 1920 Lev Kuleshov screened a series of now famous "experiments" for his film class in Moscow: experiments that isolated and revealed the *cut* as the magical interstice in which the mysteries of cinematic illusion were somehow contained. To Pudovkin, and to Kuleshov's other students, what these experiments disclosed was that the cut was an index of difference or separateness within a prevailing matrix of sameness. For the mere juncture between two strips of celluloid was enough to convince viewers that the White House stood solid and indestructible in the heart of Moscow, or that filmed details of many different women could fuse beyond the cut to corporealize a single body. Over and over the experiments revealed the primacy of spatial continuity—showing that the cut would have to wedge into it very deeply indeed before that continuity would break.

It may seem that the elementary properties of filmic illusion occupy a territory that is light-years away from the concerns of Richard Serra's sculpture. For that sculpture, with its scrupulous attention to the physical properties of material and its rigorous testimony to the procedures of its own making, is nothing if not profoundly hostile to illusionism. Nonetheless, the "cut" is a preoccupation of Serra's. It is present in the torn lead piece of 1968 and in the cutting piece of

First published in *Artforum* 10 (May 1972).

1969 or the massive *Sawing: Base Plate Measure (Twelve Fir Trees)* of 1970. Like the cut in film, Serra's cut connects materials at the same time that it physically divides them; even as the cut creates a boundary, it testifies to a primal level of coherence as the precondition to the very meaning of all boundary or contour. As such, it is a special case of Serra's use of line in sculpture.

Line is everywhere in Serra's sculpture. In the cutting and sawing pieces it is both physical edge and elemental "drawing"—a logical trajectory creating the abstract syntax that binds together the separate elements of the work. In the standing plate pieces of 1969, it is a function of the lead bar, which again cuts two ways. Physically the bar is the tool of the work's uprightness, its downward compression on the plates the visible lynchpin to the sculpture's existence. But it also functions abstractly. In *1-1-1-1* (1969), the single-point contact of plates and bar gives the work both the kind of weightlessness and the sheer connectivity of abstract line. Thus, that abstraction is read against the reality of the physical pressures of the work: its possible instability in the face of gravity. In the Pasadena *Base Plate Deflection—In It On It* (1970), line is naturalized as a function of the ground into which the piece is half-buried; and in an elevational cut piece of the same year, line again serves as both physical fact and as index of the unseen. The immense *Pulitzer Piece: Stepped Elevation* (1970–1971), which is the subject of this essay, both summarizes and deepens the earlier dualism of Serra's line. For there it is more obviously natural than ever before, and at the same time it drives ever more deeply into Serra's territory of abstraction.

Placed on a five-acre meadow on the property of Joseph Pulitzer's country home just outside St. Louis, the work consists of three rectilinear steel plates knifed into the groundswells of that field, and the fan-shaped space that spread-eagles between the three-point invasion of those plates. Roughly V-shaped, the meadow itself begins at a road running in front of Pulitzer's house and drops off gently toward a dense wood which defines the two long arms of the V. Within the broad expanse of this field, the siting of the three plates has a peculiarly dual character. In one sense the plates are conceived of as measuring the continuous drop in the level of the field, and therefore in profile they function as "steps":

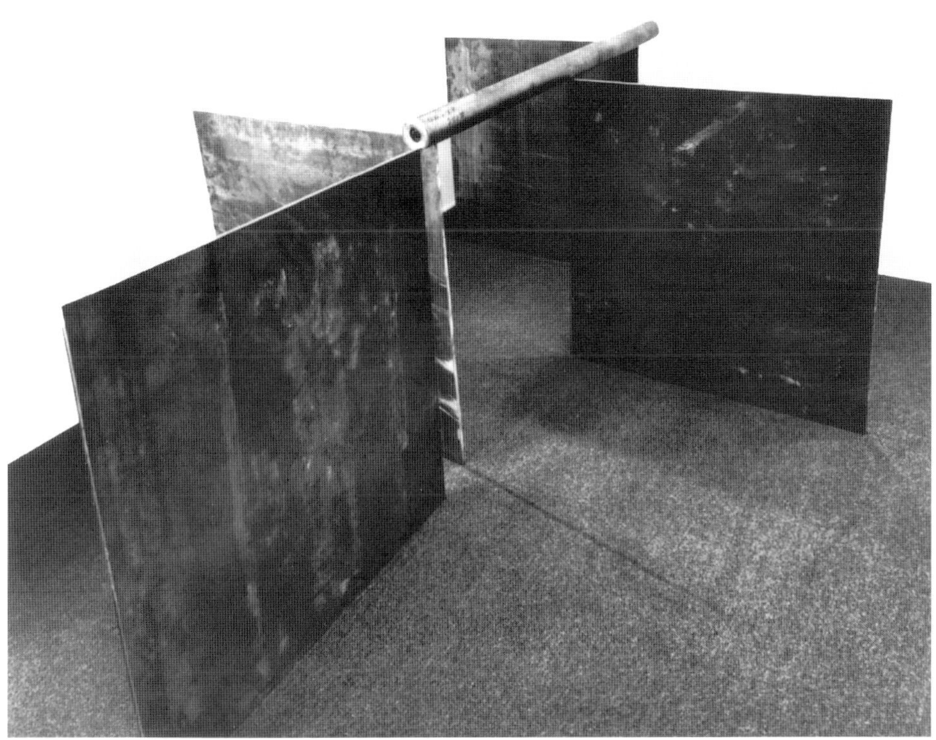

13.1 Richard Serra, *1-1-1-1,* 1969. © 2009 Richard Serra/Artists Rights Society (ARS), New York.

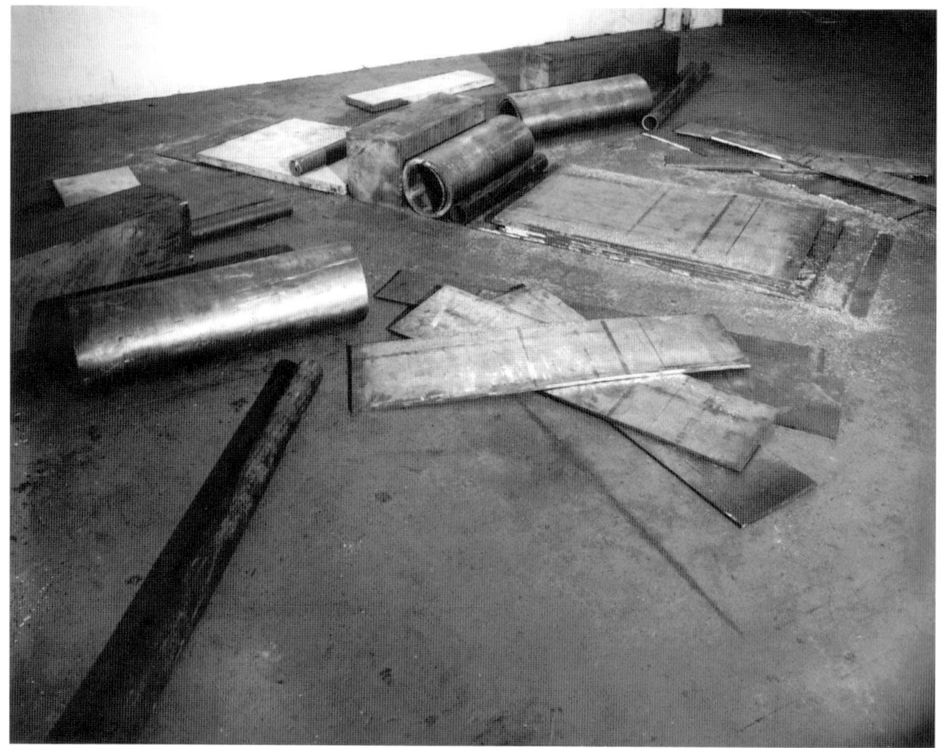

13.2 Richard Serra, *Cutting Device: Base Plate Measure,* 1969. © 2009 Richard Serra/Artists Rights Society (ARS), New York.

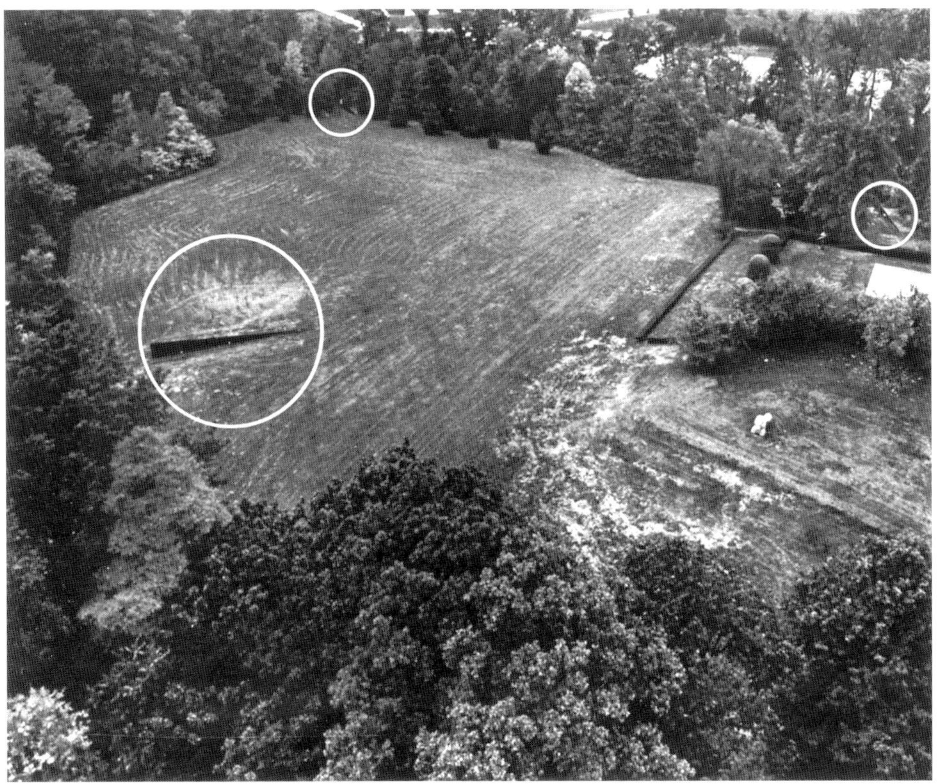

13.3 Richard Serra, *Pulitzer Piece: Stepped Elevation*, 1970 (overall view). © 2009 Richard Serra/Artists Rights Society (ARS), New York.

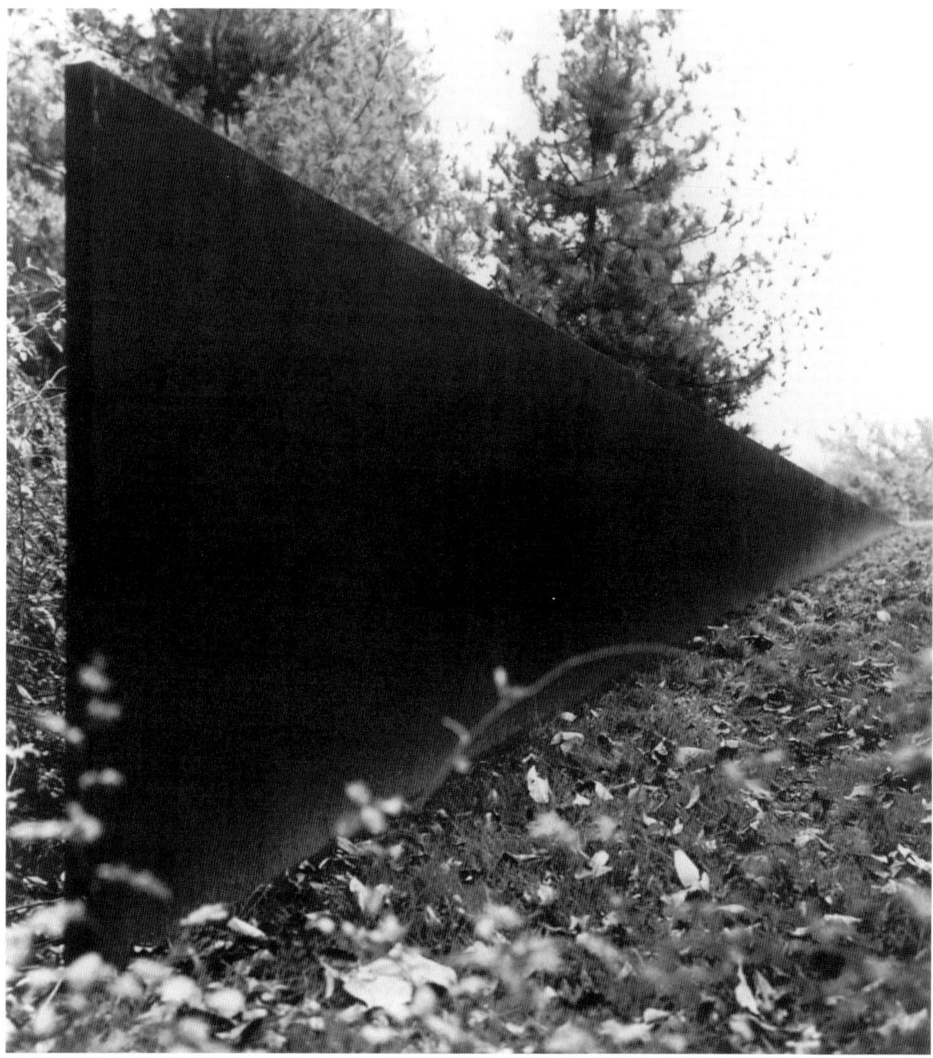

13.4 Richard Serra, *Pulitzer Piece: Stepped Elevation,* 1970 (plate 3). © 2009 Richard Serra/Artists Rights Society (ARS), New York.

each five feet high, slicing downward in succession a total of fifteen feet. The top edge of the first "step" begins level with the highest elevation in the field and extends forward forty-seven feet. At that point, the land into which the plate is wedged has dropped five feet, so that the bottom edge of the plate is no longer enveloped by the ground but rests on it, and the forward edge of the plate rises five feet into the air. At this same level in the field the top edge of the next plate begins its outward extension from point to line to plane: an extension for fifty-five feet before the land falls away the five feet necessary to expose the bottom corner of the plate. Similarly, the third plate begins where the second left off, and the land drops away before revealing the full forward profile of the sixty-foot plate. (Something of the way the steps ideally relate to one another can be read off a drawing for *Two Circular Elevational Steps,* a piece Serra did in 1971 at the L.A. County Museum.)

Although this description diagrams the actual relationship between the levels of the land and the stepped continuity of the plates, it is a description that involves a kind of telescoping or contraction of the work. In fact, about three hundred yards separates each plate from the next, so that in plan, or from the air, the three plates appear to radiate outward from an invisible central point—each one like the visible tip of a spoke that extends about 150 yards, each spoke at something like a 45-degree angle from the next. The real dispersion of the plates thus belies the conceptual continuity of a stepped succession. This dispersion documents the way the work was in fact sited or made. For after determining the site for the highest plate, Serra had to follow the contour line of the land for about three hundred yards until he found the next most abrupt point at which the ground fell five feet. The same procedure was necessary for locating the third plate. Because of this, the point of contact between one "step" and the next expanded to include the geographic fact of the long, slow arcs of the field's contours. In this three-point expansion, slope and swell are made palpable as functions of the earth which the plates both bind together and reveal. Like three stakes anchoring the soft volume of a billowing tent, the triangulated bite of the steel fins makes perceptible the shape of the land contained by their grip.

Two linear modes thus intersect within the work. Both can be known about, but neither can really be seen. One mode operates in depth, the other in breadth. The first acts through the successive stepped fall of the piece downward—the continuity of which is made totally invisible by the far-flung locations of the plates themselves. The second acts through the continuity of the contour lines to maintain the logic of the work's breadth or extension across the five acres of its "ground." Yet, within the diffuseness of the meadow's space, the actual contour lines are as imperceptible as the continuity of the slope. If this quality of the invasion of the visible by the invisible—this sense of thought's reconstruction of the real even while it is totally grounded in (rather than separated off from) the real—characterizes the entire piece, it also resonates through the experience of each individual plate. And it is in the exploration of the plates themselves that I came to understand what underlies the aspirations of this work and of Serra's other sculpture as well.

There are four mutually informing and mutually contradicting facts that shape the perceptual experience of each plate:

> 1. Line experienced abstractly in relation to depth. Standing on axis with any of the plates means taking up a position either above or below it, and this produces a sharp contraction of the enormous expanse of the plate . . . into a line. From below, the linear edge that one sees is vertical and parallel with one's own body. From above the plate, the line (now the top edge of the plate) reads as an unsupported vector shooting away from one's body into space. As such, the line inflects but does not break the continuous fabric of the space of the landscape.
>
> 2. Line understood physically as the edge of mass. Standing parallel to the face of any of the plates, one experiences its materiality, and at the same time literally loses sight of the landscape. For the wall-like plane embodied in approximately 150 square feet of 2-inch-thick steel barricades one's view of the continuous space of the plate's surrounds.
>
> 3. Mass transformed into a system of line. Standing parallel to the face of the plates, one experiences the ground or earth itself as a discrete line defining the visible shape of the plate—a meandering graphism played

off against the more rigid right angle of the exposed steel edges. The exposed shape of the plate—an elongated right triangle—is thus delineated by the line of the natural fall of the land. Gathering into itself both the immediacy of natural description and the contingency of a drafted line's attempt to record natural events, this irregular, earth-drawn hypotenuse involves the reality of the space in a kind of self-reflexive loop. Trigonometry lies suspended between its natural origins and its abstract functions.

4. Mass revealed through an implicit contour. From any angle, one is aware of the real shape of the plate even though one can never see it, and it is this invisible rectangular agent which materializes the ground as the base of each individual plate and of the sculpture as a whole. Shape itself—an invisible but knowable contour—makes the sculpture, making visible its abstract relationship and simultaneously making palpable the incredible tonnage of the entire work. Part of what the Pulitzer piece is about is the unfixable, unlocatable, indeterminate shape of mass.

Two types of shape (the visible and the implied) and two types of line (the abstract and the natural) converge in the work in a crosscurrent of inference and mutual implication. Each mode is seen as the obverse of the other, each containing within itself the potential presence of the other, each acknowledging the inextricability of its fusion with the other, each creating the possibility of the other in a continual spawn—a continuous dimensional conception. At every point, the Pulitzer sculpture testifies to the constant unfolding of the dimensions of space. On that field, dimensionality itself is understood as residing in the pure potential of line. As the leading edge of a plane set perpendicular to the visual field, line becomes the proposition of a backward cut into space; just as that plane, when rotated parallel to vision, becomes (for sight) an index of volume. And this kind of fruition of one dimension's possibilities in another—this explicit acknowledgment that space-as-perceived involves the constant intuition of depth *in potentia*—is at the heart of Serra's sculptural enterprise.

As I have tried to make clear, the Pulitzer piece simultaneously maintains line at an extreme of naturalism and an extreme of abstraction. Contained in this duality or bivalence of line is an assault on both the kind of line in sculpture that occupies space without defining it and the kind of line that defines space without occupying it. Since Serra believes occupation and definition are absolute cofunctions, the one inseparable from the other in a world that we both understand and inhabit, failure to recognize either aspect of that synthesis would be an evasion of the problem of sculpture. On the one hand, Serra's work rejects the arbitrariness of decorative drawing. On the other, it denies the kind of three-dimensional extension of the cubist grid which makes sculpture into the chess pieces on a board of ideated space.

The distinction between Serra's sculpture and that of minimalism comes in part out of his rejection of the a priori geometries of the grid. For the grid is an abstract tool describing a space that always begins at a point just in front of the person who views it. The diorama of the analytic sensibility, the grid forever leaves the viewer outside looking in. In this sense the Pulitzer work is the halfway house in Serra's push to make sculpture that articulates the way space opens out from a point within the viewer, rather than lying just beyond his first forward step.

Prefigured in the 1969 *Davidson Gate,* in which two eight-by-eight-foot plates diagonally section the cube of a gallery's space, the Pulitzer sculpture is contemporary with *Strike* (1969–1971), where a single vertical fin states the mutual dependence between the depiction of volume and the terms of dimensionality as it is lived. The eight-by-twenty-four-foot steel plate of *Strike* recapitulates with extreme simplicity the meaning of this relationship. Butted into the corner juncture of two walls for its sole means of vertical support, the steel plane transects the right-angled volume of the space. As one moves around the work, plane contracts to line (or edge) and then expands back into plane. Reciprocally, the space is blocked off and then opened out and subsequently reblocked. In *Strike,* the dimensionality of lived space once again expands from the burgeoning forth of one dimension's potential in another. Following *Strike* is a four-plate piece, *Circuit,* which will be installed at Documenta this June

[1972]. Like *Strike,* the four-plate work will occupy the closed volume of an interior space, with four twenty-two-foot plates, each eight feet high, coming out of the four corners of the room, and stopping three feet short of their mutual intersection. It is from within that three-foot-square lozenge of space, that short-circuiting of the physical presence of that piece, that the sculpture will be able to be "seen." Serra once said that *Strike* had come to mean for him an homage to Barnett Newman—to the efficiency and directness with which Newman used a sequence of plane/line/plane to walk out of the imperatives of cubist space and to simply close the door behind him.

V

Formless

My distance from Clement Greenberg had begun in the late 1960s with my "perverse" interest in surrealism. Greenberg's hostility to the movement arose from his conviction that it was merely literary and without formal interest or invention. Thanks to a Guggenheim Fellowship, I was able to dedicate myself to the work of Joan Miró from the 1920s for the exhibition "Magnetic Fields" (Guggenheim Museum, 1971), which focused on the artist's "dream paintings." William Rubin was the first to write about this work, in the catalogue for the brilliant exhibition "Dada, Surrealism, and Their Heritage" which also defied Greenberg's taboo. It was thanks to Rubin, who commissioned me to prepare a catalogue essay on the sculpture of Alberto Giacometti's relation to primitive art, that I encountered *Documents,* the magazine edited in the 1930s by Georges Bataille who developed the concept of formlessness (*l'informe*). This category became the basis of my understanding of surrealist photography. Nothing could be further from Greenberg's formal preoccupations than this welcome dependence on the formless.

Michel, Bataille et Moi

In 1927 Joan Miró made a picture of himself strolling at night in Paris accompanied by Michel Leiris and Georges Bataille. Or, since "making a picture" is something of a misstatement of how the men appear in this painting, I should say he inscribed the following words on a loose, umber wash: "Musique," in the upper left corner; "Seine" in the middle; and then, along the lower right—presumably at the spot where the quay would be—the three walkers: "Michel, Bataille et moi."

But though Miró thus indelibly penned the name of Georges Bataille into his art, no writer on that art (with the sole exception of Carolyn Lanchner, the curator of the present exhibition ["Joan Miró," Museum of Modern Art, New York, 1993]) has ever done likewise. There are two reasons why this should not surprise us. The first has to do with the extraordinary grip André Breton has had on the reception of all of surrealism, such that art historians have been entirely mesmerized by the aura of explanation he cast around it. So great has been his control that until the late 1970s neither Bataille, whom Breton openly declared his enemy, nor Bataille's magazine *Documents* figures in the indexes of any account of the surrealist movement in painting or sculpture. This is something I became acutely aware of as I was working on the relationship of Alberto

Written for a colloquium at Chantilly, 1993; first published in *October,* no. 68 (Spring 1994).

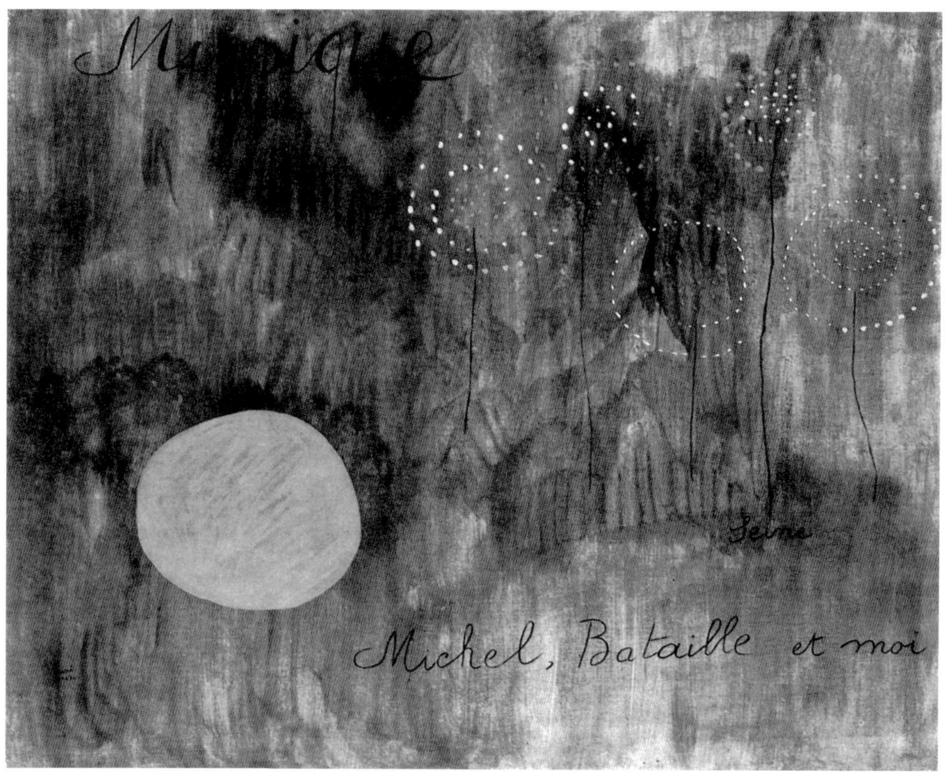

14.1 Joan Miró, *Musique: Michel, Bataille et moi,* 1927. © Successió Miró/Artists Rights Society (ARS), New York/ADAGP, Paris.

Giacometti to primitive art and I began to see the centrality of the *Documents* position for any understanding of this subject.

And yet we could say—and this brings me to the second reason—that while the sadism in Giacometti's work, its thematics of enucleation, and its drive to produce the "round phallicism" that is one avatar of the *informe* forge an open connection to the universe of Bataille's thought, there seems to be little in Miró's art that would provoke any such association. This is true whether we think of Miró under the rubric of "childishness" which has been the category of his popular success, or whether we approach him as what has been called "a painter's painter," which is the more serious form of his acceptance. Interestingly enough, *both* these descriptions were launched by Breton himself, the first when he said that he feared that Miró's development "had been arrested at the infantile stage," and the second when he stated that Miró's only desire was "to give himself up utterly to painting, and to painting alone."[1] And while Breton was employing neither characterization as a compliment, they have become the standard alternative forms of the Miró accolade.

Thus there is, on the one hand, the idea that Miró has translated a world of childlike innocence and playful spontaneity into a bestiary of excited and fantastic forms; and on the other, the notion that he has committed himself to a world of space and color, the daring and inventiveness of which other painters instantly recognize. This latter position entered the Miró literature with greatest force in 1929 by means of Michel Leiris's vivid metaphor of the tantric exercise of forming an incredibly precise mental image of a garden and then removing every leaf and twig and stone within that image—down to the very earth and sky, which are then themselves removed—so that nothing remains but the stunningly sharp experience of a void, this metaphor understood as a way of presenting those stripped-down Mirós from the mid-1920s which have come to be called "dream paintings."

By the late 1950s Leiris's idea of the void had changed in the subsequent literature on Miró to something more like the surging all-over washes and charged expressiveness of action painting, so that Miró's pictures of this time were being seen as precursors of the work of, say, Jackson Pollock. And a decade later, in my own work on the Miró of this period, which led to an exhibition called "Magnetic Fields," that Margit Rowell and I organized at the Guggenheim Museum, the dream paintings, with their monochrome blue or yellow or umber grounds interrupted by nothing more substantial than a hair-thin line more adapted to the writing of words than to the bounding of things, were placed in relation to color field painting, which is to say, an aesthetic of disembodied, dematerialized, optical space.

How, indeed, would *this* Miró, by turns the maker of children's toys and the painter of ethereal clouds, inhabit anything like the same universe as Georges Bataille? Bataille: the author of the pornographic novel *The Story of the Eye;* the theorist of formlessness and of the heterological, which is to say everything that refuses to be integrated into a world of reason and order.

And yet there is a third Miró, one who seems to be quite interested in tapping us on the shoulder, so to speak, and, like the man reaching into the inner pockets of his raincoat, offering to show us his "dirty pictures." The throbbing genitalia that enter Miró's painting in the summer of 1924 as the only palpable organic elements to be hung on his otherwise diagrammatic stick figures—whether it's the hunter gaily ejaculating in the *Catalan Landscape* or the extraordinary maternal vulva sprouting, bulblike, in the center of *The Family*—are subsumed for the most part within a kind of robust peasant admiration for fecundity and germination. But by the fall of 1924 and into the following year, Miró begins to construct an entire, somewhat spatially schematic universe through which to operate metaphoric strings of relationships based on these organs. One of the most persistent of these strings involves the equivalence that moves from the lips of the mouth to those of the labia, which with their excited aureole of hair are transmuted into a dazzling sun, whose spherical body now surrounded by tentacular flames produces the suggestion of a spider, which in turn can evoke the radiant sprays of a comet, or the stamen and corolla of a flower, and so on.

That the expressive goal of these pictures is explicitly sexual, the metaphoric substitutions driving toward a kind of stunned, explosive climax, becomes all the more obvious when we look at the group of paintings Miró made in 1925

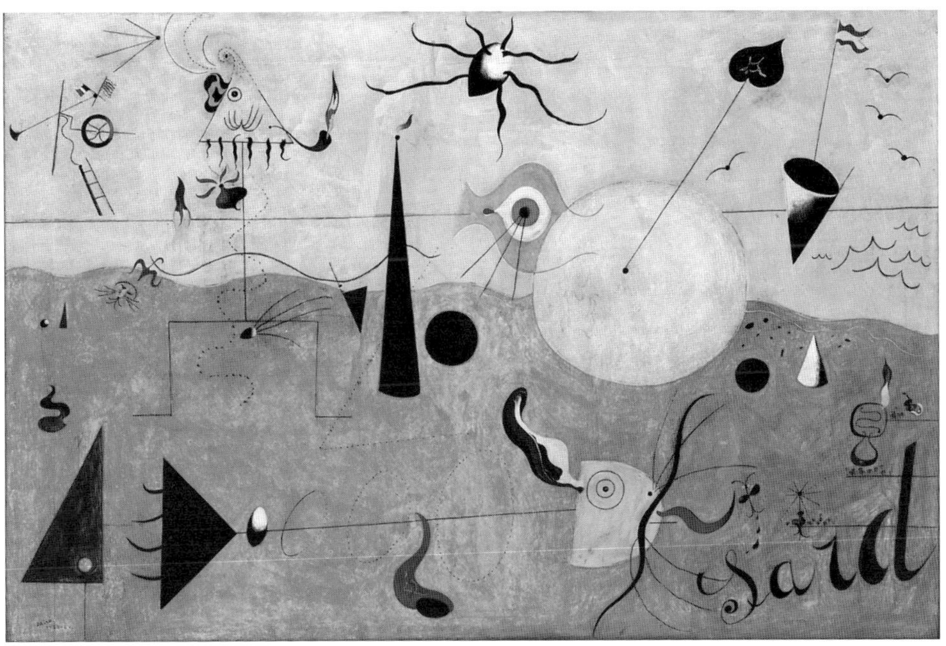

14.2 Joan Miró, *Catalan Landscape,* 1924. © Successió Miró/Artists Rights Society (ARS), New York/ADAGP, Paris.

of couples making love, this act frequently conceived as pure biological contact in which sperm meets ovum and a primitive dehiscence begins to split the single cell into two. Miró's extraordinary painting *The Kiss* delivers this copulatory sign with stunning directness, as the fission on the schematically simple level of the cell is overlaid by the far more materialized image of the contact of sexual organs achieved by the red bar that enacts the connection where male meets female and by the hair that identifies the vulva.

It must be said, of course, that an incredible prudishness dogs the literature on Miró, such that this preoccupation—this third Miró, so to speak—is consistently either ignored or shunted to one side. Jacques Dupin, Miró's most complete chronicler, describes this painting, for example, as follows:

> With *The Kiss* we have the triumph of a complete absence of premeditation and a pure form of dream writing. This kiss is inscribed on an indeterminate blue-gray ground that, perfume-like, suggests the confinement of an alcove. Two circular forms are attracted to one another to the point of joining and communicating as through the narrow neck of a vase: this is the kiss. Jubilation is expressed through the long, fine flames that escape from the interior and fly away, tapering, winding, and changing color at each turning. Around this absolutely stripped down symbol of love, only the prison of a fluctuating line, black, white or dotted, remains.[2]

The chasteness of Dupin's notion of this kiss is reinforced by his characterization of the colored ether within which it appears, as "perfume." This, we could say, is the sublimatory drive of Miró's critical reception, working consistently to purify his imagery. And yet Miró was not above specifying smells of a very different sort, as, for example, in the painting *Oh! One of These Gentlemen Who Did All That!* (1925), which the artist himself has said is about farting. And as for the ethereal character of the backgrounds of the so-called dream paintings, Miró was far more equivocal about how to characterize them. Writing to Michel Leiris in the late summer of 1924, he describes having to purge his

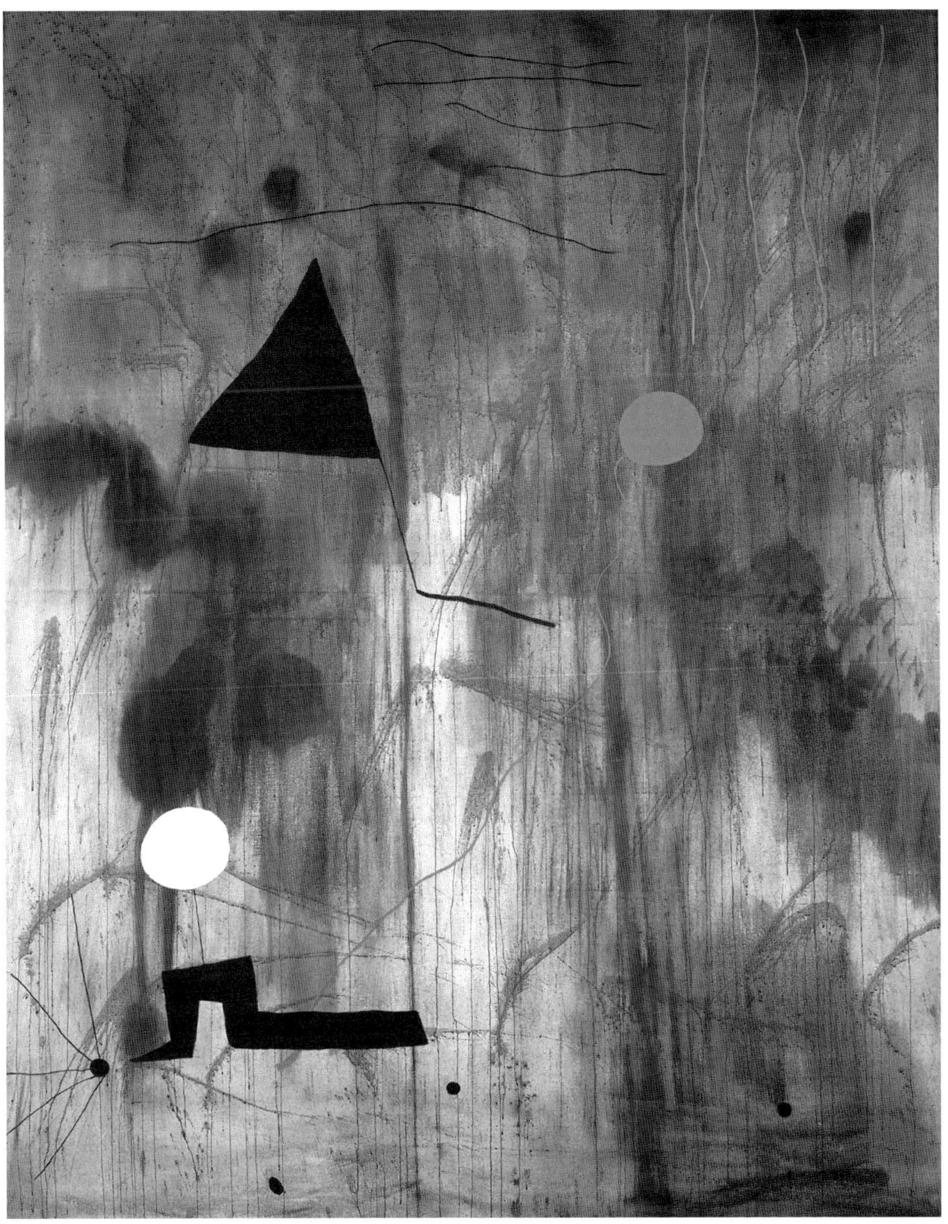

14.3 Joan Miró, *The Birth of the World,* 1925. © Successió Miró/Artists Rights Society (ARS), New York/ADAGP, Paris.

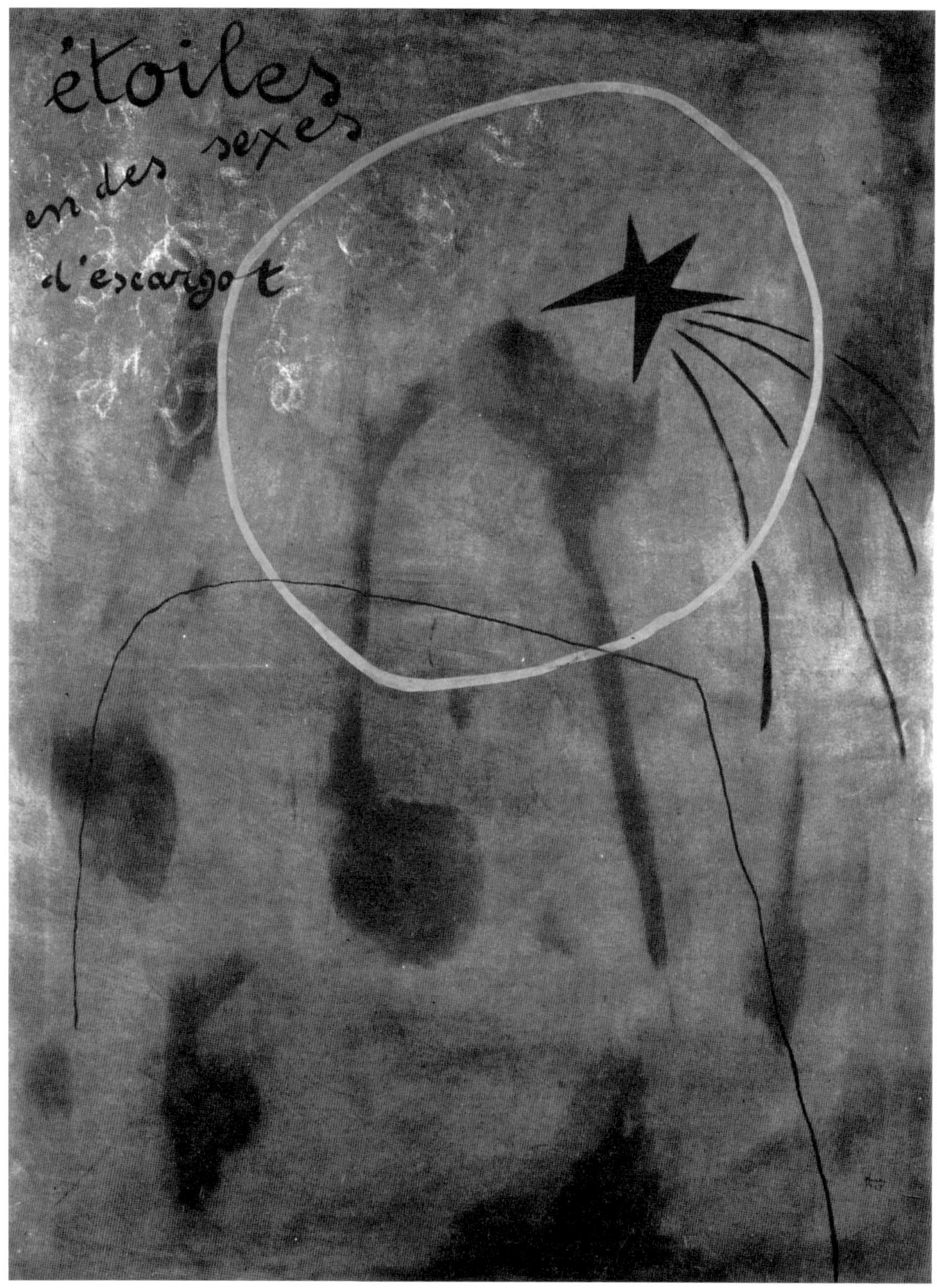

14.4 Joan Miró, *Etoiles en des sexes d'escargot,* 1925. © Successió Miró/Artists Rights Society (ARS), New York/ADAGP, Paris.

work of color, saying that "the charm and music of colors" are "the final stage of degeneration." Therefore, he says, he has decided to resort to drawing alone and admits, "This is hardly painting, but I don't give a damn." Recalling the same period in an interview in 1928, he says, "I was painting with an absolute contempt for painting. . . . I was feeling aggressive but at the same time I was feeling superior. . . . I felt contempt for my oeuvre."[3]

Accordingly, when Leiris turns away from the metaphor of the tantric exercise with which he opens his 1929 essay on Miró, and actually gets down to a direct description of the pictures from the mid 1920s, he characterizes them as seeming "not so much painted as dirtied."[4] Adopting Miró's position of attack on the medium and on color, he speaks of "These huge canvases which [are] . . . troubling like destroyed buildings, tantalizing like faded walls on which generations of poster hangers, allied over centuries of drizzle, have inscribed mysterious poems, long smears taking louche shapes, uncertain like alluvial deposits coming from god knows where, sands swept along by perpetually shifting rivers, their beds subjected to the movement of wind and rain."[5]

Thus, it is perhaps against the background of the dirty wall rather than the blue infinity of the cosmos that the transformational chains of the Miró imaginary should be seen. One of the differences this would make is that the tendency to abstract Miró's line by pushing it toward the cursive, noncorporeal quality of script, by means of the analogy many critics (including myself) have tried to set up between these works and calligrams, would meet with a certain resistance. And because of this we might begin to experience the *material* specificity of any given point in the metaphorical chain. An example might be the 1925 painting *Head of a Smoker* which has always been welcomed in the Miró literature as yet one more example of the vaporousness and fragility of the dream space, with the evanescence of the cloud of smoke resonating with and thereby reinforcing the nebulous quality of the background. Accordingly, when I wrote about this work in 1971, I compared it to Apollinaire's "Fumées," in which the cigar and its smoke seem to be subsumed, before our very eyes so to speak, into the idea of the smoke's dispersal and disappearance. And although I spoke about the phallic associations of the pipe, reproducing the apposite drawing in which a man walking along, reading a newspaper, is given a tiny pipe that is then visually rhymed with splendidly outsized genitals, I saw the transformational work of the painting as one of raising or sublimating this association—dematerializing it, so to speak. Thus I did not notice the little hairs that Miró has shown growing at the base of the puff of smoke in the painting, hairs that work to lower the relationship, to keep it fixated on the phallic half of the analogy, with the same intrusion of tactile specificity as in the little red bar of *The Kiss*. The hairs, we could say, insist that the point around which the metaphoric chains circulate is obdurately genital.

It is here that the occlusion of Georges Bataille in the Miró literature begins to take on a certain interest. Because if, in a case like this one, I didn't address the hairs that are, in a certain sense, what the painting is about, it was not so much because I didn't notice them as because I didn't know what to do with them. For it was clear they didn't fit into the "idea" idea of Miró's art.

What they *do* suggest, however, is the work of permutation that Bataille performs in his *Story of the Eye* as similar metaphoric chains are used to generate both the action of the novel and its actual linguistic texture, as well as to depersonalize the narrative, making it the adventure not so much of its characters as of its organs, the story, indeed, of an eye. Roland Barthes has described this work of permutation as the result of a kind of grid on which one axis—that of shape—allows the eye to produce the associations to eggs, testicles, and the sun. The other axis—structured on the liquid contents of these objects—produces the chain that reads: tears, yolk, sperm, urine. It is the intersection of these axes that then suggests a given episode in the story and generates the language through which it is told, as when the sun, metaphorized as eye and yolk, can be described as "flaccid luminosity," and can give rise to the phrase, "the urinary liquifaction of the sky." Barthes stresses, of course, that the *combinatoire,* used in this way as a kind of machine to produce the work, is itself a rebuke to Breton's notion of the poetic image, to his idea of the metaphorical encounter as a result of chance.[6] The calculated programming of the linguistic space of the work is thus a rejection of the aleatory, just as the focus on organs is a derisive comment on Breton's glorification of love.

And yet no matter how important we may think Barthes's analysis is of the role of the metaphorical chains in *The Story of the Eye,* we have to acknowledge that Bataille's avowed aesthetic, enunciated many times over in the essays in *Documents,* was hostile to metaphor in any form, whether poetically happenstance or coldly structuralist. When he said, in "*L'Esprit Moderne* and the Game of Transpositions," that "what we truly love, we love above all in shame," adding, "I defy any collector to love a painting as much as a fetishist loves a shoe,"[7] he is writing the manifesto of this refusal of metaphor. Bataille's fetishism is, of course, the ethnographic rather than the Freudian kind, with the fetish conceived not as above all a substitute for what is missing, but as the real power of real objects. It is this power that Bataille gives to the big toe, the essay on which ends:

> The meaning of this article lies in its insistence on a direct and explicit questioning of *seductiveness,* without taking into account poetic concoctions that are, ultimately, nothing but a diversion (most human beings are naturally feeble and can only abandon themselves to their instincts when in a poetic haze). A return to reality does not imply any new acceptances, but means that one is seduced in a base manner, without transpositions and to the point of screaming, opening his eyes wide: opening them wide, then, before a big toe.[8]

"A return to reality." This is the explicitly antisurrealist stance that will forbid metaphor just as surely as it will reject the dream. And this aesthetic is shared by the *Documents* group in general. Thus, to return once again to Leiris's Miró essay from *Documents,* we find that even with the extraordinary passage on the dirty walls and the louche configurations, these paintings come in for criticism precisely on the grounds of their dependence on metaphor. Accordingly, from the vantage of 1929, Leiris says, "If there was a time when Miró's painting posed and instantly resolved all sorts of little equations (sun = potato, slug = little bird, gentleman = mustache, spider = sex, man = sole of the foot), it seems that it is different now, and that he is not satisfied by these facile solutions." In Miró's present work, Leiris counters: "The paintings are still fascinating mysteries, but these mysteries don't fear the light of noon, and are even more disquieting in that no cock's cry can put them to flight. The ghosts he brings on stage don't vanish when the clocks strike twelve."[9] With this direct rejection of the very idea of dream painting, Leiris speaks approvingly instead of the portrait series from 1928, which he illustrates in conjunction with his essay. But in summing up the power of these works, which he admits that earlier paintings by Miró have also shared, he says: "Beautiful as snickering, or as graffiti showing the human structure in all that's particularly grotesque and horrible about it, these works are so many malicious pebbles that cause circular and vicious ripples when one throws them into the swamp of reason, where for so many years now so many nets have been rotting."[10]

In his introduction to the new edition of *Documents,* Denis Hollier has demonstrated the centrality for Bataille's aesthetic of site specificity, of the work that cannot be moved but must, instead, be consumed on the spot. The idea of an object's resistance to being uprooted and transplanted to the museum's space of aesthetic exchange and formal equivalence results, therefore, in Bataille's insistence on—as Hollier puts it—"the inexchangeable heterogeneity of a real, an irreducible kernel of resistance to any kind of transposition, of substitution, a real that does not yield to a metaphor."[11] One form this real might take is the photograph, which, like the readymade, is independent of any imaginative manipulation. Stenciled, as it were, off the world itself, it enters the space of exchange—whether that be the aesthetic space of the museum or the space of the linguistic code of a page of text—as a heterogeneous object: a splinter under the skin of meaning, a fly that lands on the lecturer's nose. And photographs were not only Bataille's major visual resource in the pages of *Documents;* he also reviewed a book of crime photography under the title "X Marks the Spot."

The deictic character of that title, its pointing gesture, its demonstrative "this," reminds us that photography belongs to that group of signs to which the semiologists give the name *index.* It is the character of the index, indeed, to mark the spot, since it is the one type of sign that is the result of a physical cause. Unlike the *icon,* a sign that relates to its referent through the axis of resemblance, or the *symbol,* where the relationship between sign and referent is arbitrary and conventional, the index has an existential connection to meaning, with the result that it can only take place on the spot. If the photograph is classified as an index, rather than as an icon, this is because it is the result of a photochemical form of causality that allows the light that falls onto the film as though it were a shadow to register the actual trace of the object that projected it. The photograph is in this sense a cast shadow—an obvious form of index—but preserved now in amber. Within language itself there are indices as well, those words like "here," "now," "this," "today," or the personal pronouns "I" and "you," that are what the linguist Émile Benveniste called "empty signs," since they too depend for their meaning on their existential relation to the person who speaks them.[12]

It is in this context that I'd like to examine *Ceci est la couleur de mes rêves* (1925), a work that has always been received as the very definition of Miró's dream paintings. It is, furthermore, a work Miró himself considered "very important"; in fact—as he told me in 1971 when I interviewed him on the subject of these paintings of the mid and late 1920s—it was "a point of departure" for the rest of his work. I must admit, however, that it was never that clear to me how this painting functioned. My assumption was that, like the calligram, the work was opening a margin between image and language within which to encounter the "idea"—that which escapes representation altogether—so that the point of the picture was that color—like dreams, like the affective lining of our inmost feelings—is fundamentally ungraspable. This reading served to help me understand how the work would be the "point of departure" for the whole of the series that was to follow, a reading consonant with what I saw as the series' exploration of color as evanescent, as what Jacques Dupin had called "perfume." But what was troubling for this interpretation was the word "Photo" that also appeared on the canvas—a word that summons up totally different associations, as it reorients the blue splotch and its accompanying text from the field of the calligram to that of the document, and as it insists on the deictic or indexical structure of the work.

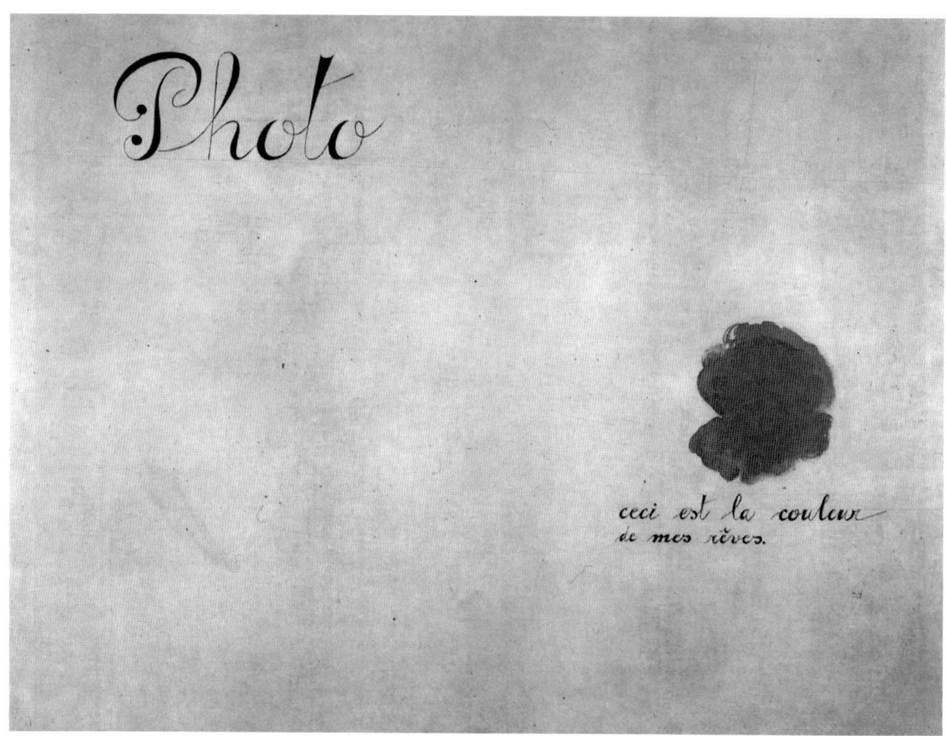

14.5 Joan Miró, *Ceci est la couleur de mes rêves,* 1925. © Successió Miró/Artists Rights Society (ARS), New York/ADAGP, Paris.

14.6 (*facing page*) Joan Miró, sketch for *Ceci est la couleur de mes rêves,* 1970. © Successió Miró/Artists Rights Society (ARS), New York/ADAGP, Paris.

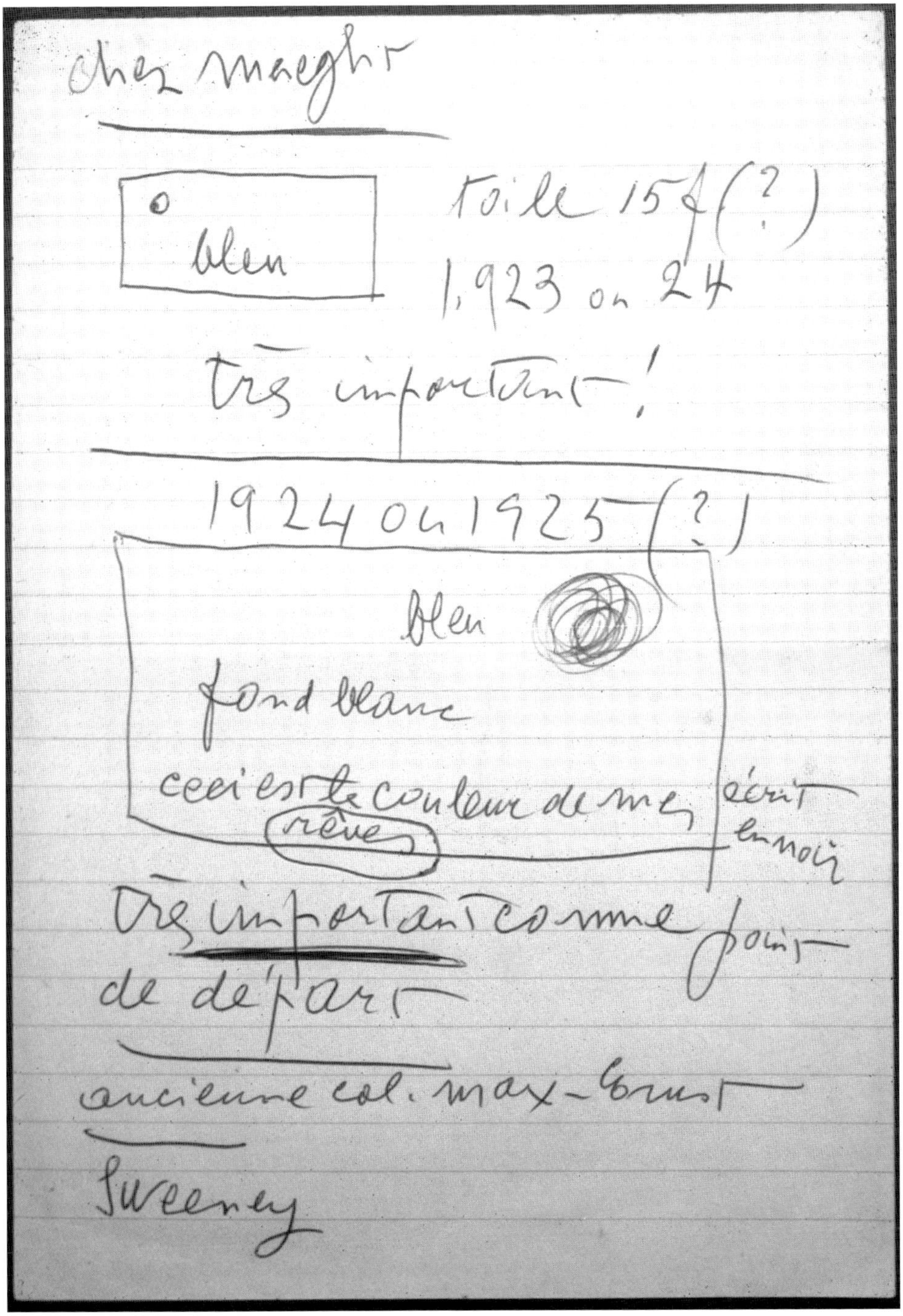

chez Maeght

o bleu

toile 15 F (?)

1923 ou 24

très important!

1924 ou 1925 (?)

bleu

fond blanc

ceci est la couleur de mes rêves

écrit en noir

très important comme point de départ

ancienne col. Max-Ernst

Sweeney

"Photo," in other words, insists on the arrival of a piece of the real into the illusionistic space of the canvas; it qualifies the cake of blue paint as heterogeneous to the picture's field, thereby making us aware of it not as a kind of generalizable idea—the color blue shared by the other paintings in the series—but as an immovable particular, the nontransposable *this* of the fly that lands on the lecturer's nose. And in this sense it is less about perfume than about Leiris's idea that the canvases in this series are not so much painted as "dirtied"; which is to say it opens up to another aspect of the work that Leiris had applauded in 1929, namely Miró's connection to graffiti.

With graffiti we encounter yet another form of heterogeneity within the field of representation, one that relates to the invasive nature of this type of mark, its criminal character, so to speak, the fact that it is defined by being a violation by the marker of a space that belongs not to him but to another. Thus, no matter what the iconic character of the configuration, the graffiti mark is, like the photograph, always structured indexically, as the trace of the marker's passage, a trace that is therefore always a signature, a sign whose signified always reads "Kilroy was here; I was here."

And in being this trace of the marker's violation of the surface, the graffiti alerts us to another feature of the index, namely its performative character. The index, in naming the particular, the "this," in making the referent erupt onto the page of writing, or onto the surface of the canvas, is not so much generating a meaning as causing something to happen. It belongs less, then, to the logic of signification than it does to the structure of events.

It is this sense of the performative that Leiris evokes when he calls Miró's paintings "malicious pebbles" tossed into "the swamp of reason," an image that stresses not only the character of the works as indexical but also a quite different meaning from the "dream painting" notion of their surfaces as evanescent. For these stones, in performing their meaning, consume themselves at the same time. Vanishing without trace, they are used up in the very act of enunciation; they are a form of object that does not outlast its use.

This insistence on use value is, as Denis Hollier has shown, the major feature of the *Documents* aesthetic. The exchange value of the object-turned-work-of-art, as it is propelled into circulation through the museological system, as it leaves the spot where it had a use, sacred or secular, this exchange value postpones that use indefinitely in favor of a kind of systematic equivalency through which it is formalized: reduced to the common denominator of style, of meaning, of beauty. The attack on exchange value was conducted by both halves of the *Documents* group, the ethnographers on the one hand as they deplored the aestheticization not only of tribal objects but of the sacred glyphs from the caves, and the avant-garde on the other, as Bataille set out to theorize that which escapes categorization altogether, that which would collapse any system of equivalency whatever.

At this point two questions undoubtedly arise, the answers to which are, I believe, extremely intertwined. The first is, given that in 1929 Leiris read Miró in terms of use value, graffiti, and the performative, and further, given that Bataille himself, in a brief notice on Miró in 1930, spoke of his work as *informe,* is such a reading a kind of pure projection that has nothing to do with how Miró himself saw his work? And second, if Miró not only welcomed this interpretation but was drawing closer and closer to the anti-aesthetic of *Documents,* why has this remained, to this day, invisible to the reception of his art?

In answer to the first, we not only have the statements Miró made in 1927 to the effect that he wanted to assassinate painting and that "Painting has been in a state of decadence since the time of the caves,"[13] but the fact that between 1928 and 1930 he was as good as his word. Not only did he start making little constructions of objects picked out of garbage cans; not only did he reinforce the indexical aspects of his work, exploiting cast shadow in the hat pin skewered to the surface of his *Spanish Dancer* (1928), for example, or the nails projecting from the constructed relief of 1930, and welcoming the performative aggressivity that this and the sandpaper surfaces of his collages embodied; but by 1930, in the very paintings Bataille chose to reproduce in *Documents* as examples of Miró's success, Miró had, in Dupin's words, "declared war" not only on painting in general but on his own gifts in particular. Calling these works "bastard, swollen, dried up," Dupin sees Miró "touching bottom." The large paintings of 1930, he says, "willed and fiercely desperate, are like cannon shots fired from a sinking ship. Miró expected too much from his energies in assuming large formats; if he had wanted to assassinate painting, he has succeeded in destroying himself."[14]

Addressing one of the pictures Bataille obviously prizes, Dupin deplores its obvious attempt to leave the domain of painting, of art, altogether: "In a *Head* on white ground of very large scale, we find furious scribblings, a shower of meteors, angry grooves striating the canvas without being able to release a true creative force. A distraught head, outlined with an awkward gesture, rises in the midst of the painting, as though stuck in the center of an impotent storm."[15] As Bataille himself discusses these precipitates of a will to kill off painting, however, he declares that "the decomposition was pushed to the point where nothing remained but some formless blotches on the cover (or, if you prefer, on the gravestone) of painting's box of tricks. Thereafter little colored and mad elements irrupted anew, after which, today, they have disappeared once more in his pictures, leaving only the trace of one knows not what disaster."[16] And the painting from 1930 that most Miró scholars and collectors now see as the one refugee from this general scene of debacle is for Bataille no different, no better or worse, than the luckless *Head*.

If there is a general agreement in the reception of Miró that 1930 is somehow a write-off in his artistic trajectory, and if we can show the cause for this in a willing collaboration with the *Documents* position, as Miró seemed, like a suicidal moth, to draw closer and closer to the flame of Bataille, why, we might ask, has the silence on this connection been so absolute? Dupin, in approaching this episode of anti-painting, needs to look back to Dada some thirteen years earlier and speculate on Miró's continuing admiration for Marcel Duchamp. "This idea of anti-painting had haunted Miró for a long time," Dupin writes, "but he only now embraced it and took it into his work so consciously and with such determination."[17] It does not occur to Dupin to open the pages of *Documents* and read Bataille.

The universal silence about this episode in Miró's work stems, I would say, from two things. The first is that if we were to take account of it, we would be forced not simply to acknowledge what it means for the two years during which

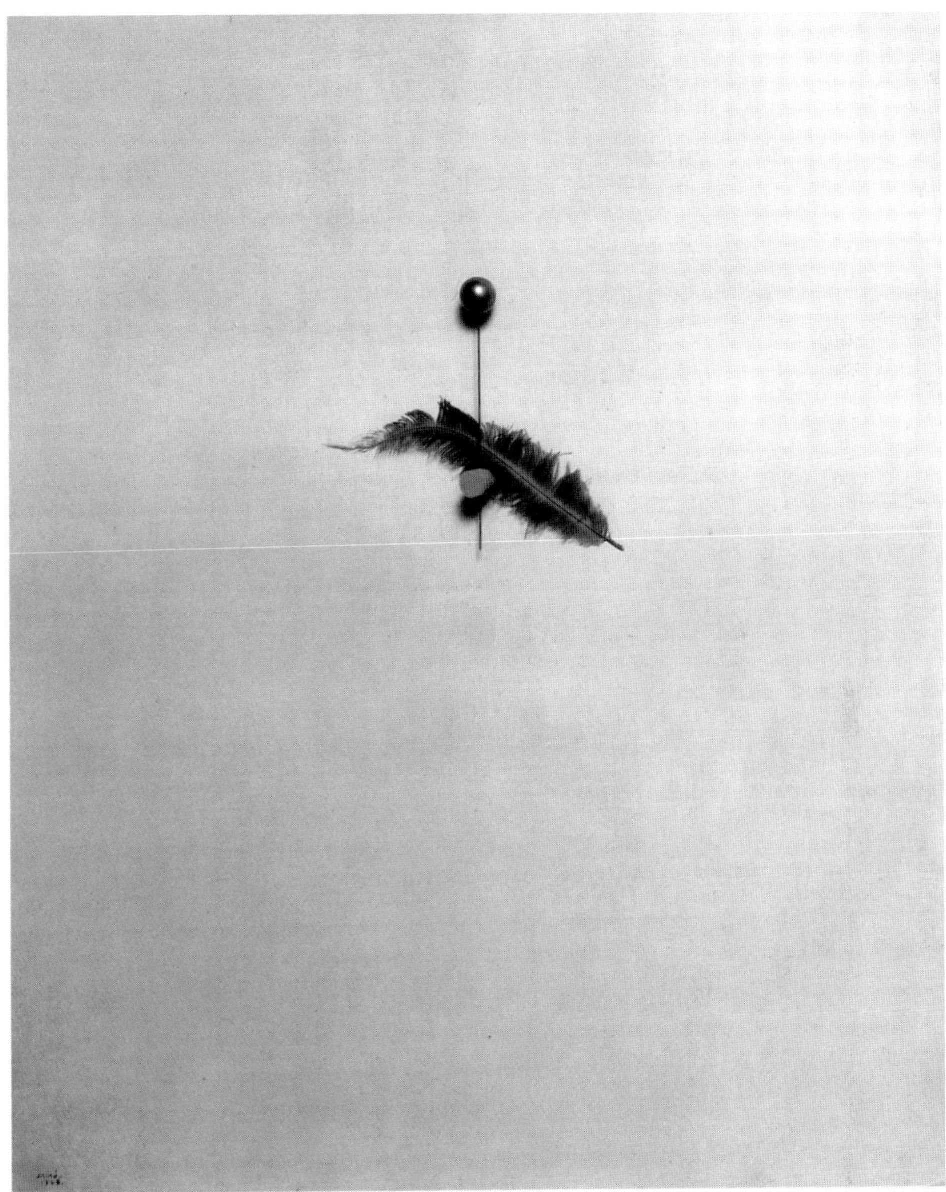

14.7 Joan Miró, *Spanish Dancer,* 1928.

Miró entered the pages of *Documents* but as well to grasp what it sanctions in the interpretation of the paintings from the mid-1920s, making them appear not so much as stain paintings, but as stains pure and simple, not so much ideograms as graffiti, not so much dreams as the aggression Miró himself claimed for them at the time.

But the second reason is that after 1933, the year in which Dupin sees Miró as having resurfaced after "touching bottom" in 1929–1930, Miró himself conspired in effacing this reading. This would explain a detail that has probably struck most of you when you looked at the drawing Miró made for me of *Ceci est la couleur de mes rêves,* and you noticed that while the painting bore the word "Photo," the sketch through which Miró remembered it does not. In speaking of the work as a "point de depart," the sketch projects, therefore, a very different series to follow from it than does the actual painting. But Miró is rewriting his past from the point of view of an artist who was determined to survive, and who must have instinctively felt that however seductive Bataille's aesthetic of the "real" might have been, however extraordinary the lure of the big toe, he could not embrace it and continue as a painter. So this is a story of a refugee who went to a strange and dangerous shore and almost foundered but was determined to come back. Whether that comeback was then a success or a failure depends, clearly, on your point of view.

As a coda to this account of a peculiarly undocumented and unrecognized passage in Miró's career, I would like to return to what I announced at the outset of this text as the one exception to this state of affairs, namely Carolyn Lanchner's willingness to write Georges Bataille into the Miró record. Pointing out that in 1930, soon after Bataille had published his essay on the big toe in *Documents* (1929), Miró filled an entire sketchbook with drawings circling around this part of the body, Lanchner goes on to say, however, that the two men's interests in the big toe "were—to borrow a children's locution—'the same but different.' "[18] This difference she sees turning, on the one hand, on Bataille's conception of the toe as that part of the human body that resists the idealizing, "humanizing" values that are read into the rest of the body's upright posture and thus—although she doesn't use the term—the toe's "base materialism," and on the other hand, on Miró's concern with the toe as "emblematic of our common humanity, male or female—the support that connects the terrestrial and the celestial. One widely quoted remark," she adds, "makes his view quite clear: 'You must always plant your feet firmly on the ground if you want to be able to jump up in the air.'"[19]

Now, with all the respect I have for Carolyn Lanchner and as much as I admire the brilliance of the exhibition she has mounted and the importance of its catalogue, I guess I would have to take issue with her claim that Miró's and Bataille's conceptions of the toe are, indeed, "the same but different." Unlike Miró's earlier exploitations of the toe for a kind of terrestrial anchoring, the placing of it into this specific context of either a formless round phallicism or an intergenital fascination—as phallic toe pushes, pseudopodia-like, from the amoebic mass of a body consistently centered around flaming vulva—surely ties these drawings to Bataille's notion of base seduction. And further, Bataille's conception of a rearranged and desublimated architecture of the human body in general seems to have had an enduring effect on Miró's imagination. So that even in the opening years of the 1930s, as he was swimming back upstream toward painting, against the tide of the *Documents* anti-aesthetic, he found himself repeating almost stroke for stroke some of Bataille's fetish objects. I have in mind particularly a drawing he made in 1933 which incorporates in an extraordinarily precise way the features of those examples of children's graffiti that Bataille published in an article on "Primitive Art," and this in the very pages of *Documents* that immediately precede his brief review of Miró in 1930.

What this absorption of Bataille's conception of the human form means for the rest of Miró's production is, I would argue, that the toe in particular becomes an organ that will no longer function in the artist's work as the hinge between the earth of peasant honesty and the sky of disembodied thought. The toe, indeed, is where Miró will locate what is most unclassifiably monstrous and aberrant, as in an extraordinary drawing of 1938 where a *Woman in Revolt*

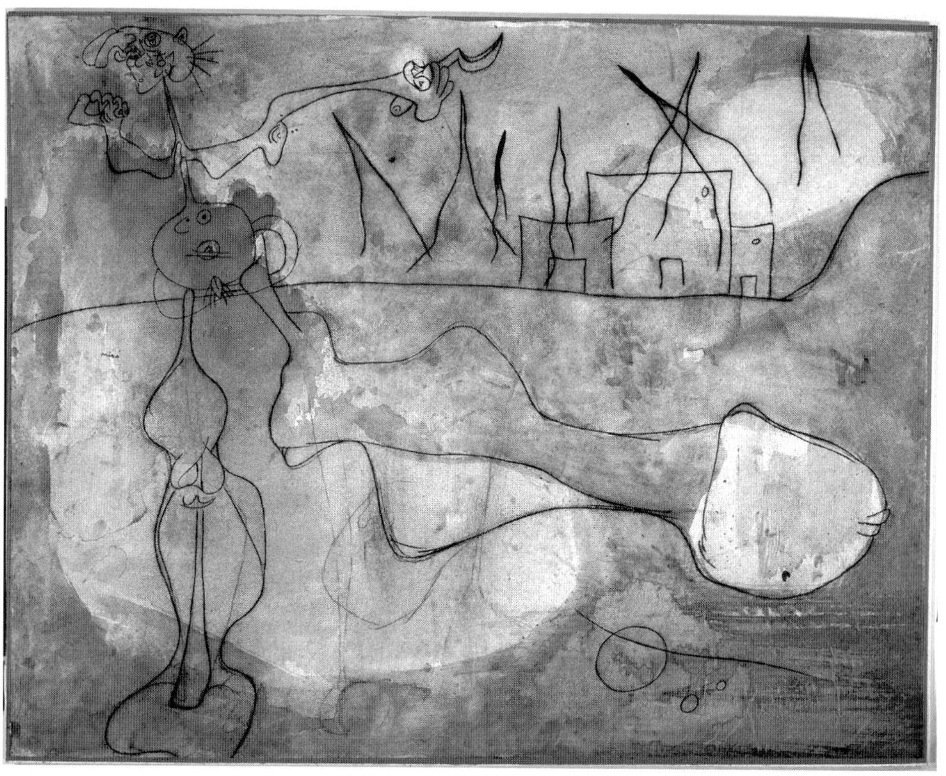

14.8 Joan Miró, *Woman in Revolt,* 1938. © Successió Miró/Artists Rights Society (ARS), New York/ ADAGP, Paris.

extends an engorged foot that will neither rest on the ground nor allow her to surmount its shackles, a foot whose grotesque toe is the woman's pure phallic appendage. It is in a detail such as this that we see the continuing reverberations of Miró's Bataille connection working away in the background of his thought but made increasingly available to him, no doubt, by the ominous political events now gathering on his horizons. It is this Bataille legacy that commands our attention and urges us to consider "Michel, Bataille et moi."

Giovanni Anselmo: Matter and Monochrome

The 1970s was the arena of a massive backlash against what was perceived as the technoindustrial complacency of minimalist sculpture—its armor-like surfaces, its assembly line composition, its sumptuous display of the artificial. On two continents, North America and Europe, this "postminimalist" backlash assumed various guises—antiform, eccentric art, earthworks—which ran parallel to one another. The major difference between them was that the European version, at least in Italy, where it was collectively named Arte Povera, was by far the more violent, activated by an urgency of protest that these artists' American counterparts could not have known. Postminimalism was, we could say, an aesthetic rejection, driven by new sets of convictions about art's history. The nature of Arte Povera, on the other hand, must be sought in the way the adjective *povera* was being deployed within cultural discourse in the postwar period of the late 1940s and 1950s. This is certainly what Germano Celant urged in his 1967 introductory essay for the burgeoning "movement":

> What has happened . . . [is that] the commonplace has entered the sphere of art. The insignificant has begun to exist—indeed, it has

Originally published as "Giovanni Anselmo: Marshall Plan Monochromes," in *Giovanni Anselmo* (Bologna: Galleria d'Arte Moderna, 2007); republished in *October,* no. 124 (Spring 2008).

> imposed itself. Physical presence and behavior have become art. . . . Cinema, theater and the visual arts assert their authority as anti-presence. . . . They eliminate from their inquiry all which may seem mimetic reflection and representation or linguistic custom in order to attain a new kind of art, which, to borrow a term from the theater of Grotowsky, one may call "poor."[1]

For the Polish stage director Jerzy Grotowski's idea of "poor theater" to enter the discursive mix at this point was to complicate the equation quite considerably. In his manifesto "Towards a Poor Theatre" (1965), Grotowski traveled a conceptual path back to the beginnings of the triumphant understanding of modernist art as the critical stripping away of superfluous aesthetic conventions in order to reveal the essential conditions of a specific medium of artistic practice. If theater is, as Grotowski argued, basically nothing beyond "the actor-spectator relationship of perceptual, direct, 'live' communion," then all the usual paraphernalia of the scenographic enterprise—costumes, makeup, lighting, sound effects, etc.—are nothing but so much "artistic kleptomania," the piracy of disparate creative disciplines, such as literature, sculpture, painting, architecture, or acting, to forge a synthetic conglomerate, one Grotowski ironically calls "Rich Theater."[2] The multisensory appeal of Rich Theater he then understands as historically driven: an attempt to outrun the "impasse presented by movies and television," in the postwar period of Spectacle Culture. Poor Theater is thus a kind of "pure" theater, cleansed of the hybrid and, of course, the inauthentic condition of its "rich" counterpart.

Here, two contradictory notions of "poor" are being used. On the one hand, the reductive, modernist, medium-specific idea of aesthetic "purity,"[3] and on the other, a resignation to the fate of technological backwardness: "poor" not as "pure" but as "Arcadian" or "artisanal."

It is difficult to map Grotowski's idea of *povertà,* crafted for the theater, directly onto the postminimalist visual arts of sculpture or painting. One vehicle for this was the idea of a direct, "live," perceptual channel, making the intersubjective axis of "communion" into the basic medium of artistic practice, in a parallel with Grotowski's "pure" theater (a parallel sounded as well by Harald Szeemann's rubric "When Attitudes Become Form").[4] Another was the embrace of nontechnological forms of energy: a "primal" form present in all aspects of life as lived directly and not mediated through representation, ideology, or codified languages. This energy was intended, on the one hand, to correspond to the basic physical forces of nature (such as gravity or electricity) and, on the other, to refer to the fundamental elements of human nature (such as vitality, memory, and emotion). "Poor" as "pure" thus also translates "poor" as "energy."

To have traveled down the Kantian road back to the "conditions of possibility" of a form of experience, and to find that for the visual arts, these are "energy" was, in the postwar years of late 1940s and early 1950s Europe, to have produced for oneself an enormous irony. With its infrastructure in ruins and its populations unemployed, Europe had become the living proof of the Second Law of Thermodynamics—without a renewal of energy, all systems are threatened with cooling down, and such a cooling-off leads to their disintegration and loss of form, tantamount to their inability to maintain the separation of their insides (figures) from their external milieu (ground). "Entropy," one possible byword for this collapse, had been clearly sounded by Robert Smithson on his side of the Atlantic. On the other side, "entropy" was given a different, economic and ethnological reading using the French philosopher Georges Bataille's notion of *dépense*. Translated as "nonproductive expenditure," *dépense* is meant to focus on the profligate release of energy necessary for organisms to maintain life once the spatial limits of their eco-support have been outgrown. The discursive displacement in Smithson's postminimalism would be, then, from "poor" to "pure" to "energy" to "entropy." This was a displacement made familiar and vivid to Italian artists by the restaging of Smithson's *Asphalt Rundown* in 1969, in Rome, by L'Attico Gallery. Smithson had been adamant about the irreversibility of entropy—once dark and light sand have been intermixed in a sandbox by the churning feet of a child running in a clockwise direction, he wrote, the reversal of the child's movement to counterclockwise will not re-sort the sand back into separate compartments. A parallel example would be the mixing of cold and hot water, with the result—tepid water—both a cooling down of the matrix and an effacement of the original difference.

In his 1967 manifesto "Notes for a Guerrilla War," Celant had developed a context within which to understand the entropic position of *Asphalt Rundown*. The guerrilla artist of Celant's war plan, marked by his refusal to add new objects to an already replete aesthet-eco-system, "does away with categorical positions (such as pop, op, or primary structures) to focus on *gestures that do not add anything* to our well-educated perception, that do not oppose themselves to life as art or lead to the creation of separate levels for the ego and the world, but exist as social gestures in and of themselves, as formative and compositive liberations which aim at the identification between man and the world."[5]

From his position in Turin in the 1960s, Giovanni Anselmo adopted entropy as his aesthetic strategy on behalf of this war. *Torsione* (1968) makes entropy visible, as the tensed spring of the work alludes to a continuing threat to its formal integrity, one that is pure illusion since the corkscrew of fabric which supports the metal bar of the sculpture has already submitted to the entropic loss of distinction to make the work, in fact, inert. *Senza titolo* (*Struttura che mangia*) (1968) presents entropy by still other means. As the head of lettuce that separates two stone plinths gradually dries out, its shrunken mass, no longer resistant to the stone's weight or the force of gravity, thus permits the collapse of the work's composite structure.

One assistance to Anselmo's formulation of entropy's connection to gravity could have been Richard Serra's *Prop* sculptures (1968–1969), made of lead plates either leaning one on the other or held up by the weight of a leaden bar pressing down. Gravity's pressure on the malleable material of the lead results in the entropic collapse of the sculptures and thus in their loss of geometric shape. In this way Serra could be embraced by Arte Povera as an antiminimalist artist. Anselmo's experience of the prop pieces might well have emerged from the 1968 New York exhibition entitled "9 at Leo Castelli," in which various American postminimalist works (including Serra's lead sculptures) shared the space with Arte Povera artists such as Anselmo himself, Paolini, Penone, Pistoletto, Prini, and Zorio.

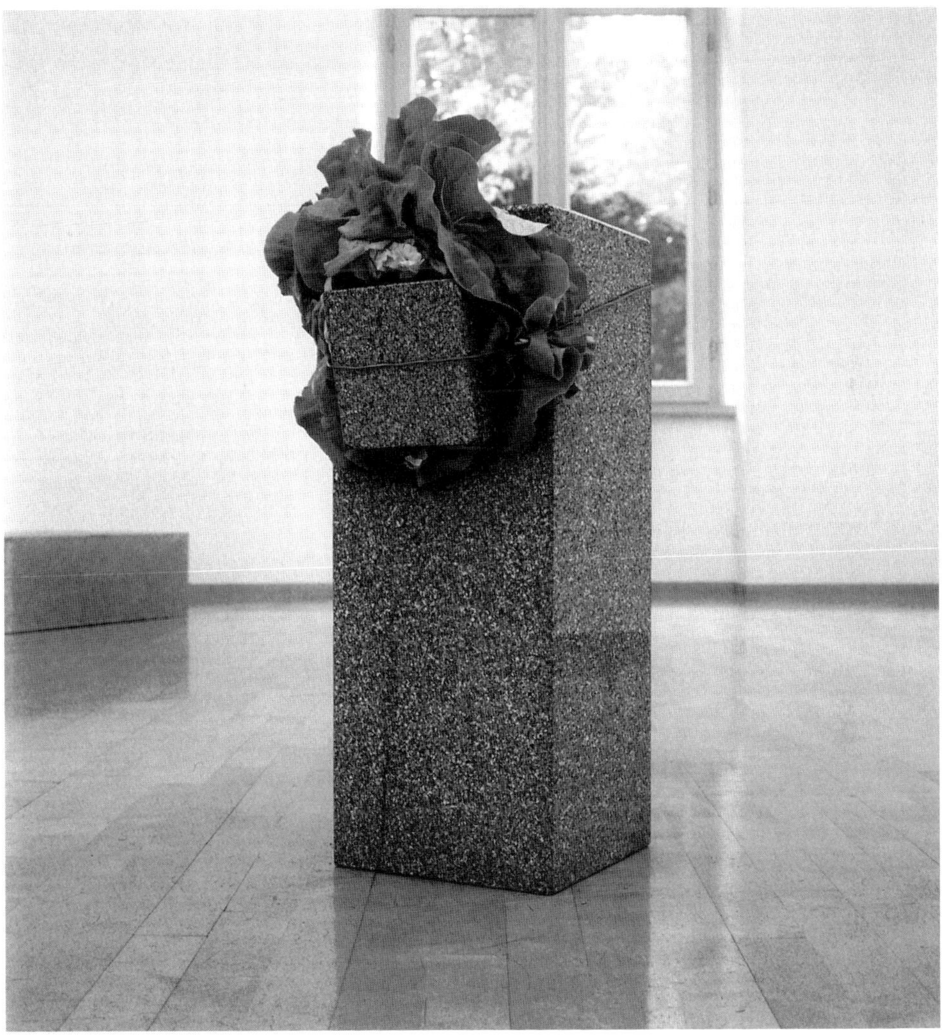

15.1 Giovanni Anselmo, *Senza titolo (Struttura che mangia)*, 1968.

If the connection between "poor" and "pure" can be triangulated by "attitudes," standing for the relation of "poor" to "entropy," history forces yet another triangulation through the guerrilla concept of *povertà*. Celant's guerrilla warrior combats the addition of any new object to an already replete aesthet-eco-system, declaring that the limits of both production and consumption have been reached.

If nothing can be added, then something must be destroyed. This is the lesson of general economics taught by Georges Bataille's *La part maudite* (*The Accursed Share,* 1949), as he looked beyond the thrift-and-savings ethos of capitalism to the almost unthinkable economic reflexes of those ancient civilizations built on the necessity to squander (*dépense*). The squander economy was *la part maudite* or "the accursed share": the requisite safety valve for an economically overheated universe. Bataille had thought his way into an economics of squander through two ethnographic examples: one of these was the profligacy of human sacrifice as practiced by the ancient Aztecs; the other was the custom of "gift exchange" which Bataille had learned about through the lectures Marcel Mauss was giving at the École des Hautes Études in Paris, which treated the ritual of *potlatch* among the Northwest Coast American Indians, such as the Tlingit, the Haida, or the Kwakiutl. *Potlatch* was understood as the violent social battle between two rival chieftains, the spoils of which was a gain in stature achieved by outspending one's competitor. Into the massive fire built by the host would be thrown vats of oil, piles of blankets, and, ultimately, the most valuable possession of all: the copper shields carved with the chief's own name. To each destruction, the guest was obliged to offer up a counterdestruction, of the same, or even higher, worth.

In 1969 Anselmo turned to the strategy of expending energy. *Respiro* (*Breath*) tightly wedges a sea sponge between two floor-bound iron bars that expand with each rise of temperature to squeeze the air out of the sponge, thereby contracting it. When the bars cool, the sponge, reabsorbing the air out of the atmosphere, expands, to ooze out beyond the gap between the bars. It is this lunglike alternation that not only mimes the sponge's "breath," but produces the image of a "waste" of energy: life's reaction to the pressures of growth.

The Accursed Share used the pressures of growth to picture the entire biosphere as a theater for *dépense,* since each biological element must collide with the limits of the space available to it, as it competes with other expanding organisms:

> As a rule the surface of the globe is invested by life to the extent possible. By and large the myriad forms of life adapt it to the available resources, so that space is its basic limit. Certain disadvantaged areas, where the chemical operations essential to life cannot take place, seem to have no real existence. But taking into account a constant relation of the biomass to the local climatic and geological conditions, life occupies all the available space. These local conditions determine the intensity of the *pressure* exerted in all directions by life. But one can speak of pressure in this sense only if, by some means, the available space is increased; this space will be immediately occupied in the same way as the adjoining space. . . . In a sense life suffocates within limits that are too close; it aspires in manifold ways to an impossible growth; it releases a steady flow of excess resources, possibly involving large squanderings of energy.[6]

Bataille extended this reflection on the "accursed share" of the biomass to the geophysics of the formation of the earth's crust:

> This first essay addresses, from outside the separate disciplines, a problem that still has not been framed as it should be, one that may hold the key to all the problems posed by every discipline concerned with the movement of energy on the earth—from *geophysics* to political economy, by way of sociology, history and biology . . . the movement I study: that of excess energy, translated into the effervescence of life. . . . But taking into account a constant relation of the biomass to the local climatic and *geological conditions,* life occupies all the available space. . . . In a sense, life suffocates within

> limits that are too close; it aspires in manifold ways to an impossible growth; it releases a steady flow of excess resources, possibly involving large squanderings of energy. . . . Without exploding, its extreme exuberance pours out in a movement always bordering on *explosion.*[7]

The form of the "squander" of energy forced on the biomass is, for example, in the explosive power of volcanic eruptions, as it is in the destructive wrath of forest fires.

Bataille speaks of "geological conditions" and of "geophysics," the former the registration or index of the compacted mass of organisms swarming at the beginnings of life.[8] Anselmo acknowledges his own fascination with these "conditions" by his frequent choice of granite for his works. The fossilized remains of early life suspended within the granite or anthracite blocks he used were, he says, "formerly, vegetable or reptile or, at any rate, something organic and animated, before the transformation of the earth's crust buried many aspects of life and drew them away from the light." The darkness of the quarry from which the blocks must be excavated "obliterates the time that has passed between us and that which, precisely, this material was then."[9]

It is in *The Stone Lifts the Canvas,* the series of granite slabs Anselmo executed in 1990, and presented as a series of surprisingly ironic versions of the fashionably modernist monochrome paintings exhibited by Manzoni and Fontana in the 1960s, that this "obliterated time" would be restored by being thrust into the verticality of the visual field.

With its long tradition of Renaissance perspective, Italian painting certainly had to be sensitive to the convention whereby the horizontal expanse of the ground or pavement is illusionistically lifted into the vertical field of the canvas and thereby onto a geometry that "measures" and "controls" it. The verticality of painting had become suspect to the Arte Povera artists, who were alert to the critiques of the New Left such as Horkheimer and Adorno's *Dialectic of Enlightenment,* where the very exercise of vision is demonized as an instrument of reason, whose relationship to power, Adorno asserts, explains the

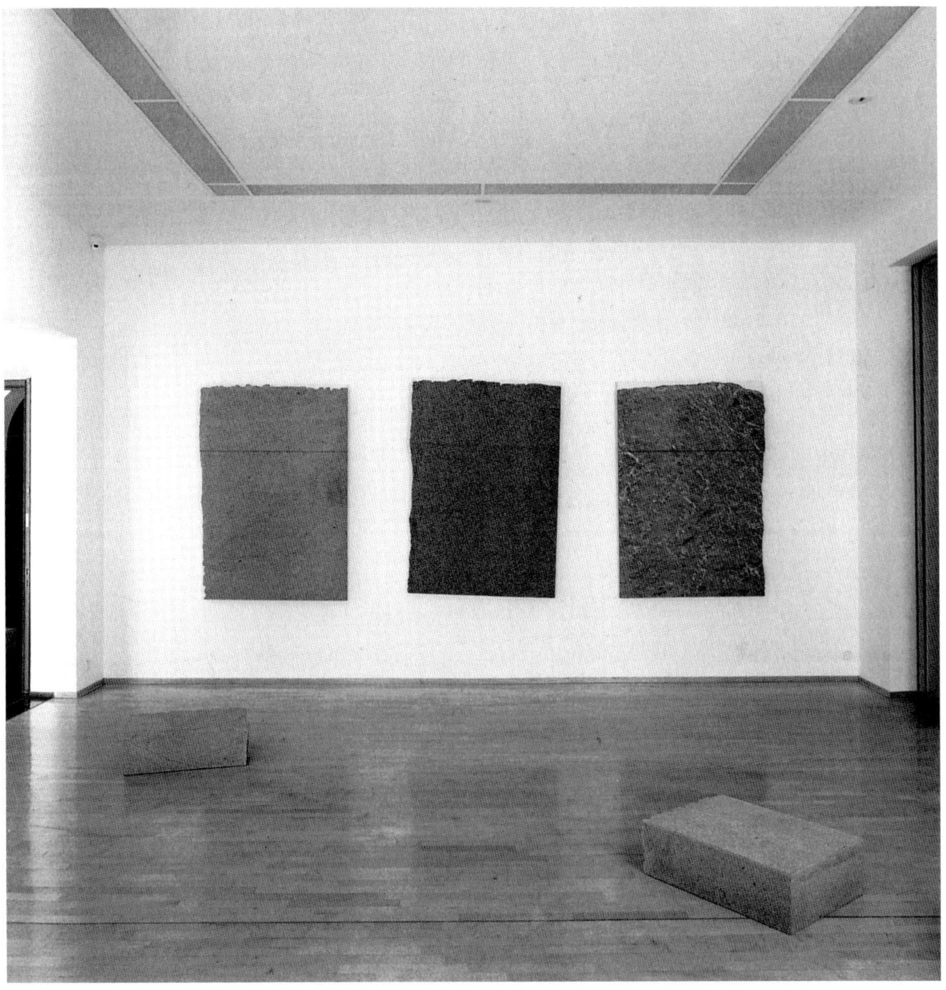

15.2 Giovanni Anselmo, *Senza titolo (La pietra solleva il canovaccio),* 1990.

development of totalitarian political systems such as fascism. The intensity of this rejection of vision as "reason" carried over to *When Attitudes Become Form* (1969), in which Harald Szeemann wonders: "is this a reaction against the geometry that has dominated over the past few years, a subjective art, a new version of Tachisme?"[10]

It is difficult to regard monochrome painting, however, as either antivisual or antigeometric. The slashes that break through the surface of Fontana's monochrome canvases seem to mime the very activity of sight as it projects itself "through" the vertical field and into the virtual space beyond it. The repetition of Manzoni's white squares asserts the very geometry of the canvas as a measurable, physical object.

Anselmo's preoccupation with luminosity and verticality is the basis of *The Invisible Shows Itself,* his series of works in which the word "visible" is projected by means of a light beam onto the vertical plane of an outstretched palm held above a horizontal stone plinth.

To "lift the stone" into the vertical field of visibility that normally belongs to the canvas is to travel through those millennia, as Anselmo put it, back to the time "before the transformation of the earth's crust buried many aspects of life and drew them away from the light." Newly restored to the light, the myriad swarm of these remains seems to radiate the heat of *dépense* into the gallery, not unlike the endless dispersal of paint resulting from Jackson Pollock's gestures, in the "intensity" to which Szeemann had referred.

That the plant and animal skeletons suspended within the quarried slabs Anselmo presents to vision are indexes, or traces, of a now-vanished life relates this series to the widespread preoccupation with the *index* itself as a medium of expression in postwar art. The source of that preoccupation was the ascendancy of Marcel Duchamp as the unrivaled exponent of the "anti-retinal" or anti-optical aesthetic position, which Szeemann had summarized as "Duchamp's preferred working method." Duchamp's most famous work, *The Large Glass* (*La mariée mise à nu par ses célibataires, même*), is a concatenation of indexes. The conical Sieves, which make up the Bachelor apparatus, are defined by the dense layer of dust that had collected on the *Glass* as it lay on the table in Duchamp's apartment. As any detective will tell you, the precipitation of dust from the air is a measure of passing time's having left its trace on the waiting surface. In the Bride's half of the *Glass* is a tripartite compartment Duchamp called the Draft Pistons, since each section bears the silhouette of a deformed geometric shape: a square of fabric Duchamp hung outside a window so that his friend Man Ray could photograph each new flaglike configuration according to how the draft altered it. Using these snapshots as templates, Duchamp transferred the wavy silhouettes from the photographic prints to the glass. Each Piston is, accordingly, the trace (or index) of the "draft," in the same way that the position of a weather vane is the index of the direction of the wind.

Monochrome painting had adopted other strategies developed by "Duchamp's way of working." The major one was the readymade, which one encounters in Yves Klein's exhibition of identical aquamarine canvases, each having been distinguished from the other only by a difference in price. Not only were these works thereby commodified, but they were likened to just those fallen objects of commerce that Arte Povera identified in the pop art it despised.

The tortured intensity of *The Stone Lifts the Canvas* cannot be accounted for, however, as just an ironic reference to monochrome painting or to the graphic strategies of Marcel Duchamp. It must be seen through the contemporary living conditions prevailing in postwar Italy and especially in Turin. This is the only way to explain a decision to execute painting in stone.

The final chapter of *La part maudite* (1949) was dedicated to the Americans' postwar Marshall Plan—which Bataille was intent on interpreting according to his model for a solar dispersal without precedent.[11] No Italian could occupy Turin, to which Anselmo moved in the 1960s, without experiencing the *miracolo italiano,* an industrial and economic reconstruction financed by the Marshall Plan's largesse of $13 billion for the loans that underwrote the rebuilt factories of Fiat and Olivetti, among others.

The gain for the Americans through the Marshall Plan was clear for all to see: the reconstructed European democracies were to be a bulwark against the spread of socialism. Further, the power of consumption by newly employed workers was to insure a positive balance of trade for the United States. The plan, then, was a form of European colonization to which Arte Povera reacted in the most hostile way possible.

In this context, "poor" is neither "pure" nor "entropic." It is a truculent form of defiance (as in Celant's "guerrilla war"—meant to resist any increase of new objects of consumption or production): with "poor" as the subversive underbelly of "squander"—the guerrilla resistance to what could be called "Marshall Plan modernism." In introducing his concept of squander, Bataille showed it applying equally to animals and plants as to the cultural phenomena of sacrifice and *potlatch.* "A living organism," he wrote, "ordinarily receives more energy than is necessary for maintaining life. If the excess cannot be completely absorbed in its growth, it must be spent, willingly or not, gloriously or catastrophically."[12]

If the relation between "poor" and pure" must be triangulated by "squander," Arte Povera's adoption of Grotowski's dismissal of the riches of modern technology (movies and television) ties it to Italy's necessary submission to American colonization and an economy not only of consumer culture but of the "kitsch" of entertainment as Spectacle.

In its attempt to shore up democratic forms of government, the Marshall Plan was meant to reinstate the Enlightenment subject as the basis of European experience. The perceptual apparatus of the centered human subject was being purchased by American largesse. The subject who consumes, Walter Benjamin taught us, is the subject who identifies with the fetish objects of his desire. The Arte Povera artists had been influenced not only by Umberto Eco's instructions about semiology in his *Open Work of Art,*[13] but by Michel Foucault's *Order of Things,* and its lesson about the creation of the modern subject by the industrial revolution. Thus armed, they were prepared for the Marshall Plan, and their parodic model of *povertà* was the form of their resistance.

The Latin Class

1 Who's Right?

So who's right, do you think? Barthes, or all the others who've written about Cy Twombly? All those for whom the Latin is serious, taken at face value, consumed as erudition, as classical humanism somehow magically surviving amidst the barbarism of the late twentieth century, a talismanic flower sprouting from a decaying Roman wall? Here it is in its most sick-making, obsequious form, written by Twombly's assiduous art-historical amanuensis, Heiner Bastian, who is compiling the catalogue raisonné of the paintings, the drawings, the sculptures, the prints. He asks:

> Who speaks through Venus and Mars, Amor and Psyche, Leda and the Swan, Achilles and Patroklos, through Achilles' grief and vengeance, through Eros' punished desires, through Orion's blind fate, through Diana, Flora, Theseus, Galatea's triumph, through Keats' Adonais, through Sesostris' sun journey, through Aurelius Commodus' madness, through Catullus, through Caesar's Ides of March: mirrors of masks as in Twombly's identification of Apollo and Mars

First published in *Artforum* 33 (September 1994).

> with the Apollonian and Dionysian principle, as indelible horizon. In *The Veil of Orpheus* the song of all that is changed, magic moment like the evening over Arcadia. Veil over the song awakening to tears the shades of the dead. Veil, time line and changing context in everything that can be captured as poetry in painting.[1]

For Barthes, it's clear that if the answer to that question is that it's Cy Twombly who speaks, it's just as clear that he can't be speaking straight. Barthes insists that Twombly's graphisms, more those of the schoolboy than the erudite, only *allude* to writing, before going off somewhere else. "When TW writes," Barthes says (having decided to refer to the artist via his own invented cipher for Twombly's name), "and repeats this one word: *Virgil,* it is *already* a commentary on Virgil, for the name, inscribed by hand, not only calls up a whole idea (though an empty one) of ancient culture but also 'operates' a kind of citation: that of an era of bygone, calm, leisurely, even decadent studies: English preparatory schools, Latin verses, desks, lamps, tiny pencil annotations. That is culture for TW: an ease, a memory, an irony, a posture, the gesture of a dandy."[2]

2 Pictorial Nominalism

And what does the *name* "call up"? For all the others, the name signals analogy, the likeness of the thing thought to be found on the surface of the painting. It functions, that is, as the title of traditional painting; it says "here is . . ." as in, here is the rape of the Sabines, the flight into Egypt, Judith beheading Holofernes. They believe that if it is written "Sunset" (as on *School of Fontainebleau* [1959]), then "here is a sun-drenched landscape," and they rush to fill in, in their imaginations, but also on the canvas onto which they project them, the places where they know Twombly has stayed: the Lake of Bolsena (although they always say the Lago di Bolsena, since that sounds so much sunnier, so much more Italian), the island of Ischia, the hills of Rome. They fill in whole narratives, as in the going mad of Aurelius Commodus, or the transformation of Narcissus. Representation, they think, is everywhere.

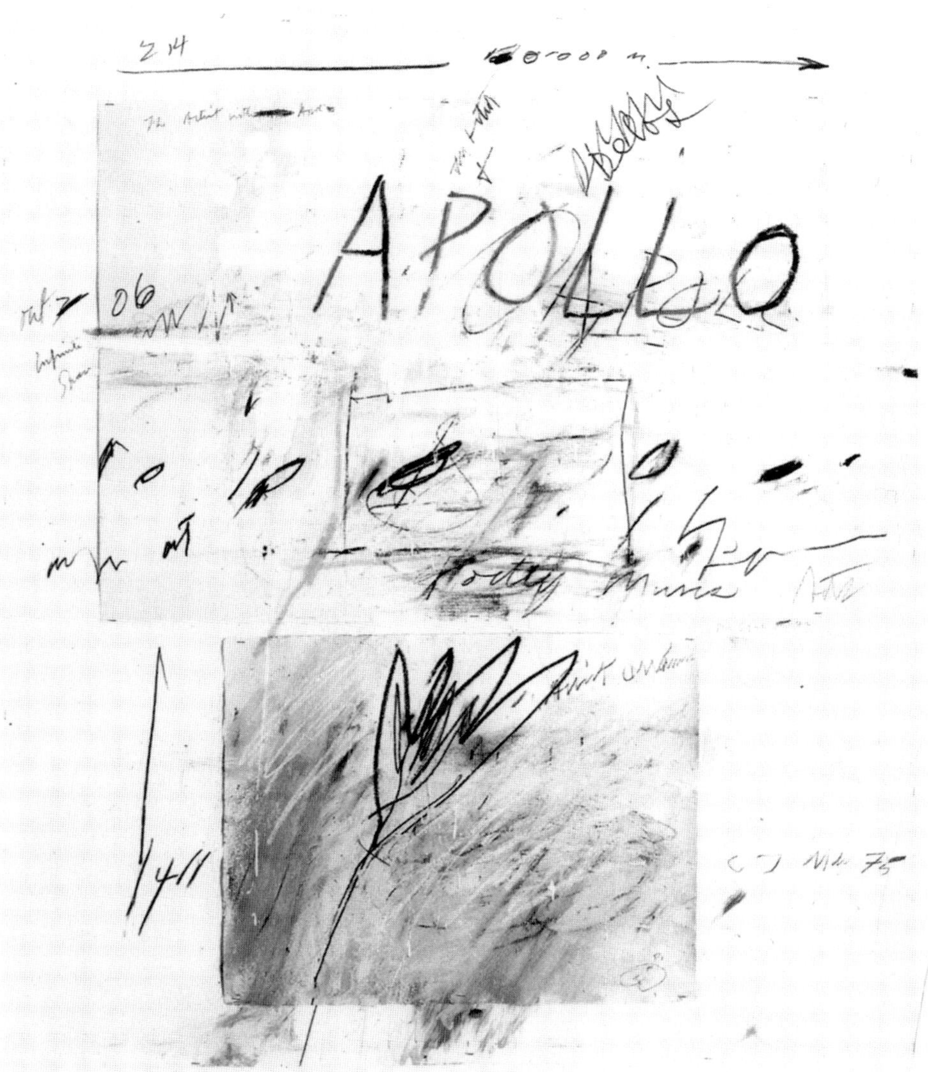

16.1 Cy Twombly, *Apollo and the Artist,* 1975.

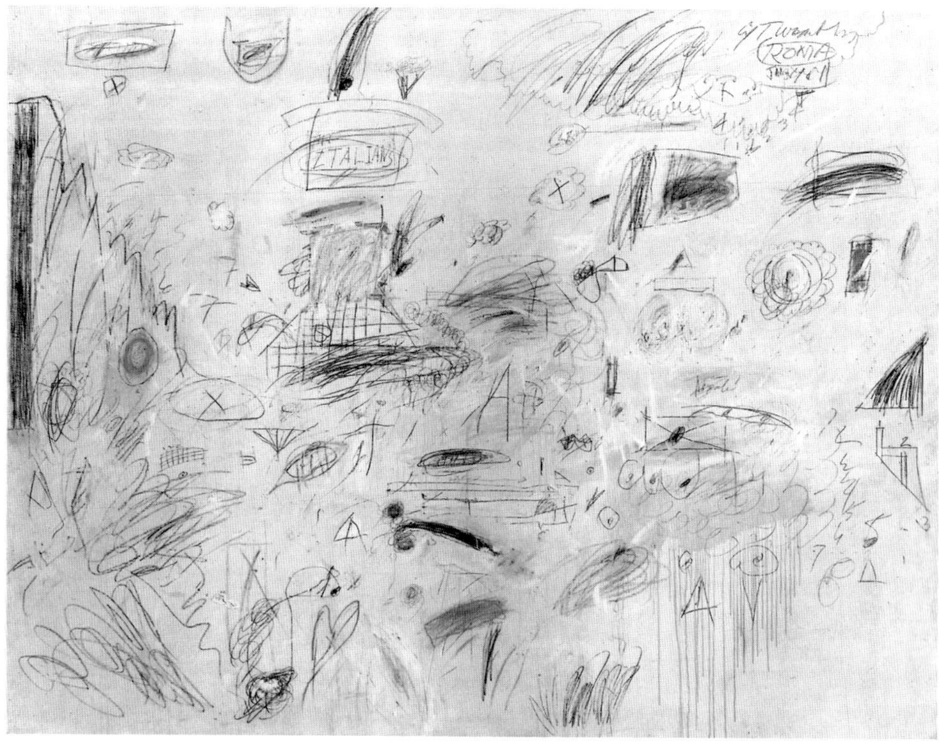

16.2 Cy Twombly, *The Italians,* 1961.

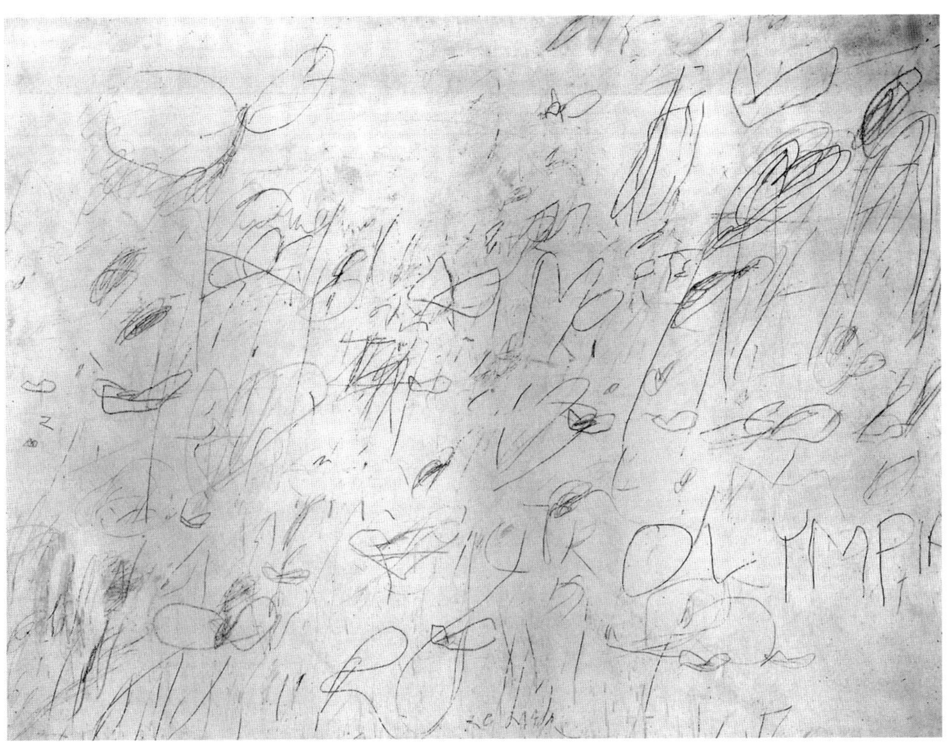

16.3 Cy Twombly, *Olympia,* 1957.

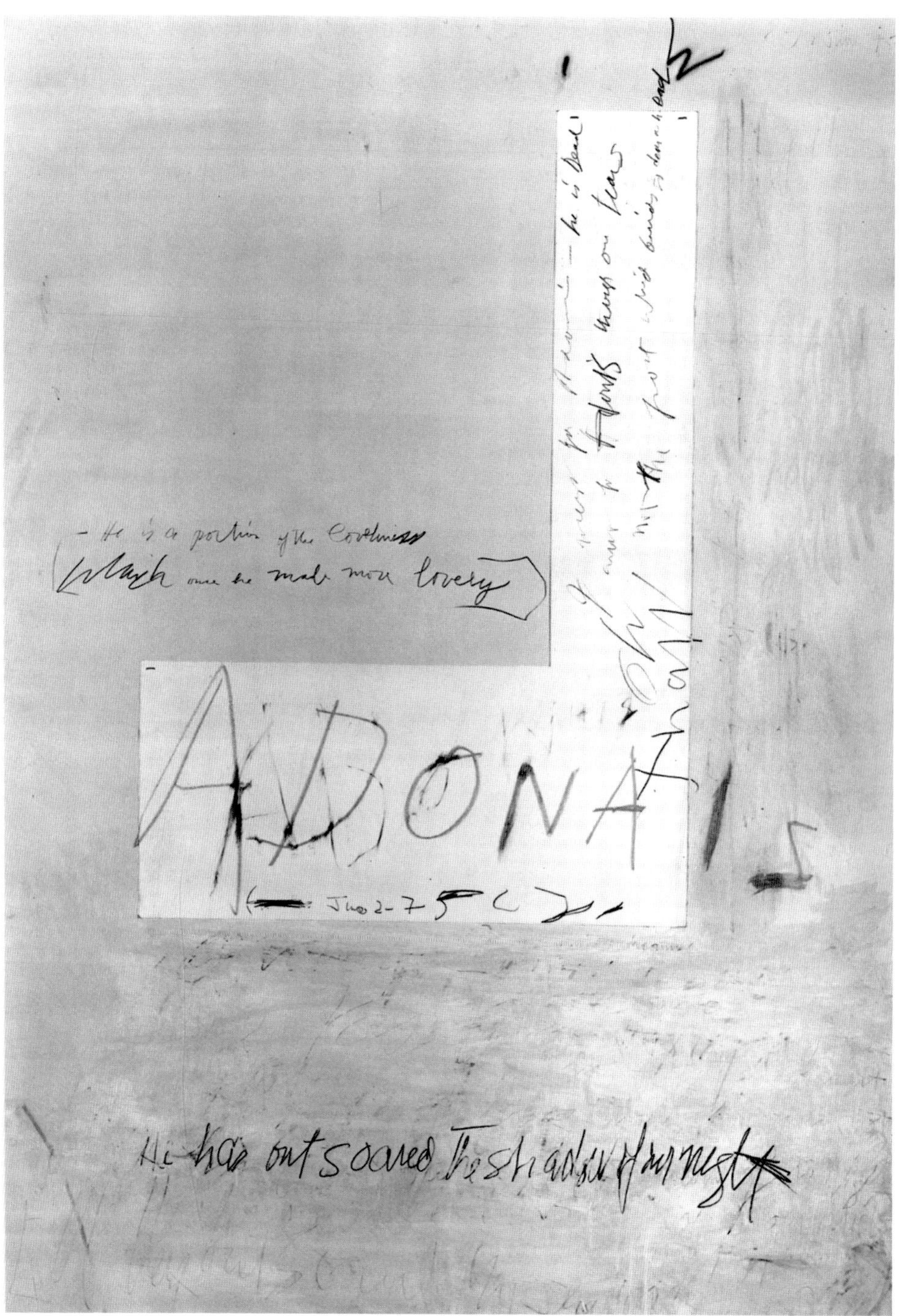
ADONAIS

Barthes is clear that Twombly's art does not work by analogy. The name is pronounced, in fact, *despite* the fact that there is no vista, no Virgil, no Leda and the Swan to be found. "In Twombly's titles, we must not look for any induction of analogy," he says. "If the canvas is called *The Italians,* do not look for the Italians anywhere except, precisely, in their name."[3]

Further, Barthes knows that if the inscription, the "pictorial nominalism," does not operate through the terms of analogy (mimesis, representation, likeness), it has another type of function, one he locates along the axis of the performative.[4] The performative is found in its purest form in those of Twombly's paintings that function as dedications: "To Valéry"; "To Tatlin." The performative is a modality of language where meaning is identified with the very performance of the statement—as in "I arrest you," "I pronounce you man and wife," "I promise," "I swear," "I toast." It is thus a linguistic operation in which reference is suspended in favor of action: not meaning something, but doing something. It is the nexus through which representation is transmuted into force (the very one Foucault invoked when he moved in 1968 to associate knowledge and power, arguing that within every seemingly neutral historical narrative, there was sequestered the discursive axis of the performative's relations of authority; hence his decision to mark the field of power by calling it discursive and its scholarly account, discourses). Even when Twombly is not actually "dedicating" a work, when he is instead only idly doodling a name on his canvas—*Leda, Mars, Bolsena*—he is operating within the field of the performative: I mark you [the canvas], I name you, I call you "painting." This is the big difference, the difference amounting to an absolute rupture of discursive intent, between the notion of the performative and that of analogy.

The others are determined to maintain analogy. Heiner Bastian insists that "Twombly sees the object and the sign that stands for it as a simultaneous unity that arises in the act of drawing," with the result that "his gesture and the breath of emotion suffuse the volatile ductus of all his forms."[5] Roberta Smith maintains that "on virtually every canvas, Twombly spells out what he has also

16.4 (*facing page*) Cy Twombly, *Adonais,* 1975.

painted and drawn." Spotting "the rapidly made vertical marks along the bottom edge of an untitled work done in Rome in 1959," which appear on either side of the scrawled name of the town "Bolsena," she elaborates what she takes to be the mimetic puzzle: "These marks could indicate blades of grass," she says, "or equally credible, some method of counting or keeping track, such as marking off the days. They are also doubtless exclamation marks, signals of an intense but unspecified emotion, whether joy or anger."[6] It never occurs to her that it is precisely this form of semiological overkill, in which she moves from one "looks-like" to another, which has the effect of undoing semiosis, of scattering and disrupting analogy, acting to perform a violence of the mark which Derrida would call dissemination: the mark reconsecrated as performative.

3 An Arena in which to Act

All the others not only welcome analogy but see it already prefigured in those works to which Twombly succeeded, as rightful heir. He and Rauschenberg and Johns perform, in their eyes, a sublation of action painting, canceling its abstract insularity but preserving its emotional intensity, and thus continuing an art of expressiveness, revealing therein abstract expressionism's own proclivities toward representation, toward landscape (Pollock), toward the body (de Kooning).

But this, I would say, is a massive misunderstanding, a refusal to acknowledge the implications of Twombly's means, the medium he adopted in 1953 and had perfected by 1955, the medium through which he drew his own conclusions about the import of abstract expressionist gesture. Turning away from an imitation of the smears and scumbles of Kline or de Kooning, which he had been practicing at Black Mountain College, Twombly took up graffiti as a way of *interpreting* the meaning of action painting's mark, and most particularly that of Pollock's radically innovative, dripped line. For graffiti is a medium of marking which has precise, and unmistakable, characteristics. First, it is performative; it suspends representation in favor of action: I mark you, I cancel you, I dirty you. Second, it is violent; always an invasion of a space that is not the marker's own, it takes illegitimate advantage of the surface of inscription, violating it, mauling it, scarring it. Third, it converts the present tense of the performative into the past tense of the index; it is the trace of an event, torn away from the presence of the marker: "Kilroy *was* here," it reads.

In this sense graffiti makes clear that the idea of the painting as the mirror of the painter—an idea suggested by Rosenberg's theory of action painting—is an impossible utopia, the dream of an art of presence. Even as the graphic lash of the graffiti strikes in the present, it registers itself as past, a mark whose violence dismembers the very idea of the image in the mirror, the whole body, Narcissus. Graffiti's character (Barthes would say its *genius*) is to strike against *form,* insuring a field in which the only way the image of the body can survive is as part object, a concatenation of obscene emblemata, the genital spatter that Twombly went on to enact in his Roman paintings from the early 1960s.

It is true that Twombly produces works that announce a connection to Pollock. He makes this unmistakable in 1955, with *Panorama,* in which he drives home the lesson of the white paintings from the same year, breaking up the loops and scrawls of the large aimless marks into a more connected "all-over" lattice, producing a kind of graffiti/skein at a monumental scale. This bow to Pollock in the regularizing and making rhythmic of the nonetheless violent mark is there as well in *Panorama*'s reprise at the end of the 1960s in the "blackboard" paintings, beginning with *Night Watch.* But this connection is not an "influence," it is a "reading," or rather, what Harold Bloom would call a strong misreading, and thus a way of declaring how Pollock's work *should* be read, at least in Twombly's eyes. Twombly "misreads" Pollock's mark as graffiti, as violent, as a type of antiform. And this misreading becomes the basis of all of Twombly's work.[7] Thus, he cannot write "VIRGIL" on a painting and mean it straight. "VIRGIL" is there as something a bored or exasperated schoolchild would carve into a desktop, a form of sniggering, a type of retaliation against the teacher's drone. And who is the teacher in this parable? Let us imagine him as Robert Motherwell, under whose "patronage" Twombly made one of his earliest public appearances.[8] The Robert Motherwell of *Mallarmé's Swan* and of the complete works of García Lorca was ever happy to sell abstract expressionism out to classical humanism, to lay claim to "philosophy" and to "literature" by means of gentrifying every loop and every splatter. This Robert Motherwell, who had the cheek to muscle in on Pollock's invention and to try to share in its inception, this narrator to whom Robert Hare referred as "the Humbert Humbert of 94th Street," wanted to domesticate Pollock, to make his work over into a lesson in symbolist lyrics.[9] It is this reading Twombly seems to protest with every means at his disposal. To rewrite "Mars" as "M / ars" is to make the deflationary, scatological, schoolroom joke: Mars = "m . . . arse." Every French second-grader wants to volunteer to spell the name of the town of Apt. "Ah-pé-té," they say, sputtering with laughter: "[il] a pété [he has farted]."

It is this deflationary gesture that Barthes sees as crucial to getting Twombly's tone. Yes, he admits, the Mediterranean light is there, as are the silence and the emptiness. And yes, there is a chain of references inscribed on the canvases that leads from antiquity to the present. He calls this the "Mediterranean effect" and says that "Twombly's inimitable art consists in having imposed the Mediterranean effect starting from materials (scratches, maculae, smears, dearth of color, no academic forms) which have no analogical relation with the great Mediterranean radiance." But he immediately adds that what takes place in each of Twombly's works is an attack on seriousness, on decorum, one which "takes on the appearance of an incongruity, a mockery, a deflation, as if the humanist turgescence was suddenly pricked."[10]

4 Who Says So?

In the unanimity of opinion on Twombly's "classicism," his reverence for the art of the past, the obeisance he pays to tradition, etc., we suspect the hand of the master at work. Heiner Bastian is, after all, Twombly's chosen mouthpiece, having published on his work since the early 1970s and having been consigned the task of gathering together the entire oeuvre. Bastian's word is the voice of the artist passed along to us as though by ventriloquy. So if Bastian says it is "a fundamental error" to think of Twombly's mark as a form of graffiti, if he dismisses graffiti as regressive and fetishistic—a collective lexicon standing "in crass opposition to the psychic activity of Twombly, for whom every line every sign is an expression of a deeply felt emotion or inner experience"—we imagine this to have been dictated by Twombly himself.[11]

Do we care? To what degree do we have to respect Twombly's self-assessment, since it is certain that Twombly himself didn't respect Pollock's? To what degree is it *our* responsibility to make an independent reading of an artist's work, acknowledging that while an artist may be a good interpreter of his or her own production, it does not follow that he or she will be its best one? No more than the analysand is the best reader of his or her dreams, motives, associations. To the contrary: The analysand is often the worst.

I have no idea which "Twombly" the Museum of Modern Art's upcoming [1994] retrospective will celebrate: Twombly's? Its own? A combination of the two? That it will be mine or Barthes's is the least likely. But one can always hope.

VI

The Subject of the Sign

Structural linguistics as well as its radical extension, poststructuralism, evacuated the idea of an autonomous subject, immediately present to itself through its independent consciousness and thought to operate as an inner voice directly addressing the subject's brain. Language was now conceived as delaying that voice through the necessities of linguistic meaning, which Derrida characterized as both difference and deferral, because of the linguistic dependence on spacing. For his part, Barthes turned to the structuralist idea of the binary or paradigm, which are functions of linguistic convention and thus not the invention of any given speaker.

Minimalism, and particularly the writings of Robert Morris, transferred the meaning of works of art from their internally articulated relations of parts to the viewer's experience of them, and of himself, in the situation in which he found them: "the concerns now are for more control of . . . the entire situation," Morris wrote. "Control is necessary if the variables of object, light, space, body, are to function. The object has not become less important. It has merely become less self-important."

The pressure this put on the subject to enter the work's signifying system forced attention to language itself and its structure of signification. "Line as Language" was an exhibition I mounted at Princeton University to analyze this development. Minimalism's drive to strip the work of art of its signifying possibilities, thus leaving it inert matter, seemed to me to raise the issues forced by analytic philosophy; the urgency of examining structural linguistics followed from this. Barthes's last class at the Collège de France dealt with *le neutre,* which became the filter through which the possible attitudes of subjects were submitted to Barthes' brilliance and rigor.

For a symposium the Getty Research Center organized to examine the subject of the biography of the artist, my thoughts naturally turned to Barthes's definitive essay "The Death of the Author" and Foucault's "What Is an Author?" For the title of my response in dismantling the very concept of biography, I borrowed the title of an important book by Eduardo Cadava: "Who Comes after the Subject?"

Line as Language

Reflecting on the wall drawings he has been making since 1968, Sol LeWitt wrote, "The physical properties of the wall, height, length, color, material, architectural conditions and intrusions, are a necessary part of the wall drawings. . . . Imperfections on the wall surface are occasionally apparent after the drawing is completed. These should be considered a part of the wall drawing."[1] The works LeWitt is describing consist of large, wall-borne networks of line, the density and direction of which are fixed by preset systems of permutation.

In acknowledging the way in which these networks—regulated by logic entirely internal to themselves—are still open to outside interference, LeWitt's statement has about it a kind of disarming simplicity. For it seems to point merely to the frailty of systems of projection: to the way, for example, a message transmitted by radio is susceptible to the intervention of static, of sounds having nothing to do with the language of its broadcast.

Yet words from his statement like "necessary" and "should" become puzzling in this context. It is not clear how the notion of necessity relates to the audible static, particularly when one thinks of it in relation to one's effort to receive meaning. And, to take an example much closer to home, it is not clear how the incidence of materials is really involved with that tradition to which

First published as catalogue text for the exhibition "Line as Language: Six Artists Draw," Princeton University Art Museum, February 23–March 31, 1974.

the wall drawings seem most closely related. In the medium of fresco, drawn and colored shapes are actually in suspension within the plaster surface of the wall, and thus wall and image are literally a part of one another. But, far from being *necessary* to the image, the imperfections of a given mural surface are not *possibly* a part of the wall painting it might bear. Whatever the damage to the wall of Santa Maria delle Grazie in Milan, for example, the stains and pitting and cracking of that surface are not conceivable as part of Leonardo's *Last Supper.* Although the illusionistic space onto which that painting opens is identified as related to the real space of the refectory, it is a relationship that is ideal rather than literal, transforming the wall itself and, by retroactive inference, transforming the room as well.

The congeries of line LeWitt describes do not project themselves out of this world and into another—into the world of an illusioned space. They are not transparent to an existence beyond the surface of the wall. LeWitt is talking about properties of material and surface that are untransformed by the agency of line, or rather of a kind of line that has been stripped of the powers of metaphor. The lines are simply elements that coexist with the surface onto which they are drawn. Hence the necessity to which LeWitt refers: the necessity of the copresence of the one with the other. And the wall with which these lines coexist is exploited as a surface whose spatial extension becomes a surrogate for the world's own extensionality, for the wall's dimensions and limits occur without knowledge of or reference to the preoccupations of art. These lines that LeWitt has forged and reforged have nothing to do with the task of projecting another world. Rather, they are part of an attempt to do something that might be characterized as an ambition to draw or mark on *this* one.

It is an ambition that in varying ways and degrees is shared by the six artists in the Princeton exhibition ["Line as Language," 1974]. Before attempting to describe the variations and differences among them, it might be well to indicate something of the history that pointed them in the direction of this project.

In locating this distinction between drawing as illusionistic projection—pointing to something beyond itself—and drawing as a species of marking on *this* world, one might consider that moment in the history of recent art when Jasper Johns performed a peculiarly radical critique of the abstract expressionist mode of drawing. What I am thinking of here is the *Target* Johns painted in 1955. In that work the drawing simply replicates the internal division of a commercially produced object; its exploitation of the design of a ready-made, flat target deprives the painting of the specific kind of interiority that had infected postwar American art. Johns's *Target* is, in this sense, not so much an attack on the "abstraction" part of the abstract expressionist sensibility as it is an act of demolition aimed at the "expressionist" aspect of that title. The very deadpan quality of *Target* becomes, in this reading, a key to Johns's own skepticism about the notion of "expression" in art.

Yet it is a skepticism that may at first seem quite peculiar. For it seems so logical to say, "Art is an expression of something," and if asked, "An expression of what?" to answer, "An expression of the artist, of what he had in mind—or an expression of the way he saw something." In the case of abstract expressionism this answer seemed particularly compelling; and it largely constituted the initial interpretations of Pollock's painting as well as de Kooning's (although it was subsequently withdrawn from formulations about Pollock's art). The early views of their work proceeded from the very logic of "expression"; every mark on their canvases was seen as asking to be read in the context of a private self from which the intention to make that mark had been directed. From this it followed that the public surface of the work demanded that one see it as a map from which could be read the privately held crosscurrents of personality—a kind of testimony of the artist's inviolable self.

Abstract expressionism was thus identified with an intense psychological privacy. "Art," wrote Harold Rosenberg, "comes back into painting by way of psychology. As Stevens says of poetry, 'it is a process of the personality of the poet.' But the psychology is the psychology of creation." And then he added, "The tension of the private myth is the content of every painting of this vanguard. The act on the canvas springs from an attempt to resurrect the saving moment in his 'story' when the painter first felt himself released from Value—myth of past self-recognition."[2] The fact that the work elicited descriptions of that sort is an index of the way certain criticism saw its task as one of simple acknowledgment of this privacy. The space on the canvas and the marks it bore were understood as referring to experience that could not be verified by consultation with anything outside itself—by checking it, so to speak, against its likeness to external data. In that sense it was the kind of space that is posited by a solipsistic reading of what Carnap called the protocol language—the language of sense impression, mental images, and private sensation. It is a reading that sees no possible outside verification of the meanings of words we use to point to our private experience—holding meaning itself hostage to that separate video of impressions registered across the screen of each individual's monitor. In terms of the private reading of the protocol language, my "green" and my "headache" point to what I see and feel, just as your "green" and your "headache" point to something you possess. Neither of us has any way of verifying the separate data to which they point and therefore of verifying their meanings.[3]

If we think about the art that issues from a necessarily unverifiable internal space—the space of the private language—we might make a connection between the way in which "expression" functions as a model in time for the same kind of things for which illusionism in painting serves as a spatial model. It is a connection that seems to account for the reaction Johns had to the space of abstract expressionism.

We can think of various kinds of illusionistic spaces: the orthogonal grid of classical perspective; the more nebulous continuum of atmospheric landscape; the undesignated, infinite depth of geometric abstraction. And in each of these pictures of the world, space itself operates as a precondition for the visibility of the pictorial events—the figures, the depicted objects—that appear within it. We consider that the ground (or background) in a painting exists somehow before the figures; and, even after the figures are placed on the ground, we understand that the ground "continues" behind them, serving as their support. In illusionistic painting, "space" functions as a category that exists prior to the knowledge of things within it. It is in that sense a model of a consciousness that is the ground against which objects are constituted. On its most abstract level, traditional picture-making is a philosophical argument about the nature of appearance, suggesting that its very possibility depends on a consciousness that is the ground for all relatedness, for all differentiation, for the constitution of perceptual wholes—and that that consciousness operates within the priorness of a mental space. The ground of Western illusionism is an entrenched Cartesianism.

Thus, just as intention can be understood as a necessarily private, because internal, mental event, which externalizes itself through the selection of objects, the objects that appear within pictorial space can be seen as issuing from an internalized, prearranged set of coordinates. As one moves within the history of painting to postwar American art—that is, to abstract expressionism—these two aspects of priorness fuse and become more nakedly the subject of the pictures themselves.

Therefore, the *meaning* of an attempt to undermine illusionism cannot be disassociated from the baggage that Western picture-making carried along with it. It is a rejection that inherently implies the disavowal of the notion of a constituting consciousness and the protocol language of a private self. It is a rejection of a space that exists prior to experience, passively waiting to be filled, and of a psychological model in which a self exists replete with its meanings prior to contact with its world. So if we wish to speak of the anti-illusionism of Johns's *Target,* we cannot limit our discourse to an ideology of form.

If Johns's *Target* combated the abstract expressionist mode of drawing (and all it implied) by the use of drawing as a species of readymade, it was clearly because of his own interpretation of the meaning of the readymade as it had surfaced in the work of Marcel Duchamp—in *Fountain,* for example, the urinal he placed on a pedestal and signed "R. Mutt/1917." For Johns saw the readymade as pointing to the fact that there need be no connection between a final art object and the psychological matrix from which it issued, since in the case of the readymade this possibility is precluded from the start. *Fountain* was not made (fabricated) by Duchamp; it was only selected by him. Therefore, there is no way in which the urinal could "express" the artist. It is like a sentence that is put into the world unsanctioned by the voice of a speaker standing behind it. Because maker and artist are evidently separate, there is no way for the urinal to serve as the externalization of the state or states of mind of the artist as he made it. And by not functioning within the grammar of the aesthetic personality, *Fountain* can be seen as putting distance between itself and the notion of personality per se. The relationship between Johns's *Target* and his reading of *Fountain*[4] is just this: the arthood of *Fountain* is not legitimized by its having issued stroke by stroke from the private psyche of the artist; indeed it could not. So it is like a man absentmindedly humming and being dumbfounded if asked whether he had meant that tune rather than another. That is a case in which it is not clear how the grammar of intention might apply.

For the art of the early 1960s, this notion of disengaging drawing (or the internal differentiations of a pictorial surface) from expression, and thus from privacy, became of paramount concern. This is true, for example, in the work of Frank Stella, whose intuitions of modernism were formed in relation to the work of Johns.

It is common enough to say of Stella's painting that it is structured deductively—that all internal differentiations of its surfaces derive from the literal aspects of the canvas edge.[5] Thus in the early black paintings, like *Die Fahne Hoch* (1959), we note the way Stella begins with the midpoints of the vertical and horizontal sides and forces the stripes into a repetitive, unbroken declaration of the expanse of the painting's four quadrants in a double set of mirror reversals. Or in the later paintings where the canvases begin to be shaped, we note that the stripes perform a more self-evident reverberation inward from the shape of that support. It seems easy enough to say this, and further to add that the effect of this surface, flashed continuously with the sign of its edge, has purged itself of illusionistic space, has achieved flatness. And that flatness, we think, is the flatness of an object—of a nonlinguistic thing. Yet we would be wrong, in the way that half-truths are wrong; for we would not have said enough.

The signs that haunt Stella's early stripe paintings are more than signifiers of their literal shapes. *Die Fahne Hoch* is deductively structured; so is *Luis Miguel Dominguin* (1971). But both paintings arrive at a particular configuration, which is the configuration of a cross. We could call this accidental, of course, just as we could conceive it as accidental that the cross itself relates to that most primitive sign of an object in space: the vertical of the figure projected against the horizon line of a nascent ground. But, in front of these pictures, one feels a necessary bond between the three types of meaning that are folded into a single act of division: the meaning of structural logic; that of representational gesture; and that of symbolic language. Thus, the three-way relationship that fuses along the striped surface of these pictures is a kind of argument for the logical connection between the cruciform of all pictoriality—of all intention to locate a thing within its world—and the way in which the conventional sign (in this case the cross) arises naturally from a referent in the world. The logic of the deductive structure is therefore shown to be inseparable from the logic of the sign. Both seem to sponsor one another and in so doing to ask one to grasp the natural history of pictorial language as such. The real achievement of these paintings is to have fully immersed themselves in meaning, and to have made meaning itself a function of surface—*of the external, the public, of a space that is in no way a signifier of the a priori, or of the privacy of intention.*

The meaning of Stella's expurgation of illusionism is unintelligible apart from a will to lodge all meanings within the conventions of a public space, and to expose illusionistic space as a model of privacy—of the self conceived as constituted prior to its contact with the space of the world.

That conception of the self had, by the late 1950s, already become an aspect of the literary experience of Samuel Beckett and of the *nouveau roman.* And it had emerged as the particularly urgent claim of the late philosophy of Wittgenstein, in which the language game was a therapy aimed at severing the connection (the logical connection) between meaning and mind. In his *Blue Book,* for example, Wittgenstein asks what it means to make the claim that we know a tune: Does it mean that before we sing it, we have quickly whistled it to ourselves silently; or that we have a picture of the score in our heads—a mental image of the tune—from which we read off the notes as we sing them? Is claiming to know the tune dependent upon having it stored up someplace inside us, like beads already positioned on a string and ready to be pulled out of our mouths? Or is it simply singing the tune, or perhaps hearing many tunes and saying, "That one just then is the right tune"?[6] The tune, and the question of just where it is stored when we claim to know it, widens out in *The Philosophical Investigations* to memory images and to the bases for all claims to know. Again and again Wittgenstein tried to sever the certainty of these claims from a picture of a mental space in which definitions and rules are stored, awaiting application. His work became an attempt to confound our picture of the necessity that there be a private mental space (a space available only to the single self) in which meanings and intentions have to exist *before* they can issue into the space of the world. The model of meaning that Wittgenstein implores us to accept is a model severed from the legitimizing claims of a private self.

The significance of the art that emerged in this country in the early 1960s is that it staked everything on the truth of that model. It is not only the meaning of Stella's art that would be missed if we read it merely as a project of formal reordering; that model of externalization operates throughout the kind of sculpture that came to be known as minimalism. One by one, artists like Donald Judd, Robert Morris, Dan Flavin, Carl Andre, and Sol LeWitt came to see that the problem of illusionist drawing was not confined to painting, but operated within the area of sculpture as well. In a three-dimensional art, drawing functions as metaphor most obviously when it serves to construct suggestive contours—converting one material into the signifier for another: stone, for example, into flesh. Or again, line in the form of edges or vectors often serves to suggest an underlying principle of cohesion or order or tension, which catalyzes the object from within. As with metaphor, the implication of this order is that it lies beyond the simple externals of the object—its shape or substance—endowing that object with a kind of intentional or private center.

Part of the effort of minimalist sculpture was to strip away that metaphorical aspect of drawing, to make the allusive qualities of edge or contour coincide exactly with the physical boundaries of the object. A cube by Judd or Morris or LeWitt becomes a function of what I have been calling the public space of this world in the same way that the surfaces of Stella's paintings manifest their signs as fully external, and therefore public. The edges of the lattices from which LeWitt composed his sculpture of the mid-1960s do not partake of an organizing system that is any different from that of the coordinates of the viewer's own space. In that sense, these lattices were composed of line understood as an existent within this world.

Once line had become this kind of fully physical element, or simple, the next step for LeWitt was to place line itself onto something that seemed more self-evidently to share in the quality of external space—namely, in its extension. For LeWitt, it was the wall surface, the wall proper, that was, like the world, simply extended, oblivious to anything like aesthetic limits or boundaries. Marking or drawing on the wall became synonymous with marking on external space. And the character of the lines that then took their place on these walls derived from the very notion of extension. LeWitt deployed the line elements as members of simple sets (one example was line as either vertical, horizontal, or forty-five-degree diagonals to the left or right), which by the operation of union could be permuted to fill out the totality of set membership. Parallelisms, oppositions, and overlays took their place on the wall, becoming a kind of evidence of logical procedure constantly insisting on externalizing and extending itself.

In giving to line this quality of evidence, the wall drawings take up that attack on the notion of a private mental space that I spoke about in relation to Stella and Johns. For the wall drawings testify to the possibility of executing any system of combination the artist can think of. One might say that they stand for the predicates of any proposition, which once made (or imagined) must be able to achieve itself physically. This attacks the notion of privacy by eating away at an idea of imagination as a special mental precinct that is truly unavailable to other minds. Insofar as imagination seems capable of postulating unverifiable fictions—"green sounds," for example—it would seem capable of withholding for itself experiences that were unimpeachably private. Yet, although "green sounds" can be named, there is a real sense in which they *cannot* be imagined, a sense in which the sound of the words sends one's thoughts running to the only place where referents for them might be found, namely, to external space. The significance of the wall as a medium for line or drawing is, then, that it becomes the ground of a refusal to separate idea from existence.

In introducing the exhibition of two recent works, *Axiom of Indifference* (1972–1973) and *Centers: Estimated and Measured* (1973) Mel Bochner used the following quotation from Piaget's *Structuralism*: "Formal grammatical systems do not furnish decision procedures . . . it [is] necessary to drop the notion of a 'basis' that contains everything in advance, and layer by layer *construction* [will] have to take the place of *axiomatization*."[7]

That remark, which has a particularly apt connection to the whole of Bochner's work, might be further elucidated by another statement from the same source:

> Since Gödel, logicians and students of the foundations of mathematics distinguish between "stronger" and "weaker" structures, the stronger ones not being capable of elaboration until after the construction of the more elementary, that is, "weaker" systems yet, conversely, themselves necessary to the "completion" of the weaker ones. The idea of a formal system of abstract structures is thereby transformed into that of the construction of a never completed whole, the limits of formalization constituting the grounds for incompleteness, or . . . incompleteness being a necessary consequence of the fact that there is no "terminal" or "absolute" form because any content is form relative to some inferior content and any form the content for some higher form.[8]

Further, Piaget's discussion revolves around the procedure of "reflective abstraction," which puts pressure on what seems to be the closed formal space of an axiomatic system—revealing the way in which its form becomes the content of a system taken from a different vantage.

Behind the disarmingly simple forms of Bochner's work, there is the drive toward this stance of "reflective abstraction." Which is to say that what had seemed to be the most absolute formal propositions of abstract art are taken to be the contents of his own work and are manipulated as such. One of these propositions concerns the nature of boundary conditions. It is a proposition asserting that within the visual field there is a formal difference between what lies inside the bounding edges of a figure and the space that lies outside or around that figure.

For Bochner, one strategy for examining the truth of this proposition was to go to systems (like metrical or logical systems) in which the spaces that lie outside figures are not subsidiary to those figures but are instead the very means of generating them. An example of this occurs in the series of works that concerns the procedures of counting. Thus, *Triangular and Square Numbers* (1965–1972) registers the fact that what counts in the formation of a square number is the repetition, in parallel rows, of the objects in a first row, the number of rows equaling the natural number of the objects in that first row. But in the formation of a triangular number, what is registered, and therefore counted, is the number of spaces between the objects or integers of a given row, the completion of the figure naturally terminating when there are no more spaces to be counted. In *Axiom of Indifference* this necessary, systematic equivalence of space inside and outside a figure's boundaries is pointed to as the conditions operating in yet another system. There, one is given the relationships that hold between certain logical conditions—one of which is the equivalence for logic of an X being "in" an area and alternatively being "not out" of the same area. What results is the perception that while these two formal situations seem quite transparent to visual experience, they are not transparent to logical operations in the same way.

In describing Bochner's enterprise, then, one might say that he is constantly mapping the axiomatic premises of a particular system onto the physical facts of the visual world in order to point to the way that what appear to be the "givens" of the one field crumble before the "givens" of another.

Theory of Painting (1970) is a work that likewise examines what happens when the ground of a figure is understood not as that which lies outside the boundaries of the figure, but rather as that thing by which figures must be generated. Through the procedures of the work a painted square is "isolated" from a ground constructed of an area (also square) of overlapping sheets of newspaper. A second figure is then generated by dispersing the same ground, thereby

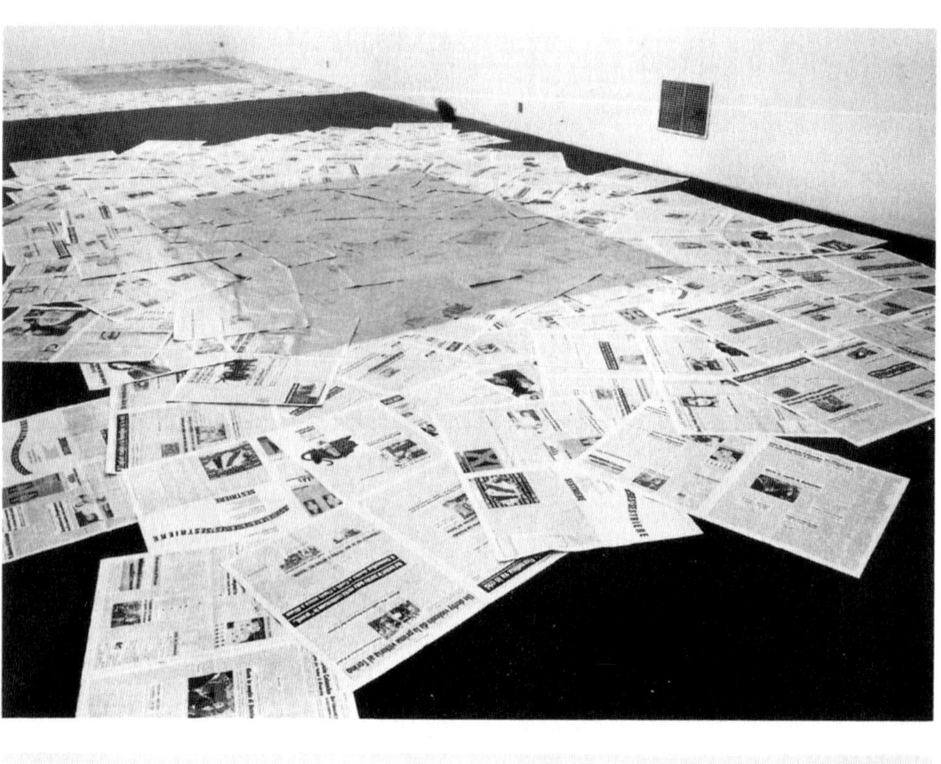

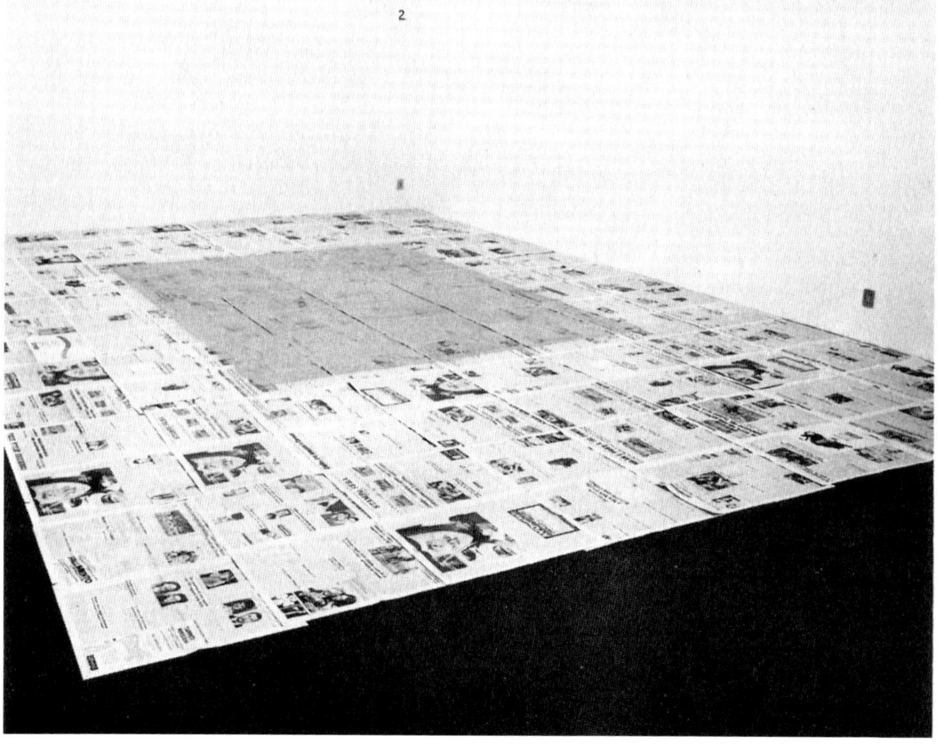

2

constructing a diffusion of the "figure" that is the self-evident product of the breaking-up of the ground. By a continuation of the process of coherence and dispersal, two remaining conditions are generated. What is interesting here—far beyond the strategy for making a particular work—is that, in investigating a theory of what constitutes a ground or background in painting (by making that ground generative rather than passive), one passes through the limits of painting considered as a formal system closed under investigation. Rather than merely asserting it, one discovers the basis for the vantage from which the formal propositions of painting become the content of a field of material operations, which one might feel forced to designate as "sculpture." But the point of the work is not *how* to deduce the conditions of sculpture from those of painting, but rather the *meaning* of the operation of such a deduction.

The use to which Dorothea Rockburne puts lines or marks is of a different order. The relationship in her work of line and wall becomes not so much a question of the application of two different orders, the one axiomatic, the other perceptual, as it is of setting up an internally generated whole that is imbedded in the space of the world and yet does not belong to it.

Neighborhood (1973), for example, consists of several sets of red, black, and graphite lines that extend onto the wall around and under a sheet of paper that has been folded twice and hung in place by two nails. The systematic relationship between paper and lines is that the lines have recorded the topological transformations of the paper as it has been reflected about the axes of its two folds. The act of folding the paper (by bringing together its two opposite corners) changes its shape from rectangular to pentagonal by making two areas of the former rectangle coincident with one another. Each act of unfolding transforms it back to its original rectangularity. On one level, the work can be seen as a result of recording the procedure of folding and unfolding, moving the paper over the surface of the wall in certain ordered patterns. In that sense the lines are the residual indicators, on a flat plane, of a set of three-dimensional operations specific to and generated by the topological space of the paper.

17.1 (*facing page*) Mel Bochner, *Theory of Painting I and II,* 1970. Galleria Toselli, Milan.

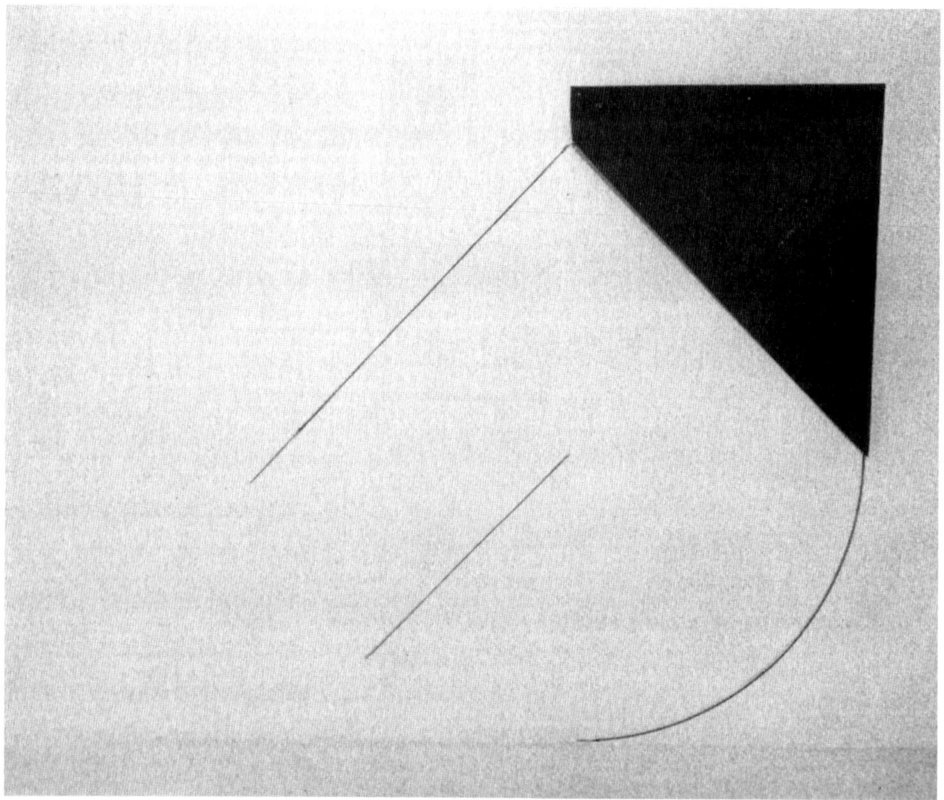

17.2 Dorothea Rockburne, *Neighborhood,* from the series *Drawing Which Makes Itself,* 1973. Carbon paper and lines resulting from the carbon paper folds. © 2009 Dorothea Rockburne/Artists Rights Society (ARS), New York.

On this level, *Neighborhood* can be seen as an outgrowth of the series *Drawing Which Makes Itself* (1973), particularly those works that employ double-faced carbon paper. There, as the carbon paper is moved into interlocking stations on the wall (or floor), the positions of its internal folds are transferred onto the wall plane by scoring the paper along the creases. The act of scoring simultaneously deposits carbon onto the wall surface and underlines the fold of the paper itself. The resultant lines or marks are read with a striking ambivalence, for they are both *on* the wall and yet are retained *within* the carbon paper that had been flipped into a new position. The act of drawing is thereby conceived as different from the traditional procedure in which a set of objects (lines) is superimposed on another, foreign object (paper). Instead, one confronts works in which the lines arise from information that is "in" the paper. And the logic of the works states the self-evidence of the fact that this information, although it could be transferred to different situations (on the wall), could not be dislodged from the mediating body of the paper that is the source of the information.

But there is another level on which *Neighborhood* can be read. There, the lines on the wall, by repeatedly marking the changing edges or limits of the paper field as it moves through its various rotations or reflections, are declarations of the boundaries or approaching limit of a changing set. For, in terms of a topological space, only those points that are within the actual field of the sheet have limits that also belong to the sheet. The limits (or neighborhoods) of the edges of the paper lie outside it. Thus the act of transcribing the changing edges of the paper, as it is folded and unfolded, is an act of recording a set of approaching limits that are in fact external to the space of the paper. It is a work that defines with striking economy and exactitude the way in which boundaries adhere, yet do not belong to the figures that generate them and that we assume they delimit. Turning its back on any kind of metaphorical explanation, and instituting line itself as a paradoxically physical element of proof, *Neighborhood* becomes a kind of metacritique—cross-examining the logic of Leonardo's remark that line does not exist in nature.

The implications of Leonardo's statement, on an intuitive level rather than on a level that relates to its mathematical consequences, are part of the subject of the wire drawings Richard Tuttle has been making since 1971. In these works, three forms of line intersect with one another. The first type of line is a distended one that is marked with pencil directly on the wall; the second is a line formed by wire attached to the two end points of the penciled line but looping out into space in a curve or configuration that is independent of the first; and the third is a linear shadow cast onto the wall by the wire—the profile of that shadow conforming neither to the pencil nor to the wire lines. All three of these "lines" begin from the same two points of origin on the wall, and all three of them intertwine within a single, visual matrix. Yet all three exist at a different level of reality and are based in, or spring from, a different conception of where to look for the ground of an object—whether the object be mark or shadow. Tuttle's work has developed in relation to questions about the way two-dimensional shapes insinuate themselves into the fabric of the visual field, thereby prodding at the categories that harden or become institutionalized by the names we use to point to aspects of that field.

With these wall- and floor-bound works we have moved very far indeed from the private space of intention and meaning that operated throughout an earlier convention of drawing. Instead, we find ourselves engaged by a projection or emptying of meaning outward—precipitating it onto the physical space of the world. What I am claiming as shared among certain artists, then, is the need to explore the externality of a propositional space and therefore of meaning. But at the same time this need has a parallel project in the work of other artists: the discovery of the body proper as an externalization of the space of the self.

That aspect of the self comes to light in what Husserl calls the paradox of the alter ego—the way in which the picture of the self as a contained whole (transparent only to itself and to the truths that it is capable of constituting) crumbles before the act of connecting with other selves, with other minds. Merleau-Ponty describes this paradox as the coexistence within an individual of separate perspectives: as the fact that for each of us—he and I—there are two perspectives, I for myself and he for himself and each of us for the other: "Of course these two perspectives, in each one of us, cannot be simply juxtaposed,

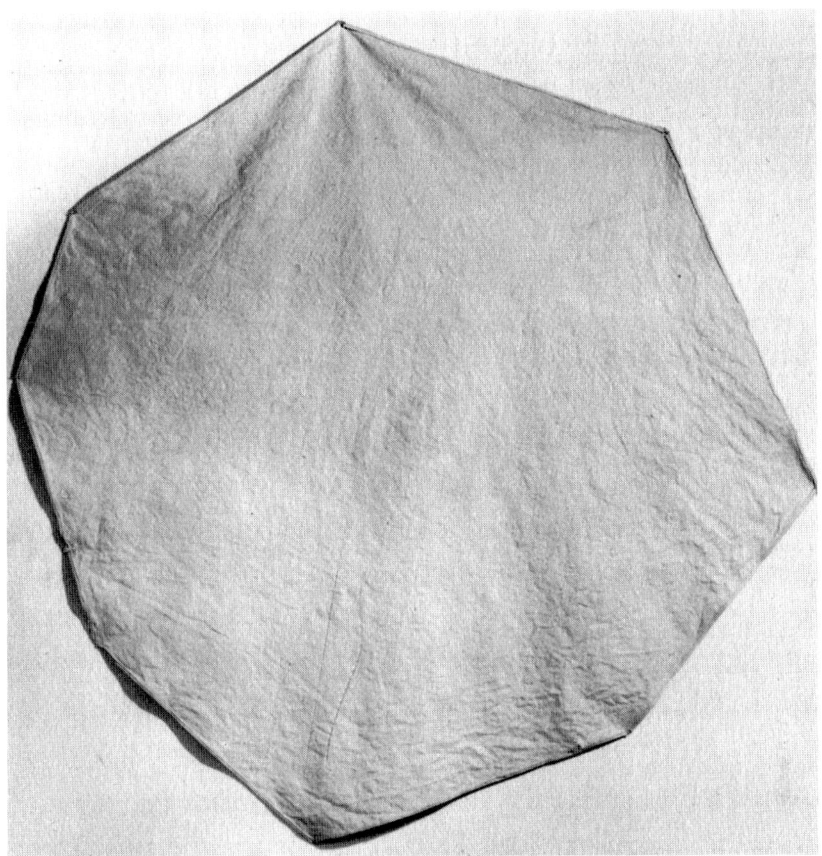

17.3 Richard Tuttle, *Even,* 1967.

for in that case it is not I that the other would see, nor he that I should see. I must be the exterior that I present to others and the body of the other must be the other himself."[9] This revelation leads away from any notion of consciousness as unified within itself. For "at the very moment when I experience my existence . . . I fall short of the ultimate density which would place me outside time, and I discover within myself a kind of internal weakness standing in the way of my being totally individualized: a weakness which exposes me to the gaze of others as a man among men."[10]

This question of shape or form as a realization of the self as it surfaces into the world is a basis for coming to terms with what is most serious in contemporary sculpture. That aesthetic of the externalized self is evident, for example, in the prop pieces that Richard Serra began to make in 1969. The special precariousness of their forms is not about imminent collapse or dissolution. Rather it suggests, by means of a metaphor of striking abstractness, a continual coming into coherence of the body. *One Ton Prop (House of Cards)* (1969) deals specifically with internal space as constantly available to external vision and as entirely defined by the perpetual act of balance by which its exterior is constituted. Interiority (the "I for myself") is clearly made a function of exteriority (the "I for others"). In assigning to this work and to the rest of the prop pieces the problematic of the double perspective, I am obviously not speaking to any specific text for which the works serve as some kind of sign. Rather, I hope to locate a certain ground from which to grasp the meaning of Serra's need in these works to achieve verticality without permanently adhering separate parts of the sculpture.

That sense of a resultant figure or shape as fully imbedded within the conditions of its own physicality—conditions that are not hidden, but are instead constantly open to inspection—forms the thinking behind Serra's 1968 lead work, *To Tear.* Here, the action of shredding a square lead sheet into a mass of line creates the boundaries of a new object while holding within those boundaries a history of transformation, within which is contained the image of the old. It is a work that seems to essentialize the experience of arriving at form through drawing understood as a continual process of exposure.

Serra's sculpture has continued to explore line as a kind of current that runs through physical space, laying that space open to a particular kind of inspection. Reversing the traditional notion of line as bounding a figure and thereby setting it off against a ground, the linear elements of a work like *Shift* (1970–1972) become vectors against which external space (space traversed along those vectors) is experienced as a configuration. In his work this relationship of line to ground is involved, then, in undermining the idea of space as a set of fixed coordinates that could possibly contain in advance a prefiguration of their meaning.

This resistance to the idea of space as something pregiven, and to a notion of the self as formed prior to experience, directed many of the strategies of minimal sculpture; Robert Morris's three L-beams (*Untitled,* 1965), for example, serve as a certain kind of cognate for this naked dependence of intention and meaning upon the body as it surfaces into the world in every external particular of its movements and gestures. For no matter how clearly we understand that the three Ls are identical, it is impossible to experience them—the one upended, the second lying on its side, and the third perched on its two ends—as the same. The L-beams have been described as "a child's manipulation of forms, as though they were huge building blocks. The urge to alter, to see many possibilities inherent in a single shape, is typical of a child's . . . vision, whereby learning of one specific form can be transferred to any variations of that form."[11] But that account seems exactly to violate one's actual experience of the work, in that what Morris refers to as "the known constant"—that ideal Cartesian unity—recedes into the ground of the sculpture as a kind of fiction, crowded out by the emergence of absolute difference within the particularity of the actual space. Situating themselves within the space of experience, the space to which one's own body appears, if it is to appear at all, the L-beams suspend the axiomatic coordinates of an ideal space. We explain space in terms of these coordinates when we think of it as an absolute grid that seems, however, to converge in depth because we are badly placed to see the three-dimensional lattice of that grid. We imagine clarity to come from thinking ourselves suspended above the grid in order to defray the distortions of our perspective, in order to recapture

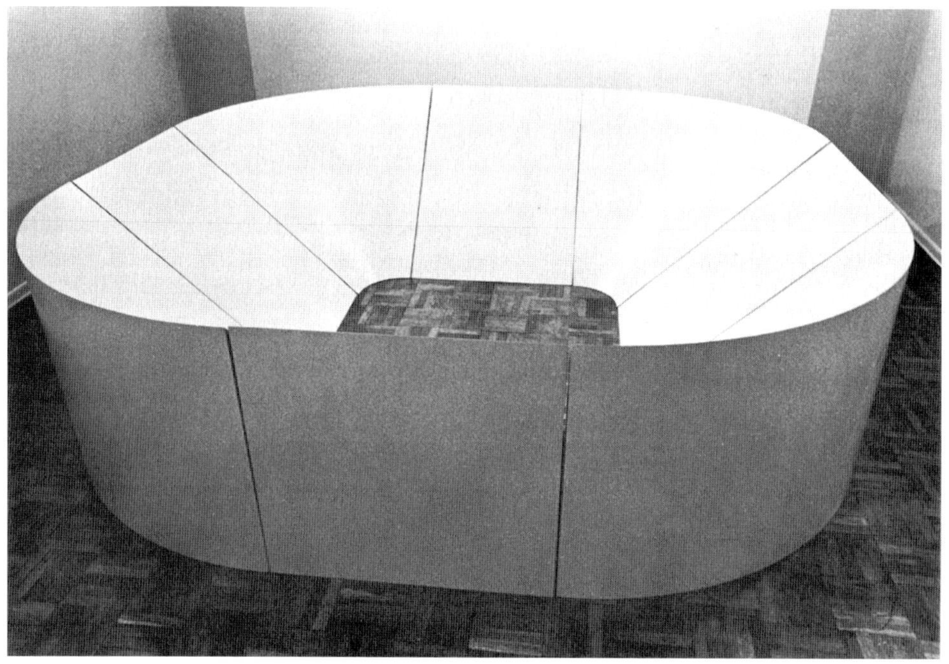

17.4 Robert Morris, *Untitled,* 1967. © 2009 Robert Morris/Artists Rights Society (ARS), New York.

the absoluteness of its total parallelism. But the meaning of depth is nowhere to be found in this suspension.[12]

Similarly, the conception of the self as an ideal, prefigured whole is challenged by the sectional fiberglass pieces that Morris made in 1967–1968. These works are constructed as transformable entities, objects that assume many different configurations. Because any particular shape the work takes has to be understood as temporary,[13] no specific configuration is allowed to become a figure against the "ground" of the object's "real" structure. The notion of a fixed, internal armature that can mirror the viewer's own self, fully formed prior to experience, founders on the capacity of the separable parts of the works to shift or to have shifted, to exist in that form only at that moment of externalization.

In a recent series of drawings (*Blind Time*), Morris has built on this notion of meaning as something projected through the body and discovered only in the act of that projection. Executed with his eyes closed, the drawings are the sensuous registrations of the artist's hands as they move across paper or wall. The tasks he performs while blindfolded vary from constructing a shape, to designating a given area, to defining the metrical components of a space.

Since he cannot see what he is doing, we might say that Morris must be guided by a mental image of the shape, the area, the points on a line. And if he *is* so guided, we might ask whether the drawings are not "representations" of those mental images—thus pushing the task of line back toward the transcription of something like private space. The answer to this is no. Morris is asking us to understand that his line, given as the outward extension of the space of his body, becomes a way for him to find out, to discover in experience, the shapes that inhabit that private space. Further, those shapes are continually stated as formed in response to outside space. It is only the body's effort to locate an area within a sheet of paper, to count up existing physical data, that prompts or gives rise to the images themselves. Most importantly, the drawings point to the outward expression of the body as the only place to which we can turn for verification of the existence of something that we are tempted to call a mental image. In this sense, an appropriate text for the drawings might be the following:

> If a blind man were to ask me "have you got two hands?" I should not make sure by looking. If I were to have any doubt of it, then I don't know why I should trust my eyes. For why shouldn't I test my eyes by looking to find out whether I see my two hands? *What* is to be tested by *what*?[14]

In 1970 Mel Bochner contributed to an exhibition a work that consisted of a sentence chalked on an area of blackboard paint. The sentence read, "Language is not transparent." Looking at the written text, one was tempted to add parenthetically, "and neither is the line that conveys it." In attempting to sketch the background from which the six artists in this exhibition work, the one constant I have found seems to be an attack on the traditional transparency of line—the way that line had always seemed to make available something that lay behind or beyond it. There are many reasons for abandoning the conventional transparency of line. One of them is the task of trying to account as accurately as possible for the grounds of one's own experience.[15]

The Motivation of the Sign

Perhaps we should start at the center of the argument, with a reading of a collage by Picasso. This object, from the group dated late November to December 1912, comes from that phase of Picasso's exploration in which the vocabulary of *papier collé* has been reduced to an austerity one is tempted to call minimalist. For in this run Picasso restricts his palette almost exclusively to newsprint. Indeed, in the work in question, *Violin* (Paris, [after December 3], 1912), two newsprint fragments, one of them bearing a dispatch from the Balkans datelined "Tchataldja," are imported into the graphic atmosphere of charcoal and drawing paper as the sole elements added to the work's surface.

Or should this rather be described as *one* piece of newsprint? For what there is to be noticed about this material, first and foremost, is that it comprises two halves of a single sheet, the jigsaw-like edges of each segment of which announce the way they could be reconnected. And further, in their very condition of being, self-evidently, two pieces of a single puzzle, the two fragments signal something more: that their present placement within the field of the collage has not simply resulted from their having been scissored apart and transported to separate sites on the visual field, but rather that one of them has had to be flipped so that what it now shows as its front was originally its reverse. And

First published in Lynn Zelevansky, ed., *Picasso and Braque: A Symposium* (New York: Museum of Modern Art, 1992).

this is to say that when these shards from the material world fluttered onto the aesthetic surface of the drawing, they did so most conspicuously by declaring the reality of literally having a front and a back.

Now if the evocation of the backs of objects, the achingly beautiful turn of a nude's or a bottle's shoulder into the place where vision ends and touch begins, has been the glory of painting from the Renaissance onward, this very turning was what was squarely at issue in cubism. In its developing, analytic years, the cubism of Picasso and Braque pronounced the impenetrable frontality of the pictorial surface more obstinately and resolutely than had any style before it, so that the little areas of modeled form that heave into relief like so many swells on the surface of a lake hit the shoals of the picture support with a finality that could only dissipate their energies into a lateral spread, never implying a further plumbing of that support into a space behind. Modeling in this sense becomes the empty trappings of an illusionist system more and more divorced from the business of illusionism, a business we could describe as using the vehicle of sight as a means of access to reality in all its carnal fullness—to its weight and density, to its richness and texture, to its heat and vaporousness, to the evanescence of its very perfume. By 1911 the asceticism of the intermittencies of cubist light and shade had almost totally renounced the possibility that the two dimensions of the visual field could ever afford its viewer direct and unmediated access to that other world of tactile completeness, the world that bodies inhabit but vision only registers by means of so many flat and frontal pictures on the retinal plane of the eye.

Collage represents the point of no return within this process. With its evacuation from the pictorial field of wave upon wave of modeling, of the cacophony of slightly canted planes, collage completely ironed out the fabric of illusionism, rendering the object's existence within the visual field as inexorably flat as an insect crushed between two panes of glass. Nothing can be seen to turn within the vise of this frontal display: there is no rotation, no obliquity, no slide from luminous highlight into the cool of shadowed depths. In collage in general, such frontality is secured by the way the paper elements glued to the surface of the sheet are literally foursquare upon that surface, an inevitable result of their actual flatness. But in the geometry of Picasso's very first series of *papiers collés,* we can see how specifically this frontality is insisted upon, for there the violin's face is figured by a square of paper whose flatfooted parallelism with the surface it joins is underscored by the rigid geometries of its alignments with other paper rectangles in the field (see Daix, nos. 517–519, and *Siphon, Glass, Newspaper, and Violin,* Paris, [after December 3], 1912).[1]

The *Violin* from November–December 1912 is indeed one of these early works, although, unlike in the very first of them, patches of modeling are readmitted to the space, albeit not enough to break the grip of the two-dimensionality established by the newspaper silhouette with the Tchataldja report. That silhouette, which both locks the notched contour of the violin into the white of the paper abutting it and lines up its own rectilinear left edge with the vertical, charcoal slash that declares the right-hand side of the object, creates at one and the same time a powerful reading of the flatness of the object as material and of its foursquareness as shape: in its material condition—that is to say, as a piece of newspaper—it produces the violin as an unbendingly opaque facade; and in its formal aspect—that is, one rectangular shape centered within the other oblong of the drawing sheet as a whole—it secures the instrument's frontality as a kind of visual absolute. For the very flatness that banishes all three-dimensionality from the field of the image declares the total presence of the two-dimensional shape to vision: held firmly parallel to the plane of the retina, the frontal shape is unassailable in its availability to the visual sense; it is nowhere dependent on the synthesis of the sense of vision with the sense of touch.

If one might argue that the experience of touch is, indeed, literally absent from the perceptual field of vision—and this is what perceptual psychology through the late nineteenth century *was* arguing, by claiming that touch is what must be inferentially added to the pictorial image in order to produce the illusion of depth[2]—then in the visual fields of these collages there is no absence, since no illusioned depth distracts us from the pure frontality of the visual screen.

No absence in the *visual* field. But the collages do indeed open another field in which absence is the essence of meaning. And that field has properly to be called "protolinguistic."

For the linguistic sign, absence is not what depletes and saps the system of representation, but rather what makes it possible. Words operate in the absence of their referents; indeed, they can be said to outrun the limits of those referents even when the referents themselves are present to the pronouncement of the word that names them. We can say the word "depth" while pointing over the side of a boat into the sea, or indicating the darkness of a shade of blue, or calling attention to the tone of someone's voice, or acknowledging the profundity of an argument. In each case the meaning of the word is not limited to the positivity of the element to which we point. Depth takes its place in a system of oppositions in which it always operates against markers of shallowness, of lightness, of highness, of banality. Like any other word, "depth" is not the name of a property but the marker in a network of relationships, relationships which the structuralists call a "paradigm," relationships produced by language not as a set of names, but as a system.[3] And it is this system that resonates behind the word as it is invoked in the total absence of anything to which it might, visually, refer.

Depth is indeed the absent element called into the field of experience, if not into the field of vision, by collage's increasing control of a kind of sign that moves very close to being linguistic. For, if cubism could not produce the illusion of depth as present, collage honored its absence through summoning it as a meaning—a signified—that would be inscribed on the pictorial surface. "Depth" would be written on this field the way "Eat me" or "Drink me" were written on the objects Alice stumbled onto in Wonderland. It would be the signified of a signifier that would not figure it forth like an image—or what the semiologist calls the "iconic sign"—but would produce it through an arbitrary set of marks—the kind of signifier which semiology terms a "symbol."[4] The earliest and most abiding form of this inscription is to be found in the *f*-holes of the collage's violin. These *f*s, so blatantly disparate in size and thickness, are what Picasso creates as the suspended emblem of foreshortening, of a plane's turning away from full view into depth so that, as it turns, its two identical incisions grow steadily unequal within our field of vision. Lifted from the foreshortened surface of a depicted violin to remain, like the smile of the Cheshire cat, a detached and weightless phantom, these wildly mismatched *f*s take their place on the insistently frontal plane of the collage's violin not to dispute that frontality in the field of vision but instead to inscribe it with the pronouncement of a depth nowhere to be seen. Become a *symbol,* the *f*s write of the instrument's body, of its turning in space, of its voluptuous fullness with the same loving irony with which Jasper Johns—stroking the words "blue" and "yellow" and "red" onto nearly monochromatic passages of paint—would write a half-century later of the color he dared not display. And this inscription of /depth/, once invented, joins Picasso's working vocabulary. Again and again he uses it for the same, evocative purpose (see *Siphon, Glass, Newspaper, and Violin,* Paris, [after December 3], 1912; *Bowl with Fruit, Violin, and Wineglass,* Paris, [begun after December 2, 1912; completed after January 21], 1913 [see figure 12.4]; and Daix, nos. 529 and 573).

Now, if one half of the newspaper element in *Violin* functions to create the intractable ground of flatness and frontality against which to inscribe the sign /depth/, the other half interlocks with it as back to front. And this, within the incredible economy of the work, serves several interrelated purposes. On the one hand, we can see it heightening the poignancy of the way depth is absent in the collage since it enacts, as an action now vanished, the very gesture which originally produced it as the reverse of its partner. On the other, we could say that in conjuring up a turning which is simply the flipping of a flat page from one frontal position to another, the gesture already heralds the reduced condition of a plenitude no deeper than a sheet of paper. Thus, in being the reverse side of the element that locates the violin's front, the second element is not only literally the paper's back but establishes the notion of /back/ or /behind/ as something that must necessarily take place in the dismantled and splayed planarity of the collage surface. Yet this marker of the nether side of the front plane of the violin galvanizes its very material surface into the marker of quite another sort of /behind/. For it is extremely clear that the same newsprint which underscores the opacity and physical resistance of the instrument's body is manipulated in the guise of its twin to break up into the intermittency of a buzz of black lettering on white paper and thereby to mimic the draftsman's various ways of creating the illusion of atmosphere and of light. We might think of the scumbled passages of Rembrandt, or the flecked highlights of Turner, or the stippled textures of Seurat; the artist's conventions for evoking atmosphere and transparency are brought into play here, so that the shower of little letters, black on white, opens this flat collage plane to the inscription of /light/ as insistently as the *f*-holes wrote /depth/ across the surface of its twin.[5]

Moreover, the relation between these two elements, which couple in their physical gesture of interlocking, creates precisely that kind of paradigmatic pair the structuralists saw as a structural prerequisite for linguistic meaning. If Ferdinand de Saussure, the founder of structural linguistics, described meaning itself as "relative, oppositive, and negative," he was insisting on this purely relational condition of signification, with *x* coming to take on meaning only insofar as it is not *y*.[6] The couple Picasso produces in these scraps of discarded newsprint perform just such a system—which in linguistic terms is described as diacritical[7]—as the one gets to speak of transparency in relation to the signified opacity of the other. This speech, this semiosis, marks the upper plane with the signified /light/, while the *f*s imprint the lower one with /depth/. But it must be stressed that both these surfaces are merely inscribed with these absent qualities, with a space and luminosity that have literally been banished from vision. And thus as the two actual planes of newsprint hold the fitful stretches of drawing that occur on the page between them in a kind of viselike grip, they never once slacken in their control of the image's presentation of frontality, in the face of which the velvety passages of charcoal drawing achieve a kind of poignant superfluousness.[8]

And just as in the case of the *f*-hole sign for /depth/, this newsprint sign for /transparency/ and /light/ becomes a staple of Picasso's collage vocabulary, appearing again and again in brilliant combinations and variations (see *Glass and Bottle of Suze,* Paris, [after November 18], 1912; *Siphon, Glass, Newspaper, and Violin,* Paris, [after December 3], 1912; *Bottle on a Table,* Paris, [after December 8], 1912; *Bowl with Fruit, Violin, and Wineglass,* Paris, [completed after January 21], 1913; and Daix, nos. 548 and 658).

If the analysis I have performed on this work seems convincing or compelling—if it seems to account, in a coherent, continuous reading, for most of the choices Picasso has made—the rest of what follows will be of some matter, for it will probably seem that a change as momentous as this one—a change not within the system of illusion from one type to another, but a conversion from one whole representational system, roughly called iconic, to another, roughly called symbolic—must be accounted for. If, on the other hand, none of this seems to have described what is going on in *Violin* or to have added up to any kind of explanatory system, then none of the rest of what will be argued here is going to mean very much, because the proofs available for what follows are, sad to say, rather thin. They only take on density in relationship to the demand one feels for this break to be explained.

The extremely small group of scholars who have, in print, called this break by the name it's been given here comprises Jean Laude, Pierre Dufour, Françoise Will-Lavaillant, Pierre Daix, Yve-Alain Bois, and myself.[9] Of these, Yve-Alain Bois has entered a suggestion for a possible cause for the switchover in late 1912 that transmutes Picasso's late analytic but still iconic vocabulary into those procedures in collage that must be called linguistic. He has proposed that the intervention of African sculpture, in the form of the Grebo mask that served as the trigger for Picasso's 1912 sculpture *Guitar,* was a precipitating agent to reorganize how Picasso conceived of the visual sign—reshaping it not just as arbitrary or conventional but as fully diacritical.[10]

While I have no doubt about the role of *Guitar* in the process of restructuring signaled by collage, and thus of the impetus performed by African sculpture, I think that the momentousness of this change cannot be explained as locally as that one encounter would suggest. Which is to say, it seems to me that something far more continuous and profound must have been at work in Picasso over a far longer period of time for such a change to be truly prepared for, or motivated.[11] And in this I would further say that Braque could be seen as a control case. For, since collage heralds no such change for him, in that Braque's use of collage elements never moves beyond the iconically structured sign toward the symbolic one (for example, *Still Life with a Violin,* Sorgues, autumn 1912), whatever is present in Picasso's earlier, analytical work that might have motivated the change in question, is probably what is missing from Braque's.

By all accounts Braque was a gentle and private person for whom outbursts of anger were rare. His irate response in 1935 to the *Autobiography of Alice B. Toklas,* called "Testimony against Gertrude Stein," seems, for this reason, rather significant.[12] Accusing Stein of getting various facts wrong—his example is that he never painted Marie Laurencin's portrait, as she said he did—and of not understanding French very well, Braque's major polemic is that Stein's account mistakes the collective nature of his and Picasso's cubism, which Braque calls their "search for the anonymous personality," turning it instead into gossip about a star—Picasso—and his followers. Gertrude Stein is, in fact, extremely demeaning of Braque, saying that the first manifestation of Picasso's cubism anyone was able to see in the Salons was the one Braque painted for him, and insisting that cubism was Picasso's invention alone.[13] Had Gertrude Stein not been more precise about what she thought Picasso invented, none of this could have had much resonance. But she was precise. She said that Picasso invented cubism in the Horta landscapes through the disjunction between the houses and their terrain.[14] Later she made this more specific when she said that the landscape was curved and the houses cut across the curve; and she added that the struggle that began cubism was "to express only the really visible things."[15] But she insisted in the famous sentences: "Once again Picasso in 1909 was in Spain and he brought back with him some landscapes which were, certainly were, the beginning of cubism. These three landscapes were extraordinarily realistic and all the same the beginning of cubism."[16]

No one really takes Gertrude Stein seriously in this claim that cubism began at Horta. Practically everyone follows Kahnweiler when he says, "During the summer of 1909 at Horta the new language of form was augmented but left essentially unchanged."[17] And the widely held assumption is that "the new language" is that which was formed the preceding year, most precociously by Braque at L'Estaque.[18] But I wish to dissent from this assumption and take Gertrude Stein more or less at her word, because what happens in Picasso's Horta landscapes does not follow Braque's L'Estaque paintings but generates an experience that needs to be seen as essentially different.

If we agree with William Rubin that the organization of the L'Estaque landscapes entails readjusting the open expanse of spatial projection to a tighter concept of bas-relief, one "which moves downward and outward towards the spectator from a back plane that closes the space," with the shallow, interlocking density of the relief maintained by a use of *passage* that allows "planes to spill or 'bleed' into adjacent ones,"[19] we can also agree that this same notion of relief is continued and intensified in the landscapes Braque made in the summer of 1909 at La Roche-Guyon.[20] And we can further say that the spatial conception is based on the creation of an even density of tilted and eliding planes over the whole of that uprighted ground, a kind of constant pressure of relief that indeed seems to respond to the evenly disseminated color stroke of certain late Cézannes.

This organization, however, could not be further from the case for Picasso in the summer of 1909. There, in the instance of the *Houses on the Hill, Horta de Ebro* (Horta de Ebro, summer 1909; see figure 12.1), although there is something we could call a relief plane—in the sense of what can be pointed to in Braque—it does not coincide with the shape of the canvas field, but instead takes the configuration of a diamond, or lozenge form, coming to a point at the lower front edge of the painting. Many of the house forms in the landscape are clearly oriented toward this diamond, reinforcing their own sense of upended frontality by declaring their relation to it, and of course establishing the visibility of its lozenge shape by doing so. The outward fan of the rooftop in the bottom center of the image thematizes, in a certain sense, the opening spread of the lower half of the diamond, the overall shape of which is made to read implicitly: (1) through the diagonal path at the lower left coupled with the treatment of the facade of the leftmost house—radically narrowing, as it does, from right to left, (2) through the silhouette of the land mass that slopes upward from the midpoint of the left side of the canvas to end in the house centered near the top edge of the frame, (3) through the downward cascade of roof lines that terminates in the horizontal which articulates the midpoint of the painting's right edge, and (4) least explicitly from a geometrical point of view but most convulsively from that of a normative sense of perspective, through the diagonal vector set up in the lower right by the right-hand eave of the near, central house.

I would argue that, if Picasso makes his relief plane from a lozenge rather than a rectangle it is because a lozenge yields most readily to another set of geometries that can be mapped onto it. The diamond shape, with its axes drawn in—and, within the shape's implicit perimeters, Picasso does indeed create a strong set of cross-axial vectors to indicate the internal geometry of the form, vertical plumb line transecting the horizontal transversal[21]—presents us with one of those visual puzzles with a long history in the game of spatial projection. It is a figure about which we can ask: Are we seeing a decorative object—four abutted triangular wedges—or are we looking at the four sloping sides of a pyramid? And if the latter, is this a concavity into which we stare, the receding walls of the spatial hollow in perspective diagrams; or is it a convexity, with the point of a solid projecting forward at us? Which is to say that Picasso's "relief plane" has, in its very origami-like configuring, a trick up its sleeve in the form of a set of possible, interpenetrating but conflicting readings; being, so to speak, a plane with a collapsible back. And when that back collapses, as it so very dramatically does in the great chasm of voluptuous darkness that opens—full-blown in its modeling and without any possible *passage*-like elision between the walls that channel this abyss—the experience for the viewer is precisely one of being centered exactly over the pyramid, suspended above it and looking directly down into its tip—the only orientation with regard to this shape that could produce the ambiguous reading one finds here.

When Gertrude Stein said that the houses cut across the landscape, refusing to fuse with it, might she not have been describing just this effect of radical disjunction that takes place between, on the one hand, the experience of shape—frontal, rising, parallel to picture and to plane of vision, the very stuff of what Leo Steinberg has (with a wink at James Joyce) called "the diaphane"[22]—and, on the other, the experience of something that imperiously, vertiginously beckons, something that excavates deep into both painting and landscape ground. And if it *is* depth into which we look, suspended over the houses at Horta and looking down—as over the reservoir (see *Reservoir at Horta,* Horta de Ebro, summer 1909)—that depth is connected to an angle of vision which is disjunct from the frontal rising field of the diaphane, the plane of vision. It is a depth which takes its cues from quite another zone of the sensorium, for it is a depth that occurs when the ground gives way below one's feet, a depth that is a function of touch, of the carnal extension of one's body.

This disjunction is, I would say, what Picasso took from Cézanne even more certainly than the lesson about the continuity of relief. For one of the anomalies registered again and again in Cézanne's work is that as the perceptual array swivels out of the strictly vertical field of the diaphane—the plane of vision parallel to the painter's upright regard—and, approaching the place where he stands, it slides away from the visual and into the ground that is beneath his very feet, the painter is then forced to drop his head and to look instead at the zone of his own body. The break thereby opened in his orientation to the array cannot but make the visual and the carnal disjunct within the unified system of the painting (see, for example, *Still Life with Plaster Cupid,* c. 1895, Courtauld Institute Galleries). And it is this discontinuity between vision and touch that is there to be seen in Cézanne, a caesura which, I would argue, affected Picasso, yet never really entered the problematic of Braque.[23]

One of the earliest examples of Picasso's working this disjunction, in all its absoluteness, into his art and tracking it systematically, so to speak, is the elaboration in 1907 of what Kahnweiler would refer to as "threadlike lines" of direction, those parallel striations of color that are often identified as marking Picasso's "African style." In Picasso's fascination with those marks, in his constant but varying recourse to them, we can see a comparison being made between the way parallel straight lines open onto two totally disjunct modalities of representation. In one, the system of Western illusionism, parallel hatching is the very mark of the oblique, of the swiveling of the plane from frontality into depth, and thus of the variation of shape in its changing relation to the angle of vision. In the second, parallel lines, etched permanently into their very ground, are a function of shape. The scarifications of the African body, they do not shift with the volume's variable relation to light, but endure beyond all visual contingency. Oscillating back and forth in relation to the significance of these striations—the frontal and immutable versus the oblique and contingent—and often using the two possibilities within the same image, although always carefully separating them, Picasso seems to be playing with the way one and the same set of marks can open onto two separate sensory tracks: one, a visual stratum, the other a tactile one; the first a registration of the frontality of the optical field, the diaphane, the second, the descriptor of all those kinesthetic cues upon which the perception of depth depends (see, for example, Daix, nos. 54 and 87). And in this oscillation what seems significant is this constant unraveling of what we can think of as the perceptual plenum, a disintegration of it into the unsynthesized possibility of two separate and separately marked sensory channels.

The idea of separate channels is supported by late-nineteenth-century associationist psychology in its insistence that the flat pictures formed on the surface of the retina are shapes indifferent to depth—like a trapezoid which can variously be read as a two-dimensional figure or as a square seen in perspective—to which remembered tactile cues must be coupled in order to aggregate the experience of a single perceptual whole. If Seurat welcomed such an idea, seeing in it the basis for conceptualizing a semiautonomous realm of vision within the human sensorium—two flat fields, retina and picture, mirroring each other's structure—Picasso, I would argue, found such a notion extremely disturbing. For, followed to its logical extreme, it seemed to be claiming that vision never has unmediated access to depth, that depth is something that in fact is never, directly, *seen*. And in this sense it brought Picasso to the very brink of an extreme skepticism about vision itself.

We can imagine a pencil held parallel to our plane of vision. What we see is a bar with a pointed end—a shape given to us as simple extension. If we turn the pencil ninety degrees, so that it is perpendicular to our visual plane, what we see is not the five or so inches that begins closer to our eyes at one end and terminates at the far end of the object; what we see is a point into which that distance has been compressed. The skeptical argument about depth reasons that vision registers extension only; that depth, because it is not a shape spread laterally across our visual field, is forever invisible. The mass of a given object, according to this argument, may be accessible to touch, but for a stationary viewer, it will forever remain the phantom property of a consciousness that must reconstruct it from intermediary sets of evidence. And thus without those added sets of clues or associations there is no way to distinguish—*directly,* from within the unmediated experience of vision—between the trapezoid and the square displayed in space.[24]

I would contend that it is this sense of the indeterminacy of the visual *as such* that accounts for the way the flattened, almost floating shapes of the *Houses on the Hill, Horta de Ebro* are set to rhyme with their diamond-shaped frame on the one hand, and the way the exaggerated, sensuously rendered experience of the free fall into depth is expressed as discontinuous with this diaphanic impression, on the other. I would further contend that this discontinuity led to the invention of *Still Life with Chair Caning* (see figure 12.2), in which the oval shape of the picture, bound as it is by a length of rope that can be alternately read as the ornate frame of a painting or as the carved edge of a table, creates the perfectly ambivalent experience of incompatible orientations: either the diaphanic, visual image to which one directs one's gaze from a vertical axis; or the table top as seen from above, one's body hunched physically over it.[25]

And if the sense of the withdrawal of the tactile or carnal from the specifically visual and frontal field was experienced by Picasso in the years succeeding *The Houses at Horta,* it was never, I would argue, manifested by Braque. If in Picasso's analytic cubism the cues that signal the two sensory strata—touch and sight—are kept rigorously separate, such a separation is a function of the logic driving this production, a logic erected on the premise that they are simply not transparent to one another. That such is not the case for Braque accounts for those stylistic differences that so many scholars have noted, even in the period when the work of the two is all but indistinguishable to the uninitiated. Braque's conception of structuring the picture through the mechanism of transparent planes—his particular use of *passage* to create a system of overlap in which vision and touch will be functions of the same interlocking network—can be seen in the painting he made of Sacré-Coeur in the winter of 1909–1910, where the pictorial thinking creates in everything but its palette a precedent for Delaunay's *Windows.* Picasso's painting of the same subject from the same place (*Le Sacré-Coeur,* Paris, winter 1909–1910), even though unfinished, makes clear how resistant he was to what would later come to be called "simultanism." For here we not only look straight on at the diaphanic veil of shapes, but were clearly going to be required to look downward also, to experience the gulfs between the buildings, when, from within another perceptual axis, the cityscape falls away from beneath us. Further, it is Braque's conception of the possible transparency between vision and touch that determines how, in 1911, he will handle the areas of stippling that appear in both his and Picasso's works from this time. For

Picasso—given the "logic" I've been describing—this stippling must continue to function as a cue for touch; it must in its close weave and density become an extension, no matter how truncated and transformed, of modeling. In this way, its dislocation from the planar profiles it abuts reads as an unmistakable evocation of touch wrenched apart from the planes whose obliquity it is "supposed" to define. But Braque's drive for transparency leads him to organize the analogous marks far more flatly and decoratively. Indeed, Braque's transparency, which William Rubin believes Picasso to have been imitating when he painted *The Accordionist* in the summer of 1911, is greatly enhanced by the use of stippling, to create not patches of chiaroscuro in the manner of Picasso but areas of a Seurat-like even fall of light. It is not surprising that when Picasso writes to Braque about the progress of this work, he refers to the stippling he will apply to it ("only at the end") as a "Signac-style treatment."[26]

If it is true that Picasso did indeed develop a position about the relationship between the painter and the visual array that is shaped by the deep skepticism about vision I have been describing, it seems also the case that this sense of a withdrawal of touch from the field of the visual was experienced by Picasso as a passionate relation to loss. That the carnal objecthood of the model was withdrawing progressively and that its loss was felt not as a triumph but as a kind of poignant tragedy is registered in Picasso's art of 1910 and 1911 by the way that work clings to the human figure, and not just to any set of figures but to those of his friends and lovers. One of the greatest monuments of this withdrawal is surely the portrait of Fanny Tellier (*Girl with a Mandolin [Fanny Tellier],* Paris, late spring 1910). Conceived in relation to the extremely beautiful Corots which Picasso saw exhibited in the fall of 1909 and which his enthusiasm led him to trade with Uhde (in which the dealer's portrait by Picasso was exchanged for a Corot lute player), the 1910 *Fanny Tellier* resonates with this sense of consternation at the thought that the extraordinary unity of the sensory plenum rendered with such directness and immediacy by Corot is no longer available to himself.[27] If we look at the displacement of the representation of velvety substance from the nude's breast—the very form that should normally carry it—to the empty space behind the figure, we are forced to compare a site of carnal pleasure now become merely a flattened, jagged shape hanging away from the body and a patch of "empty" space now endowed with the qualities of voluptuousness no longer imputed to the bodily form. And in the exquisite irony of that comparison we are led to experience something of the feelings that drove Picasso as he watched the outcome of his own visual convictions, as, that is, he watched depth and touch—what we could call the carnal dimensions—disappear, quite literally, from sight.[28]

It is in this sense that Picasso's declaration, made to Kahnweiler in June of 1912, that his "great love" for Eva Gouel will be transcribed into his work in the form of something "I will write in my paintings" is an extraordinarily charged statement.[29] For it to have gotten to the point that the carnal dimension—depth—is so unavailable to one of the most accomplished figure painters of his age that he must render his passion for a woman by *writing* it on his pictures is certainly one the great ironies in the history of illusionist painting.

But it is also one of the great watersheds.

In calling this essay "The Motivation of the Sign," I have been crossing what may seem like semiological and psychological wires. For, in semiological terms, the linguistic sign—registered by words like "jolie Eva" or "ma jolie"—is precisely *un*motivated, unlike the iconic sign which, in the axis of its resemblance to its referent, *is* motivated.[30] And if by the summer of 1912 Picasso has come to the point where what he most wants to represent in his work is the very thing he has no means to depict directly, that is the point from which he embarks on "writing" such a thing on his canvases. It is the place of embarcation on a journey into the exploration and invention for his art of the unmotivated sign.

This matter of motivating the sign, raised by my title, does not, then, refer to the import of the semiological turn heralded by collage. Rather, it addresses the specific set of signifieds that Picasso seems most insistently to organize in the opening years of his exploration of collage. Those signifieds—/depth/ and /atmosphere/ or /light/—are in no way random, but are prepared for, motivated if you will, by the experience of the preceding five years. It was the entire meaning of the oblique—touch, chiaroscuro, warmth, light—that the frontality of shape progressively occulted and marginalized, driving it from the field of visual representation. And it is this meaning that will now be inscribed on the pictorial surface through the medium of collage: /turning/, /luminosity/, /transparency/, /obliquity/. The motivation for the sign is in this sense understood as driven by that very carnality of Picasso's connection to painting and its subject which Leo Steinberg explored in the essay "The Philosophical Brothel."[31] It is not a biographical or psychological motivation—the love for this or that woman, or indeed for women—nor is it really a formal one. Let us call it a phenomenological motivation, a desire to articulate the most inwardly felt experience and to be able to objectify it at the level of the sign.

> On awakening I prepared to reply to Henri van Blarenberghe. But before doing it, I wanted to glance at *Le Figaro,* to proceed to this abominable and voluptuous act that is called *reading the newspaper* thanks to which all the unhappinesses and disasters of the universe during the last 24 hours, the battles that have cost the lives of 50,000 men, the crimes, the strikes, the bankruptcies, the fires, the poisonings, the suicides, the divorces, the painful residue of the emotions of the statesman and the actor, transmitted during our morning feast for our personal use to us who aren't even interested in them, excellently enter into relation, in a particularly exciting and tonic manner, with the recommended ingestion of several throatfuls of *café au lait.*
>
> —*Marcel Proust, "Pastiches et Mélanges," 1907*

Several scholars and critics have sought a set of concepts in structural linguistics to describe not only what happens in (Picasso's) collage but its import as well for something like a general history and theory of representation. Their position with regard to this collateral field is sharply different from that of historians seeking to "explain" cubism via *n*-dimensional geometry, the fourth dimension, X-ray photography, the ideas of Henri Bergson, etc.[32] In the latter cases, the contents of the neighboring field are understood as constituting what could be called a "master signified": an idea—of space-time; of science's access to transparency; of the notion of the *durée*—which the pictorial elements come to illustrate: "illustrate" always understood, here, in its iconic function, that of "picture." And indeed, were the terms set in train by structural linguistics—terms like "sign," "signifier," etc.—to be used in this way, we would once again confront the kind of iconological operation that those earlier sorties into the history of ideas produced. We would, that is, use the concept of the sign iconically, as a way of deciphering the referents schematically alluded to by various reductive marks occurring in a given work: the cascades of parallel curves to indicate the folded cloth of a sleeve; the long diagonal flanked by two tiny circles to convey the nose and eyes of a face.[33] But in so doing, we would have ceased to be alert to the distinction that operates at the heart of all modern semiologies, including structural linguistics.

This distinction, which cannot be overstressed, is the great gulf dividing the signified—the signifier's Siamese twin in semiology's structure of the sign—from the referent. The signified is a concept; the referent a (real) object. And the point of this difference is that the signifier/signified relationship means that the concept itself is not above the system that produces the sign as a component in a vast network of other signs; rather, the concept is a function of that same system, is affected by it. Which is to say that the signifier is not a label that gets affixed to a real-world object to produce a code name for that object (a bottle, say); instead, since the signifier and the signified are produced in one and the same operation, the meaning of a word is as much a function of the phonological considerations that produced its distinctions from its sonic neighbors (bottle, throttle, battle), as it is a result of perceptible differences in the field of reality (bottle, decanter, jar).

The condition of the "master signified," on the other hand, is that it is outside the system—like the positivist truths of science in the field of radiography, or *n*-dimensional geometry. This is in distinction to the structural-linguistic signified, which is never beyond the system and cannot be so. And the consequence of its inclusion is that meaning is always mediated by the system; it is inevitably, irremediably, irrevocably, processed by the system's own structural relations and conventions.

Thus the impulse toward structural linguistics, in the work of those writers who have acted upon it, is not the drive for a method for unpacking a style or a painting—for decoding it, so to speak—but is instead motivated by a wider consideration about the nature of representation.[34] That wider consideration is one of total resistance to a realist or a reflectionist view of art, namely, the idea that the painting or the text is a reflection of the reality around it, that reality enters the work of art with the directness of the image striking the mirror. And it is in view of that resistance that semiology is welcomed as a way of demonstrating how, specifically, the structure of any sign—whether word or image—always mediates the real, constructing not an object—a referent—but a signified.

There is thus a family of theories that the semiologically minded would be interested in, not just those bearing the names Saussure, Jakobson, Hjelmslev, or Martinet; and some of these theories were even developed as an attack on orthodox structural linguistics, although in that very attack they nevertheless maintained the integrity of representation as the construction of a signified, of meaning as something always-already mediated by the operations of the sign. Which of these theories one might turn to depends, it seems obvious, on the nature of a specific historical problem.

Now one of the problems that confronts the historian when looking at the onset of *papier collé* in the fall of 1912 is the particular choice of materials used as additions to the drawing sheet. For Braque to turn to *faux bois* wallpaper would seem merely an expansion of the painterly surfaces he had already been exploring in works of his analytic period (for example, *Homage to J. S. Bach,* Céret, winter 1911–1912).[35] It is thus less of a disruption than Picasso's choice, in November and December, of newsprint. A variety of reflectionist readings have been offered to explain this choice. One is a futurist-based reading that sees Picasso welcoming the antiestablishment associations of industrial and mass-cultural materials and objects, in all their noisy ephemerality.[36] Another is a realist reading that interprets the move as welcoming the possibility of directly including the artist's surroundings of café and studio within the picture.[37] A third—the most recent—argues that the newsprint was imported so that Picasso could speak, through it, of his attitudes toward anarchy and war.[38] All of these positions, which argue for the embeddedness of the collage material within the social context of the work, take a dim view of the structural-linguistic approach, seeing it as yet another formalism that turns its back on the object's content and the degree to which that content is motivated by the social field.[39]

But the formalism/social and materialist history battle was not invented yesterday. One only need glance at the debates waged in the 1920s in the Soviet Union to see the very same issues argued *and* with the same mutual lack of comprehension and intransigence on each of the opposing sides.[40] Except that in that earlier rehearsal of the argument there was a *third* position added, one enunciated by Mikhail Bakhtin, who called the field he wanted to articulate "sociological poetics."[41] In this rubric can be heard, of course, a strange oxymoron in the marriage between the very idea of a poetics—the attempt to define the laws internal to a linguistic form—and sociology's concern with the context of cultural production. But Bakhtin's conception of the study of art as a medium of social intercourse did involve such a marriage, although it began by cursing both the formalist and the Marxist theoretical houses. Although the opening sentence of his 1928 attack on formalism, called *The Formal Method in Literary Scholarship,* reads, "Literary scholarship is one branch of the study of ideologies," the book goes on to reject any simple, reflectionist view of art.[42] "There is no experience," Bakhtin wrote, "outside its embodiment in signs. From the outset, there cannot even be question of a radical qualitative difference between interior and exterior. . . . It is not experience that organizes expression, but, to the contrary, expression that organizes experience."[43] It was Bakhtin's position that expression—by which he meant the field of discourse (and indeed his whole theory was intended to elaborate what was meant by "discourse")—was the generator or constructor of meaning. And thus he wrote:

> It is unfortunate that Marxist criticism, which was called upon to battle Formalism on the essential issues and enrich itself in this

> battle, refused to meet Formalism on the real territory of the problems of constructive meaning. Most often the Marxists enlisted in the defense of content. In doing so they improperly contrasted what they were defending to the poetic construction as such. They simply evaded the problem of the constructive function of content in the structure of the work.[44]

Now if Bakhtin did agree with the formalists that meaning is constructed rather than given, with this construction an effect of the very medium of expression, he broke sharply with them about the nature of that medium. In the formalists' eyes, the medium was "language" and the master discipline to which they had recourse was linguistics: indeed, they looked to the Moscow circle of linguists within which figures like Roman Jakobson were developing a version of structural linguistics that paralleled Saussure's own. For Bakhtin, however, the medium was not "language" but discourse; the difference being that language is a logic, a set of grammatical and transformational laws that permit the reiteration of the same words or phrases in a multitude of contexts, or individual utterances, while discourse is, on the other hand, grounded precisely in the concreteness of the single utterance as a nonrepeatable event. From a study of the laws of how such utterances function, what followed for Bakhtin was that discourse's founding principle is that it is interpersonal. Which is to say, it is not—as the impersonal logic of the language model would have it—precipitated out of a set of linguistic rules; instead it is generated reactively, as one half of an already engendered dialogue. "All understanding is dialogical," Bakhtin would insist. "Understanding is in search of a counterdiscourse to the discourse of the utterer."[45] Or again he would say, "Meaning is personal: there is always within it a question, an appeal to, and an anticipation of, the answer; there are always two subjects in it (as the dialogical minimum)."[46] But in this question of the intersubjective grounding of meaning, Bakhtin would also make very clear that the subjects or persons he had in mind are not the subjects of psychological individualism; they are instead what he would call "semantic subjects," subjects formed in and through discourse, discourse as the ideological matrix, the very stuff of the social field. In his theory, no utterance is, then, originary; each is instead a reaction to what has already been said, or what the speaker knows to be already felt, believed, perceived, by his interlocutor—feelings, beliefs, perceptions, which form what could be called the horizon of reception. The speaker is always, in Bakhtin's terms, in an evaluative relation to that horizon, probing it, cajoling it, refusing it, seducing it. And it is that relationship between the values of the speaker and those of the receiver which fills every utterance with a condition that is communal and reactive. "No member of a verbal community," Bakhtin writes, "can ever find words in the language that are neutral, exempt from the aspirations and evaluations of the other, uninhabited by the other's voice. On the contrary, he receives the word by the other's voice and it remains filled with that voice. He intervenes in his own context from another context, already penetrated by the other's intentions."[47]

Jakobson	Bakhtin
context	object
sender . . . message . . . receiver	speaker . . . utterance . . . listener
contact	intertext
code	language

If we compare the famous graph by Jakobson of the communications model of structural linguistics with the graph that Bakhtin used to critique it, we will see both Bakhtin's agreement with the formalists' concentration on the means of expression and his disagreement with their ideas about meaning.[48] In the Jakobson model we could imagine linguistic exchange working something like the communication between two telegraph operators: one person has a content to transmit (what Jakobson refers to as "context"), and, encoding it with the help of a key, sends it through the air; if contact is established, the other decodes it with the same key, thus recovering the initial content. In refusing such a model, Bakhtin states, "Semiotics prefers to deal with the transmission of a readymade message by means of a readymade code, whereas, in living speech, messages are, strictly speaking, created for the first time in the process of transmission, and ultimately there is no code."[49] This is why Bakhtin replaces "message" with "utterance" and "code" with "language." But the substitution of "intertext" for "contact" needs some more elaboration. For Bakhtin, contact—or the opening of the channel between speaker and listener—cannot be a component of the system he is modeling, because it is the very medium of that system: without the shared horizon—spatial, lexical, ideological—there is no speech event. So the component must be the form of the dialogical relation—"the reaction that endows with personhood the utterance to which it reacts."[50] This is the intertext: the already given text to which one reacts and the reacting text being created.

There is another component to Bakhtin's notion of dialogism that needs very briefly to be mentioned. Since meaning involves community, in all the diversity of its members, dialogue will occur between types of irreducibly different discourses, and the utterance can therefore be riven by the confluence of different ages, professions, social classes, regional affiliations. This diversity Bakhtin called "heterology," and he saw power as always working to reduce this heterology and to instate homogeneous speech. "In modern times," Bakhtin's analysis ran, "the flourishing of the novel is always connected with the decomposition of stable verbal and ideological systems [church, absolute power] and to the reinforcement of linguistic heterology."[51] Modernity, in Bakhtin's eyes, thus runs toward a disruption of that unity, which in the field of literature he saw embodied in the form of poetry; the advanced guard of this disruption was the novel, which allowed for a plurality of voices.

Although this excursus into the history of literary-critical debate may seem somewhat digressive, I would like to suggest that, given the parameters of the interpretive conflict between so-called formalists and social historians of art, it might prove extremely useful to try to think about collage through the vehicle of Bakhtin's model. For that model holds out a way of analyzing the social context's immanence to the work of art: of seeing how the work, as a discursive event, interpolates the social not through an act of reflection, but through the medium of the intertext.

Suppose we follow Bakhtin in viewing any utterance, enlarged here to include aesthetic decisions—like the interjection of newsprint within the pictorial medium—as a response to another utterance. If we do so, it will not be possible for us to think of such a decision as a direct reflection of a material, such as newspaper, or of a theme, such as popular culture or the Balkan war, but rather as something always-already mediated by the voice, or utterance, or decision, of someone else: another speaking or acting subject for whom this issue—newspaper—counts. Now, on Picasso's horizon, there were in fact two such subjects. One of them was Guillaume Apollinaire, one of Picasso's most intimate companions from the opening years of cubism, and the incipient inventor of the calligram; and the other was Stéphane Mallarmé, the poet whose star was rising over the late nineteenth century to shine into the twentieth with the light of an austerely defined symbolist poetics. Because both of these had much to say on the subject of the newspaper, between the two of them we can trace a trajectory that might define the space within which Picasso's utterance can find its discursive specificity.

Mallarmé's position set the newspaper in opposition to the book, the precious object defended by him as the great medium of poetic truth. The newspaper's defects were various. Among them: that it presented to its reader column upon column of monotonous gray type; that its political vocation meant that it organized its contents into a hierarchy dictated by power—thus the lead article chases the advertising to a back page; and that (and this seems to be its worst offense) it confronts its reader with the monstrous amorphousness of an open, flat sheet, as distinct from the precious folds made available by the pages of a book.[52] And indeed Mallarmé's great poem *Un coup de dés,* organized as it is, so that poetic lines must be read across the gulf of the book's central fold, stands as an aesthetic reproach to this view of the crudeness of the newspaper form. Each of the three condemnations is, in fact, countered by the organization of *Un coup de dés,* in the way the typographic spacing and diversity refuse the monotony of the column of gray print; and the dispersal of the poem's title across the first eleven pages acts to interweave the master typography of the "headline" into the protracted body of the text. This protraction, or attenuation of a theme, held in a kind of musical suspension across wave after wave of poetic sound, establishes the analogies with music that Mallarmé wanted for his poetry (the relevant comparison would obviously be Debussy's similar kind of suspension of a single music chord or coloration throughout the length of a whole work). And when this temporal attenuation is finally collapsed at the end of the poem, where the title's boldface disappears from the last two pages and the poem conjures the image of the marks on the dice transposing themselves into the points of a starry constellation, this move is not meant to signal time's freezing itself into the rigid present of the page of text. Rather, it conjures the text's very transcendence of time through its ascension into the sphere of pure, disembodied concept.

To move from the universe of Mallarmé's book to the broadside of Apollinaire's calligram, "La cravate et la montre" (1914), is to observe the opposition to Mallarmé's poetics that had been building over the years that separate 1897 from 1914. The temporality of the calligram is not that precious distention over page upon page of sound, but instead the insistent presentness of a single page within which the watch ticks off a kind of percussive cycle of numbers—*mon coeur* is "one," *les yeux* marks "two," *l'enfant* is "three," *la main* is "five," and so forth.[53] Indeed, the poem is about the specificity of its temporal present, speaking as it does of the poet, Apollinaire (whose point of view is represented by the watch), and his friend, Serge Férat, personified in the necktie, who sit around a café table waiting for noon to strike so they can go in to lunch, with the poem's climax reading in the physical center of the page in the words, "it's 5 to 12 at last / and everything will be over."[54] Apollinaire, glorying in the very flatness of the page that Mallarmé had despised, clearly believes that the typographic revolution, already at work in the pages of the newspaper and on the surfaces of billboards and advertisements, has loosened up the sheet of print, allowing many different voices to enter, creating in fact a cacophony of tones and speakers. The space of the poem, which is also the circle of the café table physicalized by the page of the calligram in 1914, had already been mapped by the conversation poem called "Les Fenêtres," which Apollinaire wrote for a Delaunay exhibition catalogue in December 1912. There, sitting around a table, Apollinaire spoke the opening line, "From red to green, all the yellow fades," whereupon his friend René Dupuy supplied a second one by saying, "When the macaws sing in their native forests," to which André Billy added, "there's a poem to write on the bird with only one wing." The next line, which Billy added in recognition of Apollinaire's anxiety over the lateness of his text was then, "We'll send it by telephonic message."[55]

That the calligram could capture this immediacy and heteroglossia of conversation in the flat presentness of the single page, and that the newspaper itself offers a model for such a congeries of events, seems to be Apollinaire's position by the time he composed "La cravate et la montre." Indeed, as early as "Zone," the poem he wrote in the autumn of 1912 at the very moment Picasso was deciding to place newsprint inside the space of the collage, Apollinaire was declaring:

> You read the handbills, catalogues, posters that sing out loud and
> clear—
> That's the morning's poetry, and for prose there are the
> newspapers,
> There are tabloids lurid with police reports,
> Portraits of the great and a thousand assorted stories.[56]

If we now turn to that question of Picasso's decision which we are trying to track here, we might see that its inaugural gesture, the collage *Un coup de thé,* registers his decision precisely as a dialogic event—just as Bakhtin would have predicted. One of the earliest of the newsprint *papier collés,* this work punningly signals a field skewered to the surface by a headline that slyly summons forth *Un coup de dés,* in what is perhaps an ironic echo.[57] Mallarmé had thrown down the gauntlet and Apollinaire had picked it up; and collage, too, now responds to the notion of the newspaper as a medium—or *the* medium—of modernity itself. But though the Bakhtinian model encourages us to see Picasso's decision as totally mediated by the issues formulated in the terms of the Mallarmé/Apollinaire axis, the model leaves it entirely open as to which end of that axis Picasso himself supports; the dialogical response can, of course, be either a refutation or an identification.

Now, I would argue that for us to understand the specificity of Picasso's utterance—within the intertextual world of this debate—we need to do two things: to trust our eyes about how the newsprint actually looks in this first bout of Picasso's use of it; and to understand something about Picasso's attitude toward Apollinaire's embrace of the newspaper, so enthusiastically proclaimed in "Zone."

If we do the second one first, the following facts are relevant. Apollinaire's conversion to what could be called a futurist repertory of images—including the newspaper—was extremely sudden. In fact, in February of 1912 when Apollinaire reviewed the first futurist exhibition in Paris, he was rather cool to the movement—a reserve that reflected the fact that he had gone to the exhibition with Picasso and was influenced by the painter's distain for futurism's expressionist aspirations.[58] But that summer Apollinaire received what could be called a "shock of the new," delivered to him by Blaise Cendrars, an unknown poet just arrived in Paris who sent Apollinaire his poem "Pâques à New York." It was in the light of Cendrars's embrace of both the passion and the brutality of the new metropolis that Apollinaire, about to publish his own collected poetry under the projected title *Eau de vie,* suddenly realized the *arrière-garde,* lingering symbolist quality of his own work. "Zone," which he immediately set to writing and which appeared in his book as its first, explosive statement, is in fact something of a rewriting of "Pâques à New York" just as *Alcools,* the title Apollinaire would use for his book, is a revision of the much more symbolist "Eau de vie," undertaken at the suggestion of Cendrars, who had a kind of genius for these punchy futurist titles (as *Kodak,* the title of a subsequent book of his, suggests).[59] If the shock of the new catapulted Apollinaire into the newspaper as a poetic space—Cendrars's own "Transsiberian [Express]" celebrates this columnar organization by early 1913—it also changed Apollinaire's mind completely about the value of futurism as an artistic movement. Siding with Marinetti about questions of futurist poetics, Apollinaire wrote a manifesto for the journal *Lacerba* in the summer of 1913, in which he says "merde" to certain things and distributes roses to others, prominently the futurist idea of "words in freedom." And with his declaration that the adjective should be suppressed in poetry, Apollinaire gives his assent in this little broadside to Marinetti's specific attack on Mallarmé's poetics, the kind of attack that appears, for example, in the manifesto "Destruction of Syntax—Imagination without Strings—Words-in-Freedom," where Marinetti writes, "I oppose Mallarmé's choice language, his search for the unique, irreplaceable, exquisite adjective . . . [his] static ideal."[60]

But this support for futurism could not have seemed a very happy turn of events for Picasso, bringing with it as it did not only a refutation of Picasso's own aesthetic distrust of the movement but also, and closer to home, a sudden onrush of enthusiasm by Apollinaire for all those artists who had been outside the charmed circle of Picasso, Braque, and their poet-supporters. Suddenly, in late 1912, Apollinaire was living with the Delaunays, running around Paris with Léger to look at the urban iconography of billboards and street signs, and worst of all delivering, in October 1912 at the Section d'Or exhibition, a lecture called "The Dismemberment of Cubism." Having said, "Possibly it is too late to speak of Cubism. The time for experimentation is passed. Our young artists are interested now in creating definitive works," Apollinaire's praise in his lecture for Delaunay, Léger, Duchamp, and Picabia, could not have pleased Picasso.[61]

That Picasso would not have welcomed the futurism suddenly taken up by Apollinaire—who was to rebaptize it "l'esprit nouveau"—is something we might suspect at a personal level; but it is also something that is registered in the extraordinary restraint and near austerity of his first group of collages that import newsprint into their midst (see Daix, pp. 115–121 and nos. 543–550, 552–554). In fact, looking at those collages against the cacophonous model of the futurist words in freedom, we get a sense of quite another conceptual world, one ruled by symmetry, clarity, balance, indeed the very kind of austere harmonics that we would associate not with Apollinaire's position on the horizon we've been sketching, but in fact with Mallarmé's.

The suggestion that arises from the discursive space I have been filling in would lead one to conclude, I believe, that in late 1912 newsprint had initially to be recuperated by Picasso from a world of futurist abandon to which he himself was extremely hostile. Yet recuperation means here not simply siding with Mallarmé's condemnation of the newspaper, but showing that the newspaper can, to the contrary, be made to yield—for the new art—the very qualities Mallarmé condemned it for lacking. Thus without jettisoning its flatness and its columnar monotony, Picasso deploys newsprint to create, at the level of the sign, those precious aesthetic possibilities that Mallarmé had insisted were the exclusive prerogative of the book: the capacity to figure forth the fold as that metaphysical "turning" of the page that opens the work of art onto the abyss or chasm of meaning; and the ability to transmute the gray drone of the marks on the page into the very sign or constellation for light.

The intertext reveals, I think, the pressures on Picasso to embrace the materials that were now heralded by his friend Apollinaire and by many others around him as the very stuff of *l'esprit nouveau.* But it also helps us see that Picasso's very first embrace was so tremendously qualified as almost to appear a kind of rejection, as this material is reworked into what could be called a poetics of the sign. If Cendrars's slogan had become "poetry is in the streets," Picasso's response, in these incredibly balanced and patrician works, seems to be "yes, it *is* in the streets, but what we must do is to make clear the sense that what is *there* is revealed to us at the level of poetry." Thus, if at this moment Picasso's *Violin* sounds the notes of Apollinaire's "Zone," it does so by reminding his friend of the aesthetic rigor and pleasure of the transformational operations of the fold. The opening of the dialogue, at this moment in November to December 1912, is not the necktie and the pocket watch but "un coup de thé." The dialogue will continue from there and become much, much more complex. And perhaps Bakhtin can help us with this burgeoning complexity; but that is for a future discussion.

Who Comes after the Subject?

The title of this essay is borrowed from Eduardo Cadava's canny reminder of the vicissitudes through which the very concept of a subject-of-consciousness has gone since the 1960s.[1] Because authorship represents the heightened achievements of such a subject—the marshaling and mastering of intentions toward meaning and implication; the projection onto a work of that special unity and consistency that is the correlative of the continuity and coherence of selfhood—the status of authorship was vulnerable to attack by the advance guard of the poststructuralist critique of the centered subject, mounted throughout the 1960s.

The most notorious of these onslaughts was surely Roland Barthes's essay "The Death of the Author" (1968), essentially a promissory note for the magnificent study *S/Z* (1970), in which Barthes would demonstrate what he meant by that "birth of the reader" to which "the death of the author" would give rise. "A text," he explained, "is made of multiple writings, drawn from many cultures and entering into mutual relations of dialogue, parody, contestation, but there is one place where this multiplicity is focused and that place is the reader, not, as was hitherto said, the author. The reader is the space on which all the quotations that make up a writing are inscribed without any of them being lost; a text's unity lies not in its origin but in its destination."[2]

First published in Charles Salas, ed., *The Life and the Work: Art and Biography* (Los Angeles: Getty Research Institute, 2007).

In 1971, in "From Work to Text," Barthes underscored the implications of the death of the author: if the unity of the work could no longer be secured by its point of origin, it must be sought in the contrapuntal pleasures of its reception—in a burgeoning nexus that Barthes now baptized "text."

Having thus dispatched the "author," Barthes did not abandon the writers he had learned to love but continued to explore what he now called "the pleasure of the text," linking that pleasure to "the amicable return of the author." "Of course," he cautions, "the author who returns is not the one identified by our institutions (history and courses in literature, philosophy, church discourse); he is not even the biographical hero. The author who leaves his text and comes into our life has no unity; he is a mere plural of 'charms,' the site of a few tenuous details, yet the source of vivid novelistic glimmerings, a discontinuous chant of amiabilities, in which we nevertheless read death more certainly than in the epic of a fate; he is not a person he is a body."[3]

To elaborate this idea of "charms," Barthes writes:

> What I get from Sade's life is not the spectacle, albeit grandiose, of a man oppressed by an entire society because of his passion, it is not the solemn contemplation of a fate, it is, *inter alia,* that Provençal way in which Sade says "milli" (mademoiselle) Rousset, or milli Henriette, or milli Lépinai, it is his white muff when he accosts Rose Keller, his last games with the Charenton linen seller (in her case, I am enchanted by the linens); what I get from Fourier's life is his liking for *mirlitons* (little Parisian spice cakes), his belated sympathy for lesbians, his death among the flowerpots; what I get from Loyola's life are not the saint's pilgrimages, visions, mortifications, and constitutions, but only his "beautiful eyes, always filled with tears." For if, through a twisted dialectic, the Text, destroyer of all subject, contains a subject to love, that subject is dispersed, somewhat like the ashes we strew into the wind after death (the theme of the *urn* and the *stone,* strong closed objects, instructors of fate, will be contrasted with the *bursts* of memory, the erosion that leaves

> nothing but a few furrows of past life): were I a writer, and dead, how I would love it if my life, through the pains of some friendly and detached biographer, were to reduce itself to a few details, a few preferences, a few inflections, let us say: to "biographemes," whose distinction and mobility might go beyond any fate and come to touch, like Epicurean atoms, some future body, destined to the same dispersion; a marked life, in sum, as Proust succeeded in writing his in his work.[4]

One year later, Michel Foucault presented "What Is an Author?" to the Collège de France as a response to the outcry against the way he had manhandled proper names in *The Order of Things* (1969). Spinning various corpuses of work into the threads of complex fabrics he called *épistémês,* Foucault had woven together Georges Cuvier, Charles Darwin, Georges Buffon, and Carolus Linnaeus into what were decried as "monstrous families."[5]

Beginning his discussion in "What Is an Author?" with the historical conditions that gave rise to the figure of the author, Foucault asked his listeners to remember the time when most texts were anonymous and the names of their authors were invoked merely as what he called "the index of truthfulness," as when it is written: "Hippocrates said . . ." With the development of copyright law in the eighteenth century, authorship took on a juridical status and the author was institutionalized as a way of handling no-longer-anonymous texts. Authorship was now invoked "as a standard level of quality," "as a certain field of conceptual or theoretical coherence," as a form of "stylistic uniformity," and "as a definite historical figure in which a series of events converge."[6]

The author, thus constructed, Foucault concludes, is "a function of discourse,"[7] making authorship the linchpin of the organization of knowledge into separate branches or disciplines. Foucault's decision to telescope the idea of an academic discipline into the term "discourse" is related to the operations on that term mounted by the structuralist linguist Émile Benveniste, who preached the strict division of expository language into what he called "narrative," on the one hand, and "discourse," on the other. "Narrative," the term for neutral transmissions of information, such as history or biography, is marked, Benveniste pointed out, by the use of third-person pronouns and the special historical past tense, the preterite.[8] "Discourse," referring to live interchange, engages the first- and second-person pronouns and the present tense. For Foucault, the events of May 1968 enforced the special trauma of a collapse of this neat distinction, as the police were summoned into the Sorbonne at the invitation of the university's administration (something that had not happened since the Middle Ages) and the careful decorum of the university was imploded. As a consequence, discourses—whether in the form of the police interrogation or the university exam—were suddenly understood to be *disciplinary.* This was the source of Foucault's decision to organize the promulgation of knowledge (discourse) around the imposition of power (discipline). Authorship, he concludes in "What Is an Author?" is a function of disciplinary order: "The name of an author serves as a means of classification," he wrote. "The name of the author remains at the contours of texts—separating one from the other, defining their form, and characterizing their mode of existence; it does not move from the interior of a discourse to the real person outside who produced it."[9]

With these two conceptual markers—*text* and *function*—poststructuralism consolidated its moves against the biographical, empirical person of the author. Any account of this must, however, appear enigmatically arbitrary without a sense of the strong impact of Martin Heidegger's thought on French philosophy in the interwar period and of Heidegger's own assault on the legitimacy of the post-Enlightenment idea of the centered subject.[10] In Heidegger's view in "The Age of the World Picture," the source of this disruption in the concept of the subject lay in the mistranslation of the Greek word for substance—*hypokeimenon*—into the Latin word *subiectum* (subject), or relational center, with the result that man becomes the only being upon which all that is, is grounded, as regards the manner of its Being and its Truth.[11] Understanding himself as such a subject, man sets up his representations as a form of objectification: phenomena are made visible by being seen within the perspective of a ground plan, which is projected in advance, "mathematically" (as in the geometrical projection of perspective that maps out the ground plan, which Heidegger calls *Grundriss*).[12]

Organized on such a ground plan, the phenomena are grasped as a picture, such that, as Heidegger says: "The word 'picture' [*Bild*] now means the structured image [*Gebild*] that is the creature of man's producing which represents and sets before."[13]

It is in his slightly later essay, "The Question Concerning Technology" (1955), that one first finds an explanation of the malign connotations of the idea of *Gebild,* which in the analysis of technology will reappear as *Gestell,* another variant of the idea of picture, or *Gestalt.* Having decided that technology is a way of revealing, Heidegger defines it as a kind of challenging-forth that is also a storing-up, as in the way the dam on a river makes it possible to store up energy in order to call upon it later. Such storing up Heidegger calls "standing reserve," or *Bestand,* the transformatory potential of which will turn everything within its purview into a stock part, a cog in the machine of standing reserve. In addition to this reification of nature, Heidegger argues, as the administrator of the standing reserve, man himself becomes standing reserve. Further, since *Bestand* implies orderability and substitutability, objects will necessarily lose their autonomy. The system that gathers things together as standing reserve Heidegger calls *Gestell,* or enframing, and he ties this concept back to the idea of the world projected onto the ground plan and thus grasped as reified picture.

If the enframing operations of *Gestell* represent a challenging forth, which falls upon and insults objects, the opposite can be said of the poetic operations of *Gestalt,* or bringing forth, which reveal the object's connection to its projection-plan in terms Heidegger calls "rift-design" (a simultaneous distinction and connection of object and ground).

The paired opposition between *Gestell* and *Gestalt* reappears in Michael Fried's important essay "Art and Objecthood" (1967), the Heideggerian overtones of which are easy to trace and key this discussion not only to contemporary aesthetic production but also to contemporary scholarship. "Art and Objecthood" turns on the opposition between the linked terms *presence* and *presentness,* the former connected to something like the Heideggerian *Gestell* and the latter to *Gestalt.* For Fried, *presence,* like *stage presence,* is a form of gesturing to and playing for the members of an audience such that they are turned into the subjects of the inert and self-aggrandizing objects of what Fried condemns as "literalist" art (minimalism). *Presentness* counters this in ways cognate with the idea of *Gestalt: "At every moment the work itself is wholly manifest,"* Fried writes, in a "continuous and entire presentness, amounting, as it were, to the perpetual creation of itself, that one experiences as a kind of *instantaneousness*: as though if only one were infinitely more acute, a single, infinitely brief instant would be long enough to see everything, to experience the work in all its depth and fullness, to be forever convinced by it."[14]

A brief digression is needed here to open Fried's condemnation of minimalism to question, or at least to detach it from the Heideggerian parallel I have been setting up. Heidegger associates *Gestalt* with poiesis, and thus the saving destiny of art, because the contour of a form (which he also calls "rift-design") brings its context into relief, making a *socius* appear.[15] Fried's instantaneousness, by contrast, eclipses this *socius,* driving the context into permanent obscurity: Indeed, it is only minimalism (think here of Donald Judd, Robert Morris, Carl Andre, and Robert Smithson), with its demand that the viewer circulate around the object, that brings the world, or context of the object, back into experience, producing a basis for the collectivity of communal perception.

To return for a moment to "Art and Objecthood," we can see that Fried's project is at one and the same time to destroy the subject-of-presence and restore the subject-of-presentness, the viewer who, seeing everything, is able, in Fried's terms, "to experience the work in all its depth and fullness." Fried thus realizes in this essay what Barthes had called the "twisted dialectic" of the Text, as this "destroyer of all subjects" nonetheless "contains a subject to love," one that is "dispersed, somewhat like the ashes we strew into the wind after death."[16]

It is not Text, however, that is currently resurrecting the biographical subject for contemporary scholarship; rather, it is the "twisted dialectic" called trauma that is presently doing this job.

To grasp the logic of this particular set of reversals through which trauma defeats Text and resurrects the author, we must review Freud's elementary lesson on trauma from "Beyond the Pleasure Principle" (1920), in which trauma befalls a subject who was unfortunately absent—too distracted or decentered to defend him- or herself properly at the time of attack. The life story of the traumatic subject is thus the account of a fundamental absence and lack of preparation. Because of this, trauma studies is addicted to biography, which is to say, to the reconstruction of decentering and the shattering that is its result. Shoshana Felman has become the Oprah Winfrey of trauma studies; her book *Testimony* (coauthored with Dori Laub in 1992) is one account after another of the immobilization of the trauma victim, as in Paul de Man's experience of the impossibility of witnessing, Albert Camus's depiction of suicide in *The Fall,* and Walter Benjamin's suicide.[17]

For some years it has seemed that the taste for trauma would never abate and that the Shoah Business would go on forever. But trauma has mutated recently, and the form of biographical scholarship will undoubtedly run in this new direction. The latest guise of trauma studies is multiple personality disorder: a burgeoning of subjects at the site of infantile traumas. Ian Hacking's *Rewriting the Soul* (1995) is an early investigation of what the jacket copy describes as this "hot topic."[18] Reading Hacking's book makes it clear that if "who comes after the subject" is a multiple personality, nothing will restore the concept of identity, of the centered, autonomous subject, immediately present to himself, that has served us for many centuries.

Preface to *The Neutral*

As Barthes had promised in the lecture with which he inaugurated his assumption of the Chair of Literary Semiology at the Collège de France, he would pursue a "phantasmic teaching," one based on the "comings and goings of desire, which [the teacher] endlessly presents and represents. I sincerely believe," he continued, "that at the origins of teaching such as this we must always locate a fantasy, which can vary from year to year."[1]

But the fantasy on which Barthes's penultimate course "Le Neutre" is based did not "vary from year to year"; it held steady, rather, over the trajectory that took him from *Writing Degree Zero,* with the zero degree an early version of "le neutre," through all the rest of his books.

Perhaps its most touching statement is to be found in *Roland Barthes by Roland Barthes,* where Barthes traces his mature commitment to this domain back to the impulses of his early childhood, so that even while playing a version of tag in the Luxembourg Gardens, his inclination was to neutralize the exercise of power which rules an opponent "out":

> When I used to play prisoner's base in the Luxembourg, what I liked best was not provoking the other team and boldly exposing myself to their right to take me prisoner; what I liked best was to

First published in Roland Barthes, *The Neutral,* trans. Rosalind E. Krauss and Denis Hollier (New York: Columbia University Press, 2005).

> free the prisoners—the effect of which was to put both teams back into circulation: the game started over again at zero. In the great game of the powers of speech, we also play prisoner's base: one language has only temporary rights over another; all it takes is for a third language to appear from the ranks for the assailant to be forced to retreat: in the conflict of rhetorics, the victory never goes to any but the *third language*. The task of this language is to release the prisoners: to scatter the signified, the catechisms.[2]

Indeed, Barthes was obsessed by "the great game of the powers of speech," a cathexis that impelled his interest in semiology's analysis of these same powers. His image of the prisoners highlights his sense of language's coerciveness, something his lecture went so far as to call "the fascism of language."[3] For language always demands a choice, an identification of gender, of person, of desire for one or the other of two opposed values—the oppositions that structural linguistics terms "binaries," and semiology calls "paradigms." It was the position of Ferdinand de Saussure, founder of structural linguistics, that meaning itself is generated by the friction of one binary element against the other, to form the fundamental oppositions that leave the unchosen pole implicit within any speech act. Such oppositions could be white vs. black (the "versus" abbreviated by "/"), high/low, hot/cold, or in a later study by Barthes himself: *S/Z*. Barthes laments the suffering he felt at the hands of this demand for choice: "by its very structure my language implies an inevitable relation of alienation."[4] Alienating or not, however, Barthes recounts his commitment, indeed his "joy" over binaries in *Roland Barthes*:

> For a certain time, he went into raptures over binarism; binarism became for him a kind of erotic object. This idea seemed to him inexhaustible, he could never exploit it enough. That one might say everything *with only one difference* produced a kind of joy in him, a continuous astonishment.

> Since intellectual things resemble erotic ones, in binarism what delighted him was a figure. Later on he would find this (identical) figure again, in the opposition of values. What (in him) would deflect semiology was from the first the pleasure principle: a semiology which has renounced binarism no longer concerns him at all.[5]

The major binary, Male / Female, carries us to the problem of how to translate Barthes's title: should it be "The Neuter" (the third term between the genders) or "The Neutral" (which is how Barthes's most effective translator, Richard Howard, renders it in *Roland Barthes*)?[6] What Barthes himself designates as the sexual basis of the third term in the various disciplines to which he refers in his preliminary presentation (for example the drones among bees) would lead one to "neuter." But Barthes also uses the domain of international law (and Switzerland) as a basis, in relation to which only "neutral" makes sense. Furthermore, the structural linguistics of Barthes's generation, that of the Prague School, and Hjelmslev, and Greimas, in particular, was fascinated by the phonetic fact of "neutralization," which is the annihilation of opposition between sounds within certain languages: for example, the difference between *d* and *t* at the ends of words in German (with *hund* pronounced as *hunt*) or the difference between *d* and *t* in English after *s* (as in the case of *still,* which is pronounced *sdill*).

Since "neuter" is more transgressive, I was tempted to choose it; but "neutral" seemed far more apt because it has the broadest implication within structural linguistics and relates to Barthes's contempt for what he calls "The Critique Ni-ni,"[7] and in *Le Neutre,* "niniisme" (neither-norism), referring to the neutrality assumed by journalists committed to telling both sides of any story. Additionally, for structural linguistics, "neutralization" explains the action of sublation or the transcendence of difference.

In this course, Barthes calls the constancy of his commitment to a "third language" his "desire for neutral," and in *Roland Barthes,* he presents it as his dream of an "exemption from meaning":

> Evidently he dreams of a world which would be *exempt from meaning* (as one is from military service). This began with *Writing Degree Zero,* in which is imagined "the absence of every sign"; subsequently, a thousand affirmations incidental to this dream (apropos of the avant-garde text, of Japan, of music, of the alexandrine, etc.).
>
> Curious that in public opinion, precisely, there should be a version of this dream; *Doxa,* too, has no love for meaning, which in its eyes makes the mistake of conferring upon life a kind of infinite intelligibility (which cannot be determined, arrested): it counters the invasion of meaning by the *concrete*; the concrete is what is supposed to resist meaning.
>
> Yet for him, it is not a question of recovering a pre-meaning, an origin of the world, of life, of facts, anterior to meaning, but rather to imagine a post-meaning: one must traverse, as though the length of an initiactic way, the whole meaning, in order to be able to extenuate it, to exempt it. Whence a double tactic: against *Doxa,* one must come out in favor of meaning, for meaning is the product of History, not of Nature; but against Science (paranoiac discourse) one must maintain the utopia of suppressed meaning.[8]

In his lecture, Barthes returns to literature from semiology to speak of it as the practice that has access to a kind of outwitting of language's power play:

> For the text is the very outcropping of speech, and it is within speech that speech must be fought, led astray—not by the message of which it is the instrument, but by the play of words of which it is the theater. . . . The forces of freedom which are in literature depend not on the writer's civil person, nor on his political commitment—for he is, after all, only a man among others—nor do they even depend on the doctrinal content of his work, but rather on the labor of displacement he brings to bear upon the language.[9]

This raises one more knot within the flow of translation, for Barthes's idea of leading language "astray" is consistently expressed by the verb *déjouer,* which in its literal rendering as "outplay," or "outsmart," stays within the idea of language itself as a play of power. Barthes first takes up *déjouer* as a figure in his analysis of Georges Bataille's essay on the big toe, where Richard Howard translates it as "baffle," which I find both precise and economical and have adopted for the most part here.[10] Since the word relates to the field of play, Howard also uses "fake," as in "fake out." "Outwit" or "thwart" could also serve. Barthes's argument is that the big toe baffles the paradigm noble/ignoble and is thus a foretaste of his idea of the Neutral.[11]

Notes

Introduction

1. See my "Notes on the Index," in *The Originality of the Avant-Garde and Other Modernist Myths* (Cambridge, Mass.: MIT Press, 1985).

Video: The Aesthetics of Narcissism

1. The frequent use by Michael Fried of the idea of "acknowledgment" in his critical work depends on and recognizes Stanley Cavell's essay "Knowing and Acknowledging," in *Must We Mean What We Say?* (New York: Scribner's, 1969).

2. More recently, see Anne Wagner, "Performance, Video, and the Rhetoric of Presence," *October,* no. 91 (Winter 2000), for a contestation of this view.

3. For example, this completely erroneous equation allows Max Kozloff to write that narcissism is "the emotional correlate of the intellectual basis behind self-reflexive modern art." See Kozloff, "Pygmalion Reversed," *Artforum* 14 (November 1975), p. 37.

4. Sigmund Freud, *A General Introduction to Psychoanalysis,* trans. Joan Riviere (New York: Permabooks, 1953), p. 427.

5. Freud's pessimism about the prospects of treating the narcissistic character is based on his experience of the narcissist's inherent inability to enter into the analytic situation:

"Experience shows that persons suffering from the narcissistic neuroses have no capacity for transference, or only insufficient remnants of it. They turn from the physician, not in hostility, but in indifference. Therefore they are not to be influenced by him; what he says leaves them cold, makes no impression on them, and therefore the process of cure which can be carried through with others, the revivification of the pathogenic conflict and the overcoming of the resistance due to the repressions, cannot be effected with them. They remain as they are." Ibid., p. 455.

6. Jacques Lacan, *The Language of the Self,* trans. Anthony Wilden (New York: Delta, 1968), p. 11.

7. Explaining this frustration, Lacan points to the fact that even when "the subject makes himself an object by striking a pose before the mirror, he could not possibly be satisfied with it, since even if he achieved his most perfect likeness in that image, it would still be the pleasure of the other that he would cause to be recognized in it." Ibid., p. 12.

8. Ibid., p. 100. Although *moi* translates as "ego," Wilden has presumably retained the French here in order to suggest the relationship between the different orders of the self by the implicit contrast between *moi* and *je.*

9. See my "Rauschenberg and the Materialized Image," *Artforum* 13 (December 1974).

Fat Chance

1. Joan Simon, "Breaking the Silence," interview with Bruce Nauman, *Art in America* 76 (September 1988), p. 143.

2. In *Camera Lucida* Barthes says, "I wanted to learn at all costs what Photography was 'in itself.' . . . I wasn't sure that Photography existed, that it had a 'genius' of its own." Roland Barthes, *Camera Lucida,* trans. Richard Howard (New York: Hill and Wang, 1981), p. 3.

3. Rosalind E. Krauss, "Sculpture in the Expanded Field," in *The Originality of the Avant-Garde and Other Modernist Myths* (Cambridge, Mass.: MIT Press, 1985).

4. See my "Paul Sharits: Stop Time," *Artforum* 11 (April 1973). Also see Annette Michelson, "Toward Snow," *Artforum* 9 (June 1971), as cited in P. Adams Sitney, *Visionary Film: The American Avant-Garde* (New York: Oxford University Press, 1974).

5. Fredric Jameson, in "Video," *Postmodernism, or, The Cultural Logic of Late Capitalism* (Durham: Duke University Press, 1991), p. 70.

6. Stanley Cavell, "The Fact of Television," in John Hanhardt, ed., *Video Culture: A Critical Investigation* (Layton, Utah: Peregrine Smith, 1986).

7. Samuel Weber, "Television, Set, and Screen," in *Mass Mediauras: Form, Technics, Media* (Stanford: Stanford University Press, 1996), pp. 109–110.

Lip Sync: Marclay Not Nauman

1. Stanley Cavell, *The World Viewed* (Cambridge, Mass.: Harvard University Press, 1979), p. 104.

2. Michael Fried, in Hal Foster, ed., *Discussions in Contemporary Culture,* no. 1 (Seattle: Bay Press, 1987), p. 73.

3. Annette Michelson, "From a Magician into an Epistemologist," *Artforum* 9 (February 1971). In this fundamental essay on Dziga Vertov's *The Man with a Movie Camera,* Michelson tracks Vertov's obsession with reverse narrative, as finished products are shown reverting to the raw conditions from which their process toward refinement had proceeded.

4. I am referring to artists such as James Coleman, whose technical support is the slide tape, more currently embodied in the technology that underwrites 'PowerPoint; and William Kentridge, who exploits (and develops brilliantly) the support of animation. See my "'The Rock': William Kentridge's Drawings for Projection," reprinted in this volume; and "Reinventing the Medium," *Critical Inquiry* 25 (Winter 1999).

"Specific" Objects

1. Joseph Kosuth, "Art after Philosophy I and II," in Gregory Battcock, ed., *Idea Art* (New York: Dutton, 1973), p. 82; first published in *Studio International* (October–November 1969). And see Thierry de Duve, *Kant after Duchamp* (Cambridge, Mass.: MIT Press, 1996), p. 245.

2. Donald Judd, "Specific Objects," in *Complete Writings 1959–1975* (Halifax: Press of the Nova Scotia College of Art and Design, 1975), p. 181.

3. Ibid., p. 184.

4. Thierry de Duve, "The Monochrome and the Blank Canvas," in *Kant after Duchamp* (Cambridge, Mass.: MIT Press, 1996), pp. 230ff.

5. Edward Ruscha, *Leave Any Information at the Signal: Writings, Interviews, Bits, Pages,* ed. Alexandra Schwartz (Cambridge, Mass.: MIT Press, 2002), pp. 30, 32.

6. Ibid., p. 213.

7. Ibid., p. 322.

8. Ibid., p. 232.

9. Stanley Cavell, *The World Viewed* (New York: Viking Press, 1971), pp. 101–118.

10. See Stanley Cavell, "Music Discomposed," in *Must We Mean What We Say?* (New York: Scribner's, 1969), p. 200.

"The Rock": William Kentridge's Drawings for Projection

1. Written in 1982 as a direct response to the persecution of Václav Havel, to whom it is dedicated, *Catastrophe* uses the protagonist's appearance—the whitened face and gray pajamas—to call up the image of concentration camp inmates, while it mobilizes the atmosphere of total control to refer to Stalinism. When critics described the meaning of the protagonist's final gesture as "ambiguous," Beckett complained in response, "There's no ambiguity there at all. He's saying 'you bastards, you haven't finished me yet.'" (See Fintan O'Toole, "The Political Pinter," *New York Review of Books,* October 7, 1999, p. 6.)

2. In Carolyn Christov-Bakargiev, *William Kentridge* (Brussels: Palais des Beaux-Arts, 1998), p. 75; hereafter cited in the text as WK.

3. Although Kentridge speaks of using a Bolex (WK 61), he now employs a slightly more sophisticated version of the same kind of 16mm camera, an Ariflex. He has explained that he does not embrace this by-now-primitive film equipment in the same spirit as he depicts the outmoded telephones and teletype machines in his films. Rather, these simple cameras make it far more easy to shoot one, or perhaps two, frames at a time than any more technologically complex camera, whether 35mm or video.

4. I am retaining Kentridge's name for this type of coffeepot, even though French *cafetière* actually makes coffee by the drip method, not with a plunger.

5. See, for example, Elisabeth Lebovici, "Kentridge, l'art de la gomme," *Libération,* July 20, 1999, p. 25.

6. For my discussion of James Coleman's "invention" of a medium, see "'. . . And Then Turn Away?' An Essay on James Coleman," *October,* no. 81 (Summer 1997); and "Reinventing the Medium," *Critical Inquiry* 25 (Winter 1999).

7. Stanley Cavell, *The World Viewed,* enlarged ed. (Cambridge, Mass.: Harvard University Press, 1979), p. 104; hereafter cited in the text as WV.

8. Stanley Cavell, "Music Discomposed," in *Must We Mean What We Say?* (New York: Scribner's, 1969), p. 201.

9. See my "Reinventing the Medium," and *A Voyage on the North Sea: Art in the Age of the Post-medium Condition* (London: Thames & Hudson, 1999).

10. Both Cavell and Kentridge have recourse to the example of language's dependence on habit and unconscious reflexes to ballast their concepts of automatism and *fortuna.* Kentridge's references to language have been cited above; Cavell's can found in a remark such as "[A medium] provides, one might say, particular ways to get through to someone, to make sense; in art, they are forms, like forms of speech" (WV 32).

11. Cavell wrote about cartoons in 1974 in an essay addressing his critics that was added to the expanded edition of *The World Viewed.* He was thus framing his ideas about animation in terms of his own lack of awareness of the radical restructuring of the technique with the advent of video and computers. Thus, while his remarks about traditional CEL animation, as practiced by Hollywood studios and received by mass audiences well into the 1960s, are entirely relevant to the issues of animation as a medium, they don't address the historical fate of the medium that was even then appearing on the horizon. See section 6, below.

12. See Roland Barthes, "The Third Meaning," in *Image, Music, Text,* trans. Stephen Heath (New York: Hill and Wang, 1977). For the relationship between Barthes's third meaning and Coleman's use of the photo-novel for his own medium, see my "'. . . And Then Turn Away?'," pp. 12–13, 20–23.

13. *Eisenstein on Disney,* ed. Jay Leyda (Calcutta: Seagull Books, 1986), p. 21.

14. Ibid., p. 39.

15. Ibid., p. 35.

16. Walter Benjamin also took note of the weightlessness of the Disney figures: "There appears as a redemption [from the endless complications of the everyday] an existence which at every turn is self-sufficient in the most simple and simultaneously most comfortable way, in which a car does not weigh more than a straw-hat and the fruit on the tree grows round as fast as a hot-air balloon." Cited in Miriam Hansen, "Of Mice and Ducks: Benjamin and Adorno on Disney," *South Atlantic Quarterly* 92 (January 1993), p. 42; hereafter cited in the text as OMD.

17. In "The Illusion of Illusion," Keith Bradfoot and Rex Butler make this very point: "But the attempt at an ideological reading and an understanding of animation as a reified reflection of consumer society ultimately collapses for Eisenstein. This is because with animation it is impossible for the spectator to achieve the necessary distance required for critique, or inversely, for ideology, to operate. There can be no critique of the representation of capital in animation for the simple reason that animation itself is the presentation of capital." They broaden this to Deleuze's theorization of film: "With regard to cinema, Deleuze proposes that money is the obverse side of the time-image, but in animation money is the image itself. This perhaps explains why cartoon characters are the true Icons of the twentieth century . . . for in a certain sense any cartoon character is the incarnation of the ethereal spirit of the media." Bradfoot and Butler, "The Illusion of Illusion," in Alan Cholodenko, ed., *The Illusion of Life: Essays on Animation* (Sydney: Power Institute of Fine Arts, 1991), p. 272.

18. Gilles Deleuze, *Cinema 1: The Movement-Image,* trans. Hugh Tomlinson and Barbara Habberjam (Minneapolis: University of Minnesota Press, 1986), p. 4.

19. Ibid., p. 5.

20. Bradfoot and Butler, "Illusion of Illusion," p. 286.

21. Louis Hjelmslev, *Prolegomena to a Theory of Language,* trans. Francis Whitfield (Madison: University of Wisconsin Press, 1969).

22. Benjamin H. D. Buchloh, "Raymond Pettibon: Return to Disorder and Disfiguration," in Ann Temkin and Hamza Walker, eds., *Raymond Pettibon: A Reader* (Philadelphia: Philadelphia Museum of Art, 1998), p. 230.

23. Ibid., pp. 231, 232.

24. The complexity becomes clear as one listens to different accounts of the Truth and Reconciliation Commission's organization of personal memory into testimony. Kentridge himself reports: "One by one witnesses come and have their half hour to tell their story, pause, weep, be comforted by professional comforters who sit at the table with them. The stories are harrowing, spellbinding. The audience sit at the edge of their seats listening to every word. This is exemplary civic theater" (WK 125–126). Okwui Enwezor, on the other hand, applauding Kentridge's film *Ubu Tells the Truth,* dismisses these performances before the TRC as the "farcical and lengthy process of testimonies" (WK 189).

25. Walter Benjamin, "The Work of Art in the Age of Mechanical Reproduction," in *Illuminations,* trans. Harry Zohn (New York: Schocken Books, 1969), p. 236.

26. Theodor Adorno, letter to Walter Benjamin, March 18, 1936, in *Aesthetics and Politics* (London: New Left Books, 1977), p. 123.

27. In the 1920s and 1930s, Hollywood animators worked on transparent layers of celluloid, hence the term "CEL animation." This allowed the minute changes in a character's posture to be registered without the need to redraw the entirety of the background each time. It was, one could say, a primitive form of digital graphics.

28. Chuck Jones, "What's Up, Down Under? Chuck Jones Talks at *The Illusion of Life* Conference," in Cholodenko, *The Illusion of Life,* p. 64.

29. In his discussion of the weightless, disembodied condition of cartoons, Cavell adds, "In cartoons, sexuality is apt to be either epicene [either intersexual or asexual] or caricatured. I suppose this is because cartoons, being fleshless, do not veer toward the pornographic, although given a chance, they may naturally veer toward the obscene." "More of the World Viewed," in WV 172.

30. Miriam Hansen, "Benjamin and Cinema: Not a One-Way Street," *Critical Inquiry* 25 (Winter 1999), p. 343.

31. Ibid., p. 325.

32. See Friedrich Kittler, *Discourse Networks 1800/1900,* trans. Michael Metteer (Stanford: Stanford University Press, 1990); and Norbert Bolz, *Theorie der neuen Medien* (Munich: Raben Verlag, 1990).

33. Norbert Bolz, "Die Zukunft der Zeichen: Invasion des Digitalen in die Bilderwelt des Films," in Ernst Karpf, Doron Kiesel, and Karsten Visarius, eds., *Im Spiegelkabinett der Illusionen* (Marburg: Schüren, 1996), p. 57, as cited in Hansen, "Benjamin and Cinema," p. 343.

34. The relevant texts are Walter Benjamin, "A Small History of Photography," in *One-Way Street, and Other Writings,* trans. Edmund Jephcott and Kingsley Shorter (London: New Left Books, 1979); and Walter Benjamin, "Lettre parisienne (no. 2): Peinture et photographie," in *Sur l'art et la photographie,* ed. Christophe Jouanlanne (Paris: Carré 1997), p. 79.

35. See my "Reinventing the Medium," pp. 289–305. Susan Buck-Morss develops this issue in her important book *The Dialectics of Seeing: Walter Benjamin and the Arcades Project* (Cambridge, Mass.: MIT Press, 1989); see, for example, pp. 245, 293.

36. In relation to the contemporary predilection for nostalgia forms, Fredric Jameson argues that the historical past is beyond anything but aesthetic retrieval: "the attempt to appropriate a missing past is now refracted through fashion change." But he argues that a postmodernist "nostalgia" art language is incompatible with genuine historicity. Adding that in these filmic tropes, "The past is offered up mythically" through style (in Roland Barthes's use of the notion of myth), a given film will thus be redolent with 1950s-ness or 1940s-ness. Furthermore, he adds, "This mesmerizing new esthetic mode is a symptom of the waning of our historicity, of our lived possibility of experiencing history in some active way." Fredric Jameson, "The Cultural Logic of Late Capitalism," in *Postmodernism* (Durham: Duke University Press, 1984), pp. 19–21.

Allusion and Illusion in Donald Judd

1. Barbara Rose, "ABC Art," *Art in America* 53 (October–November 1965).

2. Ibid.

3. Ibid.

4. Maurice Merleau-Ponty, "Metaphysics and the Novel," in *Sense and Non-sense* (Evanston, Ill.: Northwestern University Press, 1964).

5. Rose, "ABC Art."

6. Rudolf Wittkower, "Brunelleschi and Proportion in Perspective," *Journal of the Warburg and Courtauld Institutes* 16 (1953), p. 275. In this connection Panofsky writes: "from the point of view of the Renaissance, mathematical perspective was not only a guarantee of correctness but also, and perhaps even more so, a guarantee of aesthetic perfection" (Panofsky, *The Codex Huygens and Leonardo da Vinci's Art Theory* [1940], quoted in Wittkower, p. 275).

7. Maurice Merleau-Ponty, "Cézanne's Doubt," in *Sense and Non-sense.*

8. Maurice Merleau-Ponty, *The Primacy of Perception* (Evanston, Ill.: Northwestern University Press, 1964).

9. See Michael Fried, *Three American Painters* (Cambridge, Mass.: Fogg Museum, Harvard University, 1965), and "Noland and Caro," *Lugano Review* 3 (1965).

The White Care of Our Canvas

1. Walter Benjamin, "The Storyteller, Reflections on the Works of Nikolai Leskov," in *Illuminations,* trans. Harry Zohn (New York: Schocken Books, 1969), p. 84.

2. Retort, *Afflicted Powers: Capital and Spectacle in a New Age of War* (London: Verso, 2005); T. J. Clark, *The Sight of Death: An Experiment in Art Writing* (New Haven: Yale University Press, 2006).

3. "T. J. Clark with Kathryn Tuma," *Brooklyn Rail,* November 2006.

4. Ibid.

5. Ibid.

6. Ibid.

7. Raymond Williams, *Television: Technology and Cultural Form* (London: Fontana, 1977), pp. 78–118.

A View of Modernism

1. Clement Greenberg, "Complaints of an Art Critic," *Artforum* 6 (October 1967), p. 39; reprinted in *The Collected Essays and Criticism,* ed. John O'Brian, vol. 4 (Chicago: University of Chicago Press, 1993), p. 269.

2. Michael Fried, *Three American Painters* (Cambridge, Mass.: Fogg Museum, Harvard University, 1965), p. 39; reprinted in *Art and Objecthood* (Chicago: University of Chicago Press, 1998).

3. In Barbara Rose, ed., *Readings in American Art, 1900–1975* (New York: Praeger, 1975), p. 128.

4. Alain Robbe-Grillet, *For a New Novel: Essays on Fiction* (New York: Grove Press, 1965), p. 32.

5. Ibid., p. 18.

6. Michael Fried, "Art and Objecthood," *Artforum* 5 (Summer 1967), p. 20.

7. Fried, *Three American Painters,* p. 46.

8. Fried, "Art and Objecthood," p. 22.

9. See my essay "Pictorial Space and the Question of Documentary," *Artforum* 10 (November 1971).

10. Writing, "It is the overcoming of theater which modernist sensibility finds most exalting and which it experiences as the hallmark of high art in our time. There is, however, one art which, by its very nature, *escapes* theater entirely—the movies," Michael Fried sees the automatic nature of film's escape as an impediment to its achieving the status of a modernist art. (Fried, "Art and Objecthood," p. 21.) One modernist has dealt with film: the philosopher Stanley Cavell, in his book *The World Viewed* (New York: Viking Press, 1971). But in a work dealing in part with the history of film culture, Professor Cavell manages to omit any references to Russian film of the 1920s, and in the other part dealing with modernism in cinema, he ignores experimental film entirely, speaks pejoratively of Godard, and presents Bergman and Antonioni as leading modernists.

11. Clement Greenberg, "The Necessity of Formalism," *New Literary History* 3 (1971–1972), p. 174.

12. Greenberg, "Complaints of an Art Critic," p. 39 (*The Collected Essays and Criticism,* 4:269–270).

The Cubist Epoch

1. See for example Guillaume Apollinaire, "Modern Painting" (1913), and Albert Gleizes and Jean Metzinger, "Cubism" (1912). With variations, this is the position of Apollinaire, Gleizes, Metzinger, Raynal, Allard, Hourcade, Rivière, and Salmon.

2. Reverdy and Kahnweiler spoke in the 1910s of the way cubism had transformed the painting into a self-referential and self-postulative *tableau-objet*. Greenberg's 1959 essay "Collage" (in *Art and Culture* [Boston: Beacon Press, 1961]) more strictly qualifies this notion. Rosenblum's interpretations of synthetic cubist pictures seem to reintegrate Greenberg's position with that of Kahnweiler.

3. Annette Michelson, *Robert Morris* (Washington: Corcoran Gallery of Art, 1970), p. 63.

4. Berkeley raises this issue in the 1709 *Essay towards a New Theory of Vision*; Merleau-Ponty discusses it in *The Phenomenology of Perception* in the chapter "Space." In a 1912 essay, "Conception and Vision" published in *Gil Blas,* Maurice Raynal refers to Berkeley's position. See Edward Fry, ed., *Cubism* (New York: McGraw-Hill, 1966), p. 94.

Michel, Bataille et Moi

1. André Breton, *Surrealism and Painting* (New York: Harper and Row, 1975), p. 36.

2. Jacques Dupin, *Miro* (Paris: Flammarion, 1961), p. 145.

3. Joan Miró, *Selected Writings and Interviews,* ed. Margit Rowell (Boston: G. K. Hall, 1986), p. 87.

4. Michel Leiris, "Joan Miro," *Documents* 1, no. 4 (1929), p. 264.

5. Ibid.

6. Roland Barthes, "The Metaphor of the Eye," in *Critical Essays,* trans. Richard Howard (Evanston: Northwestern University Press, 1972), pp. 240–242.

7. Georges Bataille, "L'esprit moderne et le jeu des transpositions," *Documents* 2, no. 8 (1930).

8. Georges Bataille, "The Big Toe," in *Visions of Excess: Selected Writings, 1927–1939,* ed. Allan Stoekl (Minneapolis: University of Minnesota Press, 1985), p. 23.

9. Leiris, "Joan Miro," p. 263.

10. Ibid., p. 266.

11. Denis Hollier, "The Use Value of the Impossible," in *Absent without Leave,* trans. Catherine Porter (Cambridge, Mass.: Harvard University Press, 1997), p. 131.

12. See Émile Benveniste, *Problems in General Linguistics* (Coral Gables: University of Miami Press, 1971), pp. 197–199.

13. Miró, *Selected Writings and Interviews,* p. 86.

14. Dupin, *Miro,* pp. 191, 198.

15. Ibid.

16. Georges Bataille, "Joan Miro: Peintures récentes," *Documents* 2, no. 7 (1930), p. 399.

17. Dupin, *Miro,* p. 191.

18. Carolyn Lanchner, *Joan Miró* (New York: Museum of Modern Art, 1993), p. 56.

19. Ibid., p. 57.

GIOVANNI ANSELMO: MATTER AND MONOCHROME

1. Germano Celant, "Arte povera—Im spazio," 1967, reprinted in Carolyn Christov-Bakargiev, ed., *Arte Povera* (London: Phaidon, 1994), p. 221.

2. Jerzy Grotowski, "Towards a Poor Theatre," 1965, reprinted in Christov-Bakargiev, *Arte Povera,* p. 213.

3. The notion of "purity" comes from Clement Greenberg's essay "Modernist Painting," where he speaks of the self-critical task of the artist to establish the fundamentals of the medium in which he or she works: "The task of self-criticism became to eliminate from the specific effects of each art any and every effect that might conceivably be borrowed from or

by the medium of any other art. Thus would each art be rendered 'pure,' and in its 'purity" find the guarantee of its standards of quality as well as of its independence." (Greenberg, *The Collected Essays and Criticism,* ed. John O'Brian, vol. 4 [Chicago: University of Chicago Press, 1993], p. 86.)

4. Harald Szeeman, "Zur Ausstellung," in *Live in Your Head: When Attitudes Become Form* (Bern: Kunsthalle Bern, 1969); reprinted in Christov-Bakargiev, *Arte Povera,* p. 225.

5. Germano Celant, "Art Povera: Notes for a Guerrilla War" (1967), reprinted in Christov-Bakargiev, *Arte Povera,* p. 194; emphasis added.

6. Georges Bataille, *The Accursed Share,* as cited in Daniel Soutif, "The Act of Power or Suspended Time" (1985), reprinted in Christov-Bakargiev, *Arte Povera,* p. 235.

7. Ibid., p. 30 (emphasis mine).

8. Ibid., pp. 30, 10.

9. Giovanni Anselmo, "Nel 1966 . . . ," *Data,* no. 2 (February 1972): reprinted in Christov-Bakargiev, *Arte Povera,* p. 235.

10. Szeemann, "Zur Ausstellung," p. 225. He answers his own question: "Certainly, for most of the artists shown here, Duchamp's preferred working method, the intensity of Pollock's gestures . . . "

11. Georges Bataille, *The Accursed Share,* trans. Robert Hurley (New York: Zone Books, 1988), chap. 5. I am grateful to Jaleh Mansoor, whose dissertation first brought together the Marshall Plan and the monochrome: "Marshall Plan Modernism: The Matrix of Fifties Abstraction" (Ph.D. diss., Columbia University, New York, 2006).

12. Bataille, *The Accursed Share,* p. 21.

13. Umberto Eco, *The Open Work* (1962), excerpt reprinted in Christov-Bakargiev, *Arte Povera,* p. 212.

The Latin Class

1. Heiner Bastian, *Cy Twombly: Paintings 1952–1976,* vol. 1 (Berlin: Propyläen Verlag, 1978), p. 48.

2. Roland Barthes, *The Responsibility of Forms,* trans. Richard Howard (Berkeley: University of California Press, 1985), p. 162.

3. Ibid., p. 180.

4. Ibid. For the basis of Duchamp's eventual development of painting as a form of pictorial nominalism, see Thierry de Duve, *Pictorial Nominalism: On Marcel Duchamp's Passage from Painting to the Readymade,* trans. Dana Polan (Minneapolis: University of Minnesota Press, 1991).

In his "Signature/Event/Context" (in *Margins of Philosophy,* trans. Alan Bass [Chicago: University of Chicago Press, 1982]), Jacques Derrida addresses the concept of the "performative" as developed by J. L. Austin in *How to Do Things with Words* (New York: Oxford University Press, 1962). The performative is an utterance that executes the action it pronounces, such as a judge's "I sentence you to five years in jail."

5. Bastian, *Cy Twombly,* p. 41.

6. Roberta Smith, "The Great Mediator," in Harald Szeemann, ed., *Cy Twombly* (Munich: Prestel Verlag, 1987), pp. 20, 17.

7. See my *The Optical Unconscious* (Cambridge, Mass.: MIT Press, 1993), pp. 256–265.

8. Robert Motherwell, *Notes on Cy Twombly,* exh. cat. (Chicago: Seven Stairs Gallery, 1951).

9. [David Hare], "Communication," *Art News* 66 (December 1967), pp. 8–10. This note, written as a contribution to the two-part "Jackson Pollock: An Artist's Symposium" (*Art News* 66 [April and May 1967]), was published in the above, belated and semi-anonymous form, since it was a violent attack on Robert Motherwell's accounts of the history of abstract expressionism, triggered by Motherwell's own narrative about his relations with Pollock in "Part One" of the symposium. The "Humbert Humbert" remark addresses Motherwell's repeated attempts to claim priority to the various inventions of the period (Hare calls this his "I-diddled-it-first" routine). Hare's indignation is fired by what he points to as Motherwell's outright lies: "Often Motherwell simply states that he was editor of *VVV.*" About the Pollock account, Hare asks: "Why not let Jackson Pollock alone on the floor? Why pretend he got down there with him? . . . In his *Art News* piece on Pollock, Motherwell states 'Pollock, like myself, was painting on the floor in the early 'forties.' The wording is arranged to give the impression that Pollock was following in Motherwell's footsteps. In actuality, Jackson could

not have painted in any other way.While considering the kind of work Robert was doing, it would have been totally unnecessary for him to paint on the floor." This document, which was called to my attention by Lee Krasner, deserves to be more widely known than it is.

10. Barthes, *The Responsibility of Forms,* p. 187.

11. Bastian, *Cy Twombly,* p. 48.

LINE AS LANGUAGE

1. Sol LeWitt, "On Wall Drawings," in *Sol LeWitt* (The Hague: Gemeentemuseum, 1970), p. 61.

2. Harold Rosenberg, "The American Action Painters," *Artnews* 51 (December 1952), pp. 23, 48; reprinted in *The Tradition of the New* (New York: Horizon Press, 1959).

3. Rudolf Carnap describes the protocol language: "In general, every statement in any person's protocol language would have sense for that person alone. . . . Even when the same words and sentences occur in various protocol languages, their sense would be different, they could not even be compared. Every protocol language could therefore be applied only solipsistically: there would be no intersubjective protocol language. This is the consequence obtained by consistent adherence to the usual view and terminology." Cited by A. J. Ayer, who points out that Carnap rejects this view: Ayer, "Can There Be a Private Language?" in George Pitcher, ed., *Wittgenstein* (New York: Doubleday, 1966), pp. 253–254.

4. The reason I have been stressing that *Target* represents a "reading" of the readymade that is particular to Johns (but not only to him) is that the more widely held view of *Fountain* is 180 degrees different from the one I have been describing. That view relates the readymade to the question of intention and goes as follows: the finished work of art is the result of a process of forming, or making, or creating. It is in a sense the proof that such a process has gone on, just as a footprint in soft ground is proof that someone has passed by. The work of art is thus the index of an act of creation that has at its roots the intention to make the work. "Intention" here is understood as some kind of prior mental event that we cannot see but for which the work now serves as testimony that it occurred. It is a common enough reading of the readymades that they represent or hypostatize pure intention—that since the objects in question were not fabricated by the artist but merely chosen by him, the arthood of the object

is seen as residing solely in its capacity to register that decision, to render it up, as it were, into the physical world. Through this reading, *Fountain* operates as an *expression* of Duchamp's intention to make a work.

5. Whether or not this idea is now a "commonplace," its author is Michael Fried in his *Three American Painters* (1965), reprinted in *Art and Objecthood* (Chicago: University of Chicago Press, 1998), p. 252.

6. Ludwig Wittgenstein, *The Blue Book* (New York: Harper and Row, 1960), pp. 39–42.

7. Jean Piaget, *Structuralism* (London: Routledge and Kegan Paul, 1971), p. 91.

8. Ibid., p. 140.

9. Maurice Merleau-Ponty, *Phenomenology of Perception* (London: Routledge and Kegan Paul, 1962), p. xii.

10. Ibid.

11. Marcia Tucker, *Robert Morris* (New York: Whitney Museum of American Art, 1970), p. 25.

12. Describing the problem of the meaning of depth, Merleau-Ponty writes, "When I look at a road which sweeps before me towards the horizon, I must not say either that the sides of the road are given to me as convergent or that they are given to me as parallel: they are *parallel in depth.* The perspective appearance is not posited, but neither is the parallelism. *I am engrossed in the road itself,* and I cling to it through its virtual distortion, and depth is this intention itself which posits neither the perspective projection of the road, nor the 'real' road" (*Phenomenology of Perception,* p. 261).

13. When these pieces were first exhibited in 1967, they were in fact rearranged every day by the artist into different configurations.

14. Ludwig Wittgenstein, *On Certainty* (New York: J. J. Harper, 1969), par. 125.

15. Parts of the argument of this essay were published in my article "Sense and Sensibility," *Artforum* 12 (November 1973), pp. 43–53.

The Motivation of the Sign

1. Pierre Daix and Joan Rosselet, *Picasso, the Cubist Years, 1907–1916: A Catalogue Raisonné of the Paintings and Related Works,* trans. Dorothy S. Blair (Boston: New York Graphic Society, 1979).

2. Hermann von Helmholtz summarized the positions of his *Treatise on Physiological Optics* (1866) in a popular lecture in 1867, "The Recent Progress of the Theory of Vision," in which he uses the term "unconscious inference" to describe the mechanism of association necessary to elaborate the empirical theory of vision (which "assumes that none of our sensations give us anything more than 'signs' for external objects and movements, and that we can only learn how to interpret these signs by means of experience and practice"). See *Helmholtz on Perception,* ed. Richard M. Warren and Roslyn P. Warren (New York: John Wiley and Sons, 1968), pp. 99ff. For an assessment of associationism, see Jean-Paul Sartre, *Imagination: A Psychological Critique,* trans. Forrest Williams (Ann Arbor: University of Michigan Press, 1972), pp. 19–36.

3. For a definition of "paradigm" as a structuralist concept, as well as for a basic introduction to the field of semiology, see Roland Barthes, *Elements of Semiology,* trans. Annette Lavers and Colin Smith (New York: Hill and Wang, 1967), pp. 58–88. Barthes's *The Fashion System* (trans. Matthew Ward and Richard Howard [New York: Hill and Wang, 1983]) is a full-scale attempt to articulate a paradigmatic network. More playfully, Barthes later describes the paradigm by means of the Argonauts' vessel, "each piece of which the Argonauts gradually replaced, so that they ended with an entirely new ship, without having to alter either its name or its form. This ship *Argo* is highly useful: it affords the allegory of an eminently structural object, created not by genius, inspiration, determination, evolution, but by two modest actions (which cannot be caught up in any mystique of creation): *substitution* (one part replaces another, as in a paradigm) and *nomination* (the name is in no way linked to the stability of the parts): by dint of combinations made within one and the same name, nothing is left of the *origin*: *Argo* is an object with no other cause than its name, with no other identity that its form." *Roland Barthes by Roland Barthes,* trans. Richard Howard (New York: Hill and Wang, 1977), p. 46.

4. For the semiological classification of signs, see Barthes, *Elements of Semiology,* pp. 35–38.

5. Semantics uses brackets as the notational convention for indicating the signified of a sign, as in /depth/.

6. Saussure writes, "In language there are only differences. Even more important: a difference generally implies positive terms between which the difference is set up; but in language there are only differences *without positive terms*"; or again, "putting it another way, *language is a form and not a substance*." Ferdinand de Saussure, *Course in General Linguistics,* trans. Wade Baskin (New York: McGraw-Hill, 1966), pp. 120, 122.

7. Structural linguistics uses the phonetic term "diacritical" to refer to its fundamental notion of system as the result of paired oppositions. This derives from Saussure's discussions of phonology in which the idea of a sound as such, *p* say, is rejected in favor of a concept of sound already operating in systematic opposition, for example, the voiced *p* of "put" in contradistinction to the unvoiced *p* of "up." A brilliant treatment of the systematicity of sound is Joel Fineman's "The Structure of Allegorical Desire," *October,* no. 12 (Spring 1980), 47–66.

8. That Picasso uses the collage elements to render passages of drawing—of modeling and of orthogonal marks reminiscent of perspective—superfluous needs to be made explicit. The formal rhyming, for example between the silhouette of the violin's scroll and the newspaper shape that cups it, saps the description of its illusionistic import, something that the "found" contour of the white paper on which the violin's neck is drawn constitutes as another such device. Similarly, the implacable visual parallelism between the two newsprint segments—their existence on the absoluteness of the flat surface—drains the orthogonal lines (for example the ones moving between the left and right segments) of their capacity to organize convincing foreshortening.

9. See Pierre Dufour, "Actualité du cubisme," *Critique,* nos. 267–258 (August–September 1969), pp. 809–825; Jean Laude, "Picasso et Braque, 1910–1914: La Transformation des signes," in *Le Cubisme* (Université de Saint-Etienne: C.I.E.R.E.C., Travaux IV, 1973), pp. 7–28; Françoise Will-Lavaillant, "La Lettre dans la peinture cubiste," in *Le Cubisme;* Daix, *Picasso, the Cubist Years;* Rosalind Krauss, "Re-Presenting Picasso," *Art in America* 68 (December 1980), pp. 90–96; and "In the Name of Picasso," *October,* no. 16 (Spring 1981), pp. 5–22, reprinted in Krauss, *The Originality of the Avant-Garde and Other Modernist Myths* (Cambridge, Mass.: MIT Press, 1985); and Yve-Alain Bois, "Kahnweiler's Lesson," *Representations,* no. 18 (Spring 1987), pp. 33–68, reprinted in his *Painting as Model* (Cambridge, Mass.: MIT Press, 1990).

Leo Steinberg's "The Intelligence of Picasso," though never published, is a lecture that he began to give in the spring of 1974 (at the American Academy in Rome and at the Grand Palais in Paris) and has continued to transform ever since (I heard it in 1978 at

Columbia University). Using concepts from Saussure as well as from linguistics and rhetoric generally, the lecture in part analyzes the significance for Picasso's early cubism of the difference between the analog sign (continuously traced from its referent) and the arbitrary, linguistic one.

10. See Bois, "Kahnweiler's Lesson," pp. 52–55.

11. See Yve-Alain Bois, "The Semiology of Cubism," in Zelevansky, *Picasso and Braque: A Symposium,* p. 177.

12. Georges Braque, "Testimony against Gertrude Stein," in Marilyn McCully, ed., *A Picasso Anthology: Documents, Criticism, Reminiscences* (London: Thames and Hudson, 1981), p. 84.

13. Gertrude Stein, *The Autobiography of Alice B. Toklas* (1933; New York: Vintage Books, 1961), p. 64.

14. Ibid., p. 90.

15. Gertrude Stein, *Picasso* (Boston: Beacon, 1959), pp. 15, 24. First published in French (Paris: Librairie Floury, 1938).

16. Ibid., p. 8.

17. Daniel-Henry Kahnweiler, *The Rise of Cubism,* trans. Henry Aronson (New York: Wittenborn, 1949), p. 8.

18. The fullest argument for the pioneering status of Braque's L'Estaque landscapes is given in William Rubin, "Cézannisme and the Beginnings of Cubism," in *Cézanne: The Late Work* (New York: Museum of Modern Art, 1977), pp. 151–202. The grounds for this claim were subsequently opened to question and critique by Leo Steinberg in "Resisting Cézanne: Picasso's *Three Women,*" *Art in America* 66 (November–December 1978), and "The Polemical Part," *Art in America* 67 (March–April 1979), with a response from Rubin ("Pablo and Georges and Leo and Bill") in the same issue. It was not, of course, Kahnweiler's position that cubism began in the 1908 landscapes; he had placed its origins in the right side of the *Demoiselles d'Avignon.*

19. Rubin, "Cézannisme and the Beginnings of Cubism," p. 165.

20. Ibid., p. 193.

21. Given the configuration of the lozenge, ◇ its internal axes are established by Picasso through the vectors set up by the linear elements within the array of the houses. The vertical axis is postulated through the ridge lines of the roofs of the two central houses (the one that intersects the bottom edge of the canvas at the center of that edge, and the one located immediately behind this first); the horizontal axis is indicated by roof lines located just behind this second house to its right and left.

22. See Leo Steinberg, "The Philosophical Brothel," *October,* no. 44 (Spring 1988), p. 60. James Joyce writes: "Ineluctable modality of the visible: at least that if not more, thought through my eyes. Signatures of all things I am here to read, seaspawn and seawrack, the nearing tide, that rusty boot. Snotgreen, bluesilver, rust: coloured signs. Limits of the diaphane." Joyce, *Ulysses* (New York: Vintage Books, 1961), p. 37.

23. To such a generalization about Braque, William Rubin has objected that a painting like *Harbor* (Le Havre and Paris, autumn–winter 1908–1909, p. 113) displays the same break between the foreground boats, which are seen from above, and the far houses, which rise vertically. My answer would be that though there is such a disjunction in this painting, it is a function of the subject matter and as such is an anomaly in the artist's production. Indeed, faced a few months later with a similar theme (*Harbor in Normandy* [Le Havre and Paris, May–June 1909], p. 126), Braque specifically avoids such an interruption and preserves the continuous parallelism of the representational surface with the plane of vision.

24. This paragraph is taken directly from my first attempt to sketch this notion of the role of sensory disjunction in the development of Picasso's work: "The Cubist Epoch," *Artforum* 9 (February 1971), p. 32, reprinted in this volume. There I tried to bolster the role of a skepticism with regard to vision by using Maurice Raynal's reference to Berkeleyan skepticism in his 1912 "Conception and Vision," reprinted in Edward Fry, ed., *Cubism* (New York: McGraw-Hill, 1966), p. 94.

25. This is the argument I developed in "The Cubist Epoch." It has been expanded by Christine Poggi in her chapter "Frames of Reference: *Table* and *Tableau* in Picasso's Collages and Constructions," in *In Defiance of Painting: Cubism, Futurism, and the Invention of Collage* (New Haven: Yale University Press, 1992), pp. 58–88.

26. Cited by Judith Cousins in the "Documentary Chronology" of William Rubin, *Picasso and Braque: Pioneering Cubism* (New York: Museum of Modern Art, 1989), p. 376.

27. Pierre Daix speaks of the importance of Corot for this work, in *Journal du cubisme* (Geneva: Skira, n.d.), pp. 54–55.

28. Leo Steinberg writes, "Picasso, the boy wonder, had always known how to make objects look three-dimensional and how to breathe in the space between. Such magic feats were the routine of competent students in every accredited school of art. Picasso now [in 1908] asks—and with a gathering momentum of innocence—how this thing which everyone knows how to do can be done at all." Steinberg, "Picasso's Sleepwatchers," in *Other Criteria* (New York: Oxford University Press, 1972), p. 95. The problematic of depth, that is, of foreshortening, of turning in space, of the oblique, and the implications of this for the *backs* of objects, has been a constant subject of Steinberg's work on Picasso.

29. Cousins, "Documentary Chronology," p. 395.

30. For Saussure's discussion of the arbitrariness or unmotivated character of the sign, see *Course in General Linguistics,* pp. 111–122. See as well Barthes, *Elements of Semiology,* pp. 50–51. Section 25 ("The Vestimentary Sign") of Barthes's *The Fashion System* contains a subsection headed "The Motivation of the Sign," from which my own title is drawn.

31. The culmination of Steinberg's analysis of Picasso's *Demoiselles d'Avignon* reads, "The space of the *Demoiselles* is a space peculiar to Picasso's imagination. Not a visual continuum, but an interior apprehended on the model of touch and stretch, a nest known by intermittent palpation, or by reaching and rolling, by extending one's self within it. Though presented symbolically to the mere sense of sight, Picasso's space insinuates total initiation, like entering a disordered bed" (Steinberg, "The Philosophical Brothel," p. 63). Steinberg's analysis has often been read as license to elaborate an erotic iconography for the painting. It would seem less an iconographic analysis, however, than a phenomenological one (see my "Editorial Note," *October,* no. 44 [Spring 1988], p. 5).

32. See Linda Dalrymple Henerson, "A New Facet of Cubism: 'The Fourth Dimension,' and 'Non-Euclidean Geometry' Reinterpreted," *Art Quarterly* 34 (Winter 1971), pp. 410–433, expanded in her *The Fourth Dimension and Non-Euclidean Geometry in Modern Art* (Princeton: Princeton University Press, 1983). Bergson and duration enter discussions on cubism as early as Albert Gleizes and Jean Metzinger's *Du cubisme* (1912), particularly when they speak of changing "quantity into quality": translated in Robert Herbert, ed., *Modern Artists on Art* (Englewood Cliffs, N.J.: Prentice-Hall, 1964), p. 7. For later literature, see Timothy Mitchell, "Bergson, Le Bon, and Hermetic Cubism," *Journal of Aesthetics and Art Criticism* 36 (Winter

1977), pp. 175–183; and Robert Mark Antliff, "Bersgon and Cubism: A Reassessment," *Art Journal* 47 (Winter 1988), pp. 341–349. For the question of X-ray photography, see Linda Dalrymple Henderson, "X Rays and the Quest for Invisible Reality in the Art of Kupka, Duchamp, and the Cubists," *Art Journal* 47 (Winter 1988), pp. 323–340.

33. For a lengthier discussion of this point, see Bois, "The Semiology of Cubism," in Zelevansky, *Picasso and Braque: A Symposium.*

34. Limiting references here just to those of us who have written on cubism, our further concern with representation as such has led to semiological considerations of abstract art, as in Yve-Alain Bois, "Piet Mondrian, *New York City,*" *Critical Inquiry* 14 (Winter 1988), pp. 244–277, and the introduction to his *Painting as Model,* or my "Reading Jackson Pollock, Abstractly," in *The Originality of the Avant-Garde and Other Modernist Myths*, pp. 221–243.

35. As Christine Poggi argues regarding Braque's wood-grained paper, in *In Defiance of Painting,* pp. 98–105.

36. Tom Crow, "Modernism and Mass Culture in the Visual Arts," in Benjamin H. D. Buchloh, Serge Guilbaut, and David Solkin, eds., *Modernism and Modernity* (Halifax: Scotia: Press of the Nova Scotia College of Art and Design, 1983), pp. 215–264.

37. Robert Rosenblum, "Picasso and the Typography of Cubism," in Roland Penrose and John Golding, eds., *Picasso in Retrospect* (New York: Icon Editions), pp. 33–48.

38. Patricia Leighton, *Re-Ordering the Universe* (Princeton: Princeton University Press, 1989), chapter 5. This is a presentation of the material in her earlier essay, "Picasso's Collages and the Threat of War, 1912–1913," *Art Bulletin* 67 (December 1985), pp. 653–672. David Cottington's essay "What the Papers Say: Politics and Ideology in Picasso's Collages of 1921," *Art Journal* 47 (Winter 1988), pp. 350–359, insists that any literalist reading of the newspaper reports must be mediated through a conflicting social fact of the situation in which Picasso found himself in the early teens, namely, the restriction of his patronage to a small group of bourgeois collectors, and the effect this has on the thematic tenor of the collages. See as well his essay "Cubism, Aesthetics, Modernism," in Zelevansky, *Picasso and Braque: A Symposium.*

39. Leighton has been the most explicit about this. See *Re-Ordering the Universe,* p. 11; her "Editor's Statement: Revising Cubism," *Art Journal* 47 (Winter 1988), p. 273; and her attack on this essay as presented at "Picasso and Braque: A Symposium," at the Museum of Modern

Art in 1992: "Cubist Anachronisms: Ahistoricity, Cryptoformalism, and Business-as-Usual in New York," *Oxford Art Journal* 17 (1994), pp. 91–102.

40. The attack on the Russian formalist school of poetics was opened in 1924 by Trotsky in "The Formalist School of Poetry and Marxism," in his *Literature and Revolution* (Ann Arbor: University of Michigan Press, 1971).

41. The best introduction to the work of Bakhtin is Tzvetan Todorov, *Mikhail Bakhtin: The Dialogical Principle,* trans. Wlad Godzich (Minneapolis: University of Minnesota Press, 1984). Discussing Bakhtin's intervention in the debates between the formalists and the Marxist critics in the 1920s, Todorov says, "In the preface to *Problems of Dostoevsky's Work* (1929), Bakhtin indicates that his objective is to go beyond 'narrow' ideologism' as well as 'narrow formalism'; he uses almost the same phrase in the preamble to 'Discourse in the Novel': 'The guiding idea of this work is that the study of verbal art can and must overcome the breach between an abstract "formal" approach and an equally abstract "ideological" approach'" (p. 35).

42. M. M. Bakhtin and P. M. Medvedev, *The Formal Method in Literary Scholarship: A Critical Introduction to Sociological Poetics,* trans. Albert J. Wehrle (Cambridge, Mass.: Harvard University Press, 1985), p. 3.

43. V. N. Voloshinov, *Marxism and the Philosophy of Language,* trans. L. Matejka and I. R. Titunik (New York: Seminar Press, 1973), p. 101; cited by Todorov, *Mikhail Bakhtin,* p. 43.

44. Bakhtin and Medvedev, *The Formal Method in Literary Scholarship,* p. 67.

45. Voloshinov, *Marxism and the Philosophy of Language,* p. 122.

46. Bakhtin also writes, "I call meaning the *answers* to the questions. That which does not answer any question is devoid of meaning for us. . . . The answering character of meaning. Meaning always answers some questions," in Todorov, *Mikhail Bakhtin,* p. 54.

47. Mikhail Bakhtin, *Problems of Dostoevsky's Poetics,* trans. Caryl Emerson (Minneapolis: University of Minnesota Press, 1984), p. 131.

48. This analysis is based on that of Todorov, *Mikhail Bakhtin,* pp. 54–55.

49. Ibid., p. 56.

50. Bakhtin, *Dostoevsky's Poetics,* p. 246.

51. Mikhail Bakhtin, "Discourse in the Novel," in *The Dialogic Imagination,* ed. Michael Holquist, trans. Caryl Emerson and Michael Holquist (Austin: University of Texas Press, 1981), p. 182.

52. Stéphane Mallarmé, "Le Livre, instrument spirituel," in *Oeuvres complètes* (Paris: Gallimard, 1945), pp. 378–382. Christine Poggi summarizes Mallarmé's objections to the form of the newspaper in an essay that insists on a specifically futurist embrace of commercial materials (including newsprint) by Picasso, for his collages, and thus a pointed rejection of Mallarmé's symbolist position. See Poggi, "Mallarmé, Picasso, and the Newspaper as Commodity," *Yale Journal of Criticism* 1 (1987), pp. 133–151. My rather different conclusions are developed below.

53. See Tom Conley, "Lyrical Ideograms," in Denis Hollier, ed., *A New History of French Literature* (Cambridge, Mass.: Harvard University Press, 1989), pp. 847–849.

54. "Il est—[moins] 5 enfin/Et tout serra fini."

55. Francis Steegmuller, *Apollinaire, Poet among the Painters* (New York: Farrar, Straus, 1963), pp. 236–238.

56. Tu lis les prospectus les catalogues les affiches qui chantent tout haut
Voilà la poésie ce matin et pour la prose il y a les journaux
Il y a les livraisons à 25 centimes pleines d'aventure policières
Portraits des grands hommes et mille titres divers.

Guillaume Apollinaire, "Zone," in *Oeuvres poétiques,* ed. Marcel Adéma and Michel Décaudin (Paris: Gallimard, 1956), p. 39.

57. Robert Rosenblum was the first to make this connection, echoed ever since in the literature on cubism ("Picasso and the Typography of Cubism," pp. 35–36). Rosenblum was careful to include a source for Picasso's knowledge of *Un coup de dés,* which was not published in book form until 1914. It had been published, however, in the May 1897 issue of *Cosmopolis,* where most Apollinaire scholars agree the young Apollinaire would have encountered it. Since many of Apollinaire's activities (for example his position in 1908–1909 as critic on *La Phalange,* a literary review edited by the Mallarméan Jean Royère) connected him not just with symbolism in general but with the Mallarméans in particular, this youthful encounter was undoubtedly prolonged. The fame of *Un coup de dés* was such that Thibaudet's 1913

book on Mallarmé focused on its analysis. See Scott Bates, *Guillaume Apollinaire* (New York: Twayne Publishers, 1967), p. 76; Cecilly Mackworth, *Guillaume Apollinaire and the Cubist Life* (New York: Horizon Press, 1963), pp. 16, 96.

As he did in the discussion following this paper, Kirk Varnedoe—in his catalogue text for *High and Low*—objects to the overly literary cast of the idea of a reference to *Un coup de dés* by Picasso here: "Or (since Picasso's French at the time was laughable, and the chances that he had read this poem, as opposed simply to knowing its title, are slim) the strategically omitted letters may have conjured something more prosaic, associated with café consumption: a cup (*coup*[*e*]), or in slang a 'hit' or 'dose' (*coup*) of tea." Kirk Varnedoe and Adam Gopnik, *High and Low: Modern Art and Popular Culture* (New York: Museum of Modern Art, 1990), pp. 37–38. Since Varnedoe's suggestion has already been picked up and enthusiastically repeated by at least one writer (Arthur Danto, in his review of *High and Low* in the *Nation,* November 26, 1990), it seems necessary to address its probability. Simply put, *un coup de thé,* used to mean something like "a spot of tea," is impossible in French. The parallel Varnedoe is invoking is with *un coup de rouge* (a hit of red [wine]), which has very specific class and use connotations, ones in which workers slugging back a glass of wine conjure up a situation in which the physicality of *coup* (hit) is possible. Since the drinkers of *un coup de rouge* would never be caught dead drinking tea, there is no possibility of a French association between wine and tea in this expression. Instead, the literal use of *un coup de thé* would be more like someone picking up a handful of tea leaves and hurling it in someone else's face, both an improbable idea and a non-French construction. Since, throughout the decade leading up to this collage, Picasso attended the weekly poetry readings at the Closerie de Lilas, his French—although putatively "laughable"—left him nonetheless with a taste for the literary.

58. See Steegmuller, *Apollinaire,* p. 262. In *L'Intransigeant* (February 7, 1912), Apollinaire wrote of the futurists: "'The simultaneity of states of mind in the work of art: that is the intoxication of our art.' This declaration by the Italian Futurist Painters reveals both the originality and the weakness of their painting. They want to paint forms in movement, which is a perfectly legitimate aim, and at the same time, they share the mania of the majority of *pompiers* who want to depict states of mind. . . . Boccioni's best canvas is the one most directly inspired by Picasso's recent works." *Apollinaire on Art,* ed. Leroy Breunig, trans. Susan Suleiman (New York: Viking Press, 1972), p. 199.

59. For the relationship between Apollinaire and Cendrars, see Jay Bochner, *Blaise Cendrars: Discovery and Re-creation* (Toronto: University of Toronto Press, 1978), pp. 43–55. The

Apollinaire scholars are often insistent that the "Pâques à New York"/"Zone" influence ran the other way (see Bates, *Guillaume Apollinaire,* p. 182).

60. F. T. Marinetti, "Destruction of Syntax—Imagination without Strings—Words-in-Freedom" (1913), trans. in Umbro Apollonio, ed., *Futurist Manifestos* (New York: Viking Press, 1973), p. 105.

61. Steegmuller, *Apollinaire,* p. 235.

Who Comes after the Subject?

1. See Edouardo Cadava, Peter Connor, and Jean-Luc Nancy, eds., *Who Comes after the Subject?* (New York: Routledge, 1991).

2. Roland Barthes, "The Death of the Author," in *Image, Music, Text,* trans. Stephen Heath (New York: Hill and Wang, 1977), p. 148.

3. Roland Barthes, *Sade, Fourier, Loyola,* trans. Richard Miller (New York: Hill and Wang, 1976), p. 8.

4. Ibid.

5. Michel Foucault, "What Is an Author?," in *Language, Counter-Memory, Practice,* trans. Donald F. Bouchard (Ithaca: Cornell University Press, 1977), p. 114.

6. Ibid., pp. 126, 128.

7. Ibid., p. 124.

8. Émile Benveniste, "The Nature of Pronouns," in *Problems in General Linguistics,* trans. Mary Elizabeth Meek (Coral Gables: University of Miami Press, 1971), pp. 217–222.

9. Foucault, "What Is an Author?," p. 123.

10. Heidegger's impact on French philosophy is especially clear in Jacques Derrida's consideration of the subject. See Jacques Derrida, "The Double Session," in *Dissemination,* trans. Barbara Johnson (Chicago: University of Chicago Press, 1981), pp. 173–286; Jacques Derrida, "The Violence of the Letter," in *Of Grammatology,* trans. Gayatri Chakravorty Spivak (Baltimore: Johns Hopkins University Press, 1974), pp. 101–140; and Jacques Derrida, *Speech and*

Phenomena: And Other Essays on Husserl's Theory of Signs, trans. David B. Allison (Evanston: Northwestern University Press, 1973).

11. On *hypokeimenon,* see Martin Heidegger, "The Age of the World Picture," in *The Question Concerning Technology and Other Essays,* trans. William Lovitt (New York: Harper and Row, 1977), p. 128.

12. Ibid., p. 119.

13. Ibid., p. 134.

14. Michael Fried, *Art and Objecthood* (Chicago: University of Chicago Press, 1998), p. 167; italics in original.

15. In "The Age of the World Picture," p. 133, Heidegger writes: "The interweaving of these two events, which for the modern age is decisive—that the world is transformed into picture and man into *subiectum*—throws light at the same time on the grounding event of modern history, an event that at first glance seems almost absurd, namely, the more extensively and the more effectually the world stands at man's disposal as conquered, and the more objectively the object appears, all the more subjectively, i.e., the more importunately, does the *subiectum* rise up, and all the more impetuously, too, do observation of and teaching about the world change into a doctrine of man, into anthropology. It is no wonder that humanism first arises where the world becomes picture."

16. See Barthes, *Sade, Fourier, Loyola,* pp. 8–9.

17. Shoshana Felman and Dori Laub, *Testimony: Crises of Witnessing in Literature, Psychoanalysis, and History* (New York: Routledge, 1992), 137, 157, 165–167; and Shoshana Felman, "Benjamin's Silence," *Critical Inquiry* 25 (1999), pp. 201–234.

18. Ian Hacking, *Rewriting the Soul: Multiple Personalities and the Sciences of Memory* (Princeton: Princeton University Press, 1995).

PREFACE TO *THE NEUTRAL*

1. Roland Barthes, "Lecture," trans. Richard Howard, *October,* no. 8 (Spring 1979), p. 15.

2. Roland Barthes, *Roland Barthes by Roland Barthes,* trans. Richard Howard (New York: Hill and Wang, 1977), p. 50.

3. Barthes, "Lecture," p. 5. Reacting to a remark by Ernest Renan on the French language's inoculation against reaction, Barthes said, "But language—the performance of a language system—is neither reactionary nor progressive; it is quite simply fascist; for fascism does not prevent speech, it compels speech."

4. Barthes, "Lecture," p. 5.

5. Barthes, *Roland Barthes by Roland Barthes,* p. 51.

6. Ibid., p. 132.

7. Roland Barthes, *Mythologies*, trans. Annette Lavers (New York: Noonday Press, 1972), pp. 81–83.

8. Barthes, *Roland Barthes by Roland Barthes,* p. 87.

9. Barthes, "Lecture," p. 6.

10. Roland Barthes, *The Rustle of Language,* trans. Richard Howard (New York: Hill and Wang, 1986), p. 242.

11. See Bernard Comment, *Roland Barthes, ver le neutre,* chapter titled "Politique: Déjouer tout pouvoir" (Paris: Christian Bourgois, 1991), pp. 219–254.

Index

Page numbers in boldface indicate illustrations.